C000116417

Strategic Control of Marketing Finance

Strategic Control of Marketing Finance

DAVID HAIGH

FINANCIAL TIMES

PITMAN PUBLISHING

PITMAN PUBLISHING
128 Long Acre, London WC2E 9AN

A Division of Longman Group UK Limited

First published in Great Britain 1994

© David Haigh 1994

British Library Cataloguing in Publication Data
A CIP catalogue record for this book can be obtained from the British Library.

ISBN 0 273 60231 4

All rights reserved; no part of this publication may be reproduced, stored
in a retrieval system, or transmitted in any form or by any means, electronic,
mechanical, photocopying, recording, or otherwise without either the prior
written permission of the Publishers or a licence permitting restricted copying
in the United Kingdom issued by the Copyright Licensing Agency Ltd,
90 Tottenham Court Road, London W1P 9HE. This book may not be lent,
resold, hired out or otherwise disposed of by way of trade in any form
of binding or cover other than that in which it is published, without the
prior consent of the Publishers.

Typeset by PanTek Arts, Maidstone, Kent
Printed and bound in Great Britain by
Biddles Ltd, Guildford and King's Lynn

The Publisher's policy is to use paper manufactured from sustainable forests.

CONTENTS

To Cherry

FOREWORD

After agreeing to write this book, the contract remained in my in-tray for months. Committing myself to producing a book was relatively easy. Getting around to writing it was more difficult. Signing the contract was even harder; so it kept being moved to the bottom of the pile.

One of the particular problems came in deciding what should be in the book and what the tone of voice should be. I began with an ill-defined view of what might be interesting to the mythical Managing, Marketing and Finance Directors who might want to know something about the subject without reference to turgid textbooks. I visited various business bookshops and was horrified to see just how many books there were on the subject. However, I felt that despite the large number of texts already weighing down the shelves there was a place for a topical book, dealing with current trends across the whole area of marketing finance. The text is not meant to be comprehensive because in the space available this would be impossible. It is supposed to cover many of the areas where significant changes are occurring and where directors should be considering the position of their companies.

The intention was to give practical guidance, to give descriptions of important techniques and to draw conclusions which might help individual directors steer company thinking. It was also my intention wherever possible to draw on the thoughts of major practitioners in the different areas covered rather than to pontificate too much myself. Several people suggested that there should be plenty of examples and case studies. I hope I have managed to fulfil these intentions and pieces of advice in the final text.

As the book was written I included material which fitted what seemed the most topical issues in the marketplace. One event which occurred during the writing of the book was the Marketing Forum aboard the SS Canberra. Several hundred marketing directors and managers met for three days and discussed issues of current concern. The organisers, Richmond Events, kindly allowed me to reproduce the results of their delegate research which highlights the importance of many issues dealt with in the book.

There was a wide spread of marketeers present on board the SS Canberra, with 30 per cent of delegates responsible for up to £1 million of marketing expenditure, and 11 per cent responsible for £30 million or more, with a wide range of budgets in between. Delegates represented companies ranging in turnover from under £10 million to over £500 million. The areas of greatest concern to the 253 marketing decision-makers who completed the detailed delegate questionnaire were: changing consumer behaviour patterns – 67 per cent; product development and evolution – 48 per cent; legislation – 42 per cent; IT – 36 per cent; expanding Europe – 30 per cent; environmental issues – 30 per cent; changes in available media – 26 per cent; and integrated marketing – 25 per cent.

Although this latter point is apparently of less concern many delegates are actively engaged in the process of integrating their marketing functions. There has been an increase in the integration of internal functions including marketing, sales, IT, operations, human resources and so on. Twenty-six per cent of delegates already have this type of integration in place, and 23 per cent are in the process of implementing an integrated marketing strategy.

In addition, there has been a move towards greater external integration and a gradual shift of budgets below the line. Within such a sample of delegates there are inevitably huge variations. However, some broadbrush indicators can be defined. For example, the average marketing budget split among those polled was 45 per cent above the line and 55 per cent below the line, a significant departure from received wisdom, which suggests that the majority of a marketing budget should be disposed above the line. The average spend in different areas was as follows:

Press advertising	21 per cent
Television	16 per cent
Radio	1 per cent
Outdoor media	2 per cent
Exhibitions	6 per cent
Direct marketing	15 per cent
Sales promotion	16 per cent
Sponsorship/hospitality	4 per cent
PR	8 per cent
Market research	6 per cent
Other	5 per cent

Not only has there been an increase in below the line disciplines in recent years but there has been a very clear trend towards external integration in one form or another.

Within the sample, expenditure on Information Technology for marketing differed dramatically. Forty-three per cent of delegates spent under £100,000 on IT while 3 per cent spent over £5 million. Concern for IT may be lower than for the changing consumer but this is an area which will dramatically increase in significance in coming years.

In terms of agency provision, 61 per cent of SS Canberra delegates used a full service agency, 22 per cent used creative services only while 14 per cent did not use an agency at all. Fifty-five per cent review agency relationships annually or more frequently. In terms of agency remuneration 8 per cent of delegates now incorporate some form of payment by results. Four per cent pay for ideas, 53 per cent pay straight fees and only 43 per cent pay on the conventional commission system. In this context 39 per cent of delegates polled felt the the squeeze on agency remuneration had gone far enough while 61 per cent felt that it had not yet gone far enough. Some worrying facts about client perceptions of the agency process. It is clear that the process of change in the agency business, driven by client expectations, is by no means over.

These and many other issues are dealt with in the book and other areas are dealt with that marketing decision makers are apparently in the dark about. For example, many marketing and finance people believe that the arguments about brand valuation have run their course and that the whole issue of brand valuation is now rather passé'. In fact, nothing could be further from the truth as Interbrand gears itself up for a whole new series of applications for its brand valuation methodology. Interbrand argues that brand valuations for intercompany royalty payments and for tax planning will boom in the 1990s. Several large blue-chip companies are already using brands held off-shore as a way of reducing tax levels in high tax operating areas. Yet many marketeers are unaware of the opportunities which exist in this area.

I asked Richmond Events to include specific questions on this topic in their questionnaire. Only 16 per cent of responding delegates were even aware that it is possible to hold brands offshore in low tax areas and to charge royalties back to operating subsidiaries in high tax areas. Of those who were aware of the technique only 38 per cent are currently taking advantage of the opportunity. This is staggering in relation to the opportunity to add value to the company by legitimately avoiding taxes.

Hopefully, this and a number of other issues discussed in the book will suggest courses of action to busy Managing, Marketing and Finance Directors which might not otherwise have occurred to them.

In preparing the book I have been given a great deal of help by many people in the marketing business who agreed to be interviewed, by other authors who allowed me to quote from their works, from various Institutions which allowed me to quote from their research and publications, from my colleagues and family who have been extremely helpful and long suffering. I would just like to say thank you to everyone who has helped produce the text.

David Haigh

1

GROWING SIGNIFICANCE OF MARKETING FINANCE

'God is on the side not of the heavy battalions but of the best shots'
Voltaire

INTRODUCTION

Marketing is a subject on which there is no shortage of text books, but few deal with current trends in the relationship between marketing and finance. This book attempts to fill that gap, providing an indication of the trends which are making the relationship critical in many companies. It looks at the economic, environmental, demographic and competitive changes which are making marketing more risky and expensive. It looks at how marketing can be made more responsive and productive by harnessing the relationship between the two disciplines. It looks at current developments which may be of interest and practical value to directors of marketing organisations, both large and small.

The book begins by looking at the changing world and the threats and opportunities it presents. Subsequent chapters consider the background, training and interface between personnel in the two disciplines, the impact of Information Technology (IT), at pricing, costing, distribution, New Product Development (NPD), budget allocation, campaign planning, agency management, project control and evaluation and above all the development of corporate and marketing strategies. As far as possible the book attempts to be topical and relevant. The views of leading practitioners in each area have been incorporated together with current examples and thoughts for the future. It does not attempt to cover all subjects in minute detail but to stimulate a broad awareness of and interest in major developments.

The presiding theme of the book is the need for more effective financial understanding of and interest in marketing issues. As Voltaire suggested, victory will go to the best shots rather than the heavy battalions. But to be the best shots marketers need to be able to see the targets with sights they can rely on. It is the financial function which will help define the targets and calibrate the sights. Hopefully, this book will help in that process.

Competitive pressures

In recent years the importance of a marketing culture has grown in many organisations which previously took their markets for granted. Competitive pressures have affected not only conventional fast moving consumer goods (FMCG) companies but also industrial, professional, charitable, governmental and financial organisations which used to be immune to such vulgarities! Increasing consumer expectations, deregulation, the accelerating pace of technology, the rapid rate of new product development, the increasing power of retailers and distributors, and the creation of world markets, have all raised the stakes for many organisations.

It has always been true that organisations with a production rather than a customer focus were vulnerable to competition, but in many cases significant barriers to market entry reduced the threats. However, cultural differences, structural barriers, restrictive trade practices and protectionist government policies have gradually reduced, resulting in greater risks for companies which are slow to adapt. For example, deregulation is in vogue in many developed countries, most notably in the US and the UK, where traditional public services are being opened up through privatisation, management buyout, the creation of quasi-commercial agencies, and competitive tendering. As a result, schools, hospitals, doctors and even prisons are getting to grips with marketing concepts for the first time.

Protectionist trade barriers are also being eliminated on an international scale. The recent GATT agreement is expected to add $130 billion to the world economy. While GATT and the world's free trade blocks may not be perfect there is an inexorable economic trend towards more open markets. This issue is particularly relevant in Europe where duplication and over-capacity across the EC mean that significant rationalisation will inevitably result as the single market becomes a reality.

Fragmentation

In terms of communicating with target audiences, companies are now faced with the decline of mass consumer media and the growth of niche media opportunities, as the media marketplace fragments. This results in greater opportunities to target specific audiences, but a reduction in the ability to reach mass audiences. Marketing approaches need to be far more intelligently directed, both in terms of products and services offered to consumers, and in the ways such products and services are promoted to a series of discrete audiences.

The ability of brands, other than market leaders, to survive and thrive will more frequently come into question. To break out of a cycle of decline, innovative marketing strategies will be required and more efficient ways of using available marketing budgets will become essential.

In an increasingly fragmented market, the ability to interpret and exploit relevant information will be crucial. However, there has been an information explosion, both internal and external, and many marketing people have already experienced a tendency towards 'analysis paralysis'.

Professionalism

The number and complexity of tasks which the average marketing person is expected to grasp, and to be expert in, also expands by the day, from media targeting to database manipulation, from distribution to finance.

One result has been a rapid move towards professionalism in the marketing discipline. Gone are the days when gifted or creative amateurs could hold their own at senior levels. The marketing function in many companies is evolving from a simple pyramid to a much flatter structure as serious marketing organisations opt for fewer but better qualified, senior operators. The granting of a Royal Charter to the Institute of Marketing, the massive upsurge in internal training programmes and academic courses all point to the increasing need for professional knowledge.

A similar pattern can be seen in the finance area, which is coming to accept that specialist skills are needed of those finance people who form the bridge with the marketing function. The Chartered Institute of Management Accountants, in particular, is pioneering the development of specific marketing accountants, to service the increasingly complex task.

This change in structure is having an effect on the type of agency and consultancy which is servicing the marketing departments of major companies. As internal marketing teams get leaner and more professional there is an increasing need for agencies and consultancies of a similar complexion. Despite the recession there has been an upsurge in the number and complexity of consultancies servicing the marketing business. The fragmentation of conventional agency services and the involvement of specialists looks set to increase.

Accountability

There is also more of a requirement for a genuine client/agency partnership, a demand for greater professionalism from consultancies and an increasing demand for accountability in all areas of external agency activity.

Marketing is now recognised by many organisations as the cockpit of the business. Marketing decisions are taken at a far higher level than in the days when marketing and promotion meant one and the same thing to many Chief Executives. Marketing strategy is, more than ever before, fundamental to corporate strategy. The risks are greater and the resources required to be successful have also increased.

Against this background, speed and intelligence of response to new market conditions is becoming increasingly critical to corporate survival. Project approval, control and evaluation is being much more carefully monitored and controlled. Pressure is also growing to use marketing budgets more effectively. Unfortunately, increasing competitive pressures coincide with a period of worldwide recession, which the UK may finally be leaving, but which much of the developed world is only just entering. This has created an environment where accountability is not just a slogan but a prerequisite of corporate survival.

Inevitably perhaps, the finance function is now much more likely to put marketing expenditures under the microscope. Marketing activity is coming under ever greater scrutiny from financial people who have all heard Lord Leverhulme's comments, about not knowing which half of the advertising spend is actually working, and who enjoy passing opinions about marketing activities before wielding the axe over such a large, discretionary, 'overhead' budget.

Changing relationships

There is a growing recognition that changes are needed in a number of fundamental areas of the marketing discipline itself, and in the nature of the interface between marketing, finance and the other key management disciplines within many organisations. This book attempts to explore some of the major trends involved in this process and to contribute to the developing relationship between marketing and finance.

THE IMPACT OF RECESSION

The progress of the UK recession has been well documented; the decline in Gross Domestic Product (GDP), the rise in unemployment, the housing crisis, the government funding deficit. Recessions seem to hit the UK on a rough ten year cycle, although the shape of the recession differs from decade to decade. This time round inflation is more under control but at the cost of much higher unemployment and government borrowing.

It is also well known that recession hit the UK 18 months to two years before the rest of Continental Europe. The slump is now well under way in Germany and France while the UK is tentatively emerging from the depths of gloom. High manufacturing costs, and the structural costs of integration, threaten to make the German decline a sharp and painful one. It seems that the pain will be exacerbated by high interest rates, to maintain the value of the Deutschmark and keep out inflation. The French economy is also receding after a long period of growth, and most other European economies are moving in sympathy with these central economies.

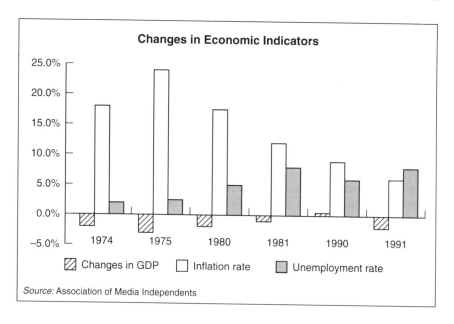

Figure 1.1

It seems that Europe as a whole is set for a difficult period. The virtual col-
lapse of the Exchange Rate Mechanism (ERM) indicates the sort of
pressures bearing on all EU countries as they try to square the need to stimulate their flagging economies, with the plan to create a more unified Europe.
If lower interest rates and devaluation create a short-term economic stimulus, as they have in the UK, since 'Black Wednesday' in September 1992,
many countries will find it politically impossible to ignore the option. So
there may be a prolonged period of dislocation as individual economies go
their own way.

In the UK a number of aspects of the recession have been particularly significant for marketing decision makers. Much of the economic growth of the
eighties was stimulated by the rising housing market and the boom in consumer credit. Savings ratios were at an all-time low and house prices
reached an all-time high, as a proportion of average salaries. From an historic average of somewhere around three times earnings house prices rose to
nearer five times, a level which proved unsupportable. The subsequent drop
in house prices created the 'negative equity' crisis, the overhang of property
foreclosures and a major loss of consumer confidence. The resurgence of
high unemployment levels, coupled with low levels of pay growth, has had a
similar effect.

All recessions have damaging effects on consumer confidence but the
contrast between the euphoria of the late eighties and the present situation

has changed a number of fundamental consumer attitudes, which will continue for some time after the economy recovers. The changes can be summarised as follows:

- increased consumer conservatism
- increased loyalty to proven brands
- the demise of the conspicuous consumer
- the growth of a 'value for money' culture
- the decline of the 'house worshipper'
- a continued interest in savings.

Not only tight financial circumstances but also a more conservative consumer mood will affect many markets for some time to come.

THE ACCOUNTABILITY REVOLUTION

One impact of the recession has been a huge upsurge in financial accountability. It is a cliché that the finance director's role moves up the pecking order during a recession, when the corporate emphasis moves from expansionary growth to cost cutting. However, in this recession the need to explain value for money at all levels has been particularly pronounced; of expenditure within companies, of costs to trade customers, of product and service prices to consumers, and of performance to share and stakeholders. The days of aggressive takeovers holding bad management to account may have waned but the internal cultures of many organisations have absorbed the lessons of the eighties.

The need for financial literacy

There has never been a time when the impetus to explain and analyse costs, and value for money, has been stronger. As a result, the need for non-financial people to understand and use financial disciplines has increased dramatically.

Social accountability

There also seems to be a wider social trend underlying the accountability revolution. The narrow financial consequences of the trend have been complemented by a move towards much greater social accountability. The Citizen's Charter is just one expression of the belief that the individual has a right to good service, value for money and an explanation when they are not received. The concept of *open government* seems to have hit the mark, at least at the sloganeering level. Perhaps this is a reaction to the excesses and the failures of governmental and regulatory systems in the 1980s.

The debate about *corporate governance*, the demand for more non-executive directors, audit and remuneration committees are all manifestations of this trend in the business world. A more open business culture fits with both this change in moral climate and with the need to break down barriers to maximise competitive advantage.

Transparency

At its most practical level the accountability revolution means that both trade customers and consumers expect and demand transparency and clear explanations, particularly of costs. This is a fact which has impacted recently on the advertising agency business where the perception, if not the reality, of overcharging has seriously damaged agency/client relationships.

THE INFORMATION EXPLOSION

The massive decrease in the cost of computing power has resulted in a huge and growing impact on the conduct of all business disciplines including marketing. In all business areas there are now huge, accessible databases which provide more and more useful information. At the consumer level more public information is available to make informed purchasing decisions.

Some of the issues posed by this information explosion are:

- is new software capable of sensibly manipulating the data?
- how is it possible to integrate the different data sources?
- are individuals skilled in interpreting and specifying required information?
- how can marketing users avoid analysis paralysis?

One of the major problems facing *marketeers* is that with all the data now available from Electronic Point of Sale (EPOS) and other sources there is a danger that retailers or competitors could be making better, more strategic decisions, simply because they are able to interpret and use the avalanche of data in a more meaningful way.

GROWTH IN CONSUMER SOPHISTICATION

The iconoclast

There has been a steady decline in respect for traditional values and institutions; government, church, marriage, the family. Consumers no longer respond well to authority or accept conventional wisdom. Smaller, more personal peer groups and the media have much more influence, and consumers often have to be persuaded at a more individual level.

The individual consumer

As technology creates the ability to make products in a multiplicity of different forms the needs of the individual consumer are becoming all-important. At present, many technically advanced and consumer-oriented organisations are responding to the demand for individuality, even within highly automated production processes. Some of the best examples are Japanese. For example, the constant innovation in product lines to fit customer needs, at electronics companies like Sony.

Or, the constant model changes and modifications being produced by Japanese car makers. In the days of Henry Ford the consumer could have any colour of car 'as long as it was black', and cars were the archetype of mass production. Today we live in an age of diversification. There is apparently no limit to the amount of differentiation and diversity of preferences. Judging by the rapid rate of model changes, Japanese car makers seem to have taken the view that if they do not keep pace with the growth of this diversity they are bound to decline.

The 'professional' consumer

While Eastern Europe and the developing world may be typified by impulsive and ill-informed new consumers, the developed world has become cynical and well-informed. First world consumers are increasingly aware of manufacturing, marketing and communications issues. They are switched-on to advertising and consumer imagery. They are media literate. They know their consumer rights. They are not bamboozled by false or competing product claims and simply cannot be condescended to.

The discriminating consumer

Gone are the days when consumers in the developed world could easily be persuaded to make the impulse purchase, based on new technology or a new communications campaign. As the population ages and as wealth increases this discrimination becomes ever greater.

For example, The Henley Centre 'Planning for Social Change' Survey, 1992 found the following profile of responses to the proposition that 'I don't rush out and buy new products just because they are new' (see Figure 1.2).

Consumers increasingly buy to satisfy their own genuine and considered needs. In many cases this implies a different style of product design, delivery and communication.

The global consumer

There is a growing tendency for consumers to belong to 'global tribes' rather than to nationally-based consumer groups. For example, many execu-

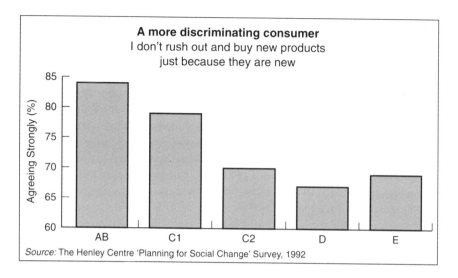

Figure 1.2

tive audiences have more in common with their peers around the world than with other socio-economic groups in their own countries. This has probably always been the case to some extent, but we are now in an era when communication with narrow groups across national boundaries is becoming a realistic possibility.

SHIFTING DEMOGRAPHICS

Many social and cultural changes will no doubt occur in the next decade. In developed markets there will be a gradual increase in household numbers and incomes, a reduction in family sizes and further declines in traditional family structures. However, a small number of major demographic trends are likely to have a much more significant impact on corporate and marketing strategies. They impact on the size and preferences of the customer base, the nature of products and services provided, the composition of the workforce and the location of manufacturing and production facilties.

Middle-age spread

One of the main factors affecting the economic structure of the developed world in the nineties will be an increase in the number of older, retired people depending upon a declining number of younger, working people. In demographic terms society's midriff is bulging.

UK Population trends in England and Wales, 1950–2000

TOTAL 000	1950 50,616	1960 52,383	1970 55,811	1980 56,330	1990 57,745	2000 59,050	% point change 1950–2001
Men	48.6%	48.2%	48.7%	48.7%	48.8%	49.1%	+0.5%
Women	51.4%	51.8%	51.3%	51.3%	51.2%	50.9%	−5.0%
0–4	8.6%	7.9%	8.3%	6.0%	6.8%	6.7%	−1.9%
5–14	13.7%	15.4%	15.7%	15.0%	12.3%	13.6%	−0.1%
15–19	6.6%	6.8%	6.9%	8.3%	6.8%	6.2%	−0.4%
20–24	7.0%	6.3%	7.8%	7.4%	8.0%	5.9%	−1.1%
25–34	14.6%	12.8%	12.5%	14.2%	15.3%	13.8%	−0.8%
35–44	15.3%	13.6%	11.9%	11.9%	13.7%	14.9%	−0.4%
45–54	13.3%	14.0%	12.3%	11.2%	11.3%	13.0%	−0.3%
55–64	10.2%	11.5%	11.8%	11.0%	10.1%	10.4%	+0.2%
64+	10.7%	11.7%	12.8%	15.0%	15.6%	15.5%	+4.8%
TOTAL	100.0%	100.0%	100.0%	100.0%	100.0%	100.0%	

Data may not be equal due to rounding

Source: Mintel

Figure 1.3

For example, the percentage of people in England and Wales over 64 grew from 10.7 per cent in 1950 to 15.6 per cent in 1990. Between 1990 and the year 2000 the population is expected to age further as the 'babyboomers' of the 1950s reach middle age. There is expected to be a continued decline in the percentage of the population between 15 and 34, down from 30.1 per cent in 1990 to only 25.9 per cent by the year 2000, equivalent to a decease in absolute terms of 2.1 million individuals.

This is a trend which affects all the affluent nations of Europe.

Medical rationing

As healthcare technology becomes ever more powerful, and as life expectancies lengthen, the demands of the more dependent sections of the population will continue to grow at the expense of the younger, wealth-creating groups. The cost of healthcare is rapidly rising and the lifestyle expectations of an ageing population are also increasing. These trends are already beginning to have a number of impacts on society.

In both the US and UK there is a growing debate about the ability of healthcare systems to deliver up to the level of consumer expectations. In the UK the growing realisation that the NHS cannot provide full cover for all medical conditions and interventions has stimulated a growing debate about the allocation of budgets and the need for explicit '*medical rationing*'. This has come as a shock to many who had always assumed that the very best and latest treatments could and should be universally available on demand.

Flexible retirement

There is a growing trend towards flexible retirement dates. Increasingly active, older people need something to occupy their 'third age', and the opportunity to earn more for longer. The undesirable side to this in the UK is a whispered debate, currently in progress between politicians, about the scope for deferral of statutory retirement ages and the curtailment of state pension rights, to limit future costs.

However, it seems that many organisations are increasingly willing to accept older employees and 'second career' makers, particularly women returning to the workforce. This latter fact may go some way to explain Mintel's prediction, in its 'Special Report on British Lifestyles', 1992, that the percentage of employed men within the UK working population will decrease from 59 per cent to 54 per cent between 1990 and the year 2000, while the percentage of employed women will increase from 41 per cent to 46 per cent.

Part-timing

Many of the additional members of the workforce will be part-timers. It is predicted that by the year 2000 nearly half of all employed women in the UK will be part-time workers. The percentage of employed men working part-time is also expected to increase substantially from the current level of just over 5 per cent.

The 'fascism of youth' declines

The relaxation of traditional prejudices towards older staff will partly be stimulated by a need to fill the gap of available and qualified workers, and partly by the demands of older consumers who may feel more comfortable with older service staff. An increased emphasis on service delivery in sectors as diverse as motor vehicles, airlines, computers, financial services and retailing is already apparent, and, as many companies will be catering for an older consumer profile, demand for older staff will increase. Service represents an increasingly important part of economic activity in developed countries and is becoming a more integral part of the consumer proposition, even in conventional product markets. The development of service jobs in the UK between 1950 and the year 2000 will be seen as quite startling.

The re-emergence of fashion models from the sixties and the popularity of geriatric rock stars all point towards the gradual erosion of the 'fascism of youth' in many areas of consumer marketing. The development of marketing consultancies like Third Age Marketing, which specifically targets this increasingly important group of older consumers, are signs of demographic change.

The 'haves' and 'have nots'

For while at the macro-economic level the ageing population may be increasingly dependent upon a decreasing number of younger workers, at the micro-economic level many 'third agers' will have significant assets and incomes. A growing distinction will become apparent between the *haves* and the *have nots* within the older age groups. The wealthier segment, the much vaunted 'grey panther' market, is already being eyed greedily by many organisations, particularly in the healthcare, financial services, leisure and premium product sectors.

The adolescent world

In contrast to this demographic shift in the developed world many parts of the developing world have population profiles heavily biased towards the young (see Figure 1.5).

As developing countries increase their standards of living, and quality of life, demographic profiles will inevitably level out. For example, Singapore reached the point some years ago where concern about declining birth rates led to the introduction of policies designed to maintain population levels and thereby provide one of the key ingredients in its economic miracle – people. However, for some time to come there will be a significant demographic disparity between the developed and the developing world.

Shifting sands – into town . . .

A second demographic issue of major significance over the coming decade will be population shift. Within the UK there is a well established pattern of population migration from rural areas to towns and cities, and from declining, peripheral regions to the affluent South and Southeast.

Similar shifts have been experienced in other EU countries, as rural populations have moved towards wealthier conurbations. As the EU gradually becomes more integrated there will be an increasing level of population shift, particularly among those with specialist technical skills and among the more educated sections of the population.

Working population trends in England and Wales, 1950–2000

Working Population 000	1950 23,068	1960 25,010	1970 25,675	1980 26,838	1990 29,774	2000 32,550
Agriculture	9.3%	7.6%	3.5%	2.8%	2.1%	1.8%
Industry	46.5%	45.4%	46.6%	38.2%	29.1%	25.4%
Services	44.2%	47.0%	49.9%	59.0%	68.8%	72.8%
Employed men	69.0%	66.0%	64.0%	60.0%	59.0%	54.0%
Employed women	31.0%	34.0%	36.0%	40.0%	41.0%	46.0%
Unemployed	0.1%	1.3%	2.2%	2.2%	5.6%	3.2%

Source: Mintel

Figure 1.4

Out of town?

One interesting question will be to what extent the advent of more flexible working patterns and new technology will lead to the movement of people back out of cities to rural areas in wealthier regions. Many of the factors are in place for such a migration, including increasingly sophisticated teleworking technology, and a strong consumer interest in living in the country.

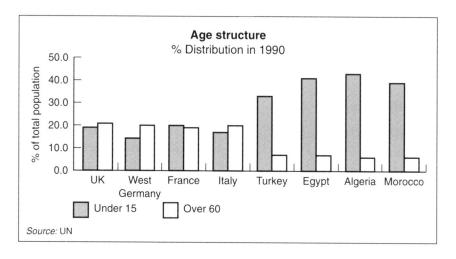

Figure 1.5

UK regional population trends, 1951–2001

	1951 000	1961 000	1971 000	1981 000	1991 000	2001 000	% change 1951– 2001
Scotland	5,096	5,179	5,244	5,180	5,061	4,999	−2
North England	3,137	3,250	3,296	3,104	3,069	3,050	−3
North West	6,447	6,567	6,743	6.414	6,400	6,350	−2
Yorkshire & Humberside	4,522	4,635	4,799	4,860	4,975	5,125	+13
East Midlands	2,893	3,100	3,390	3,819	4,049	4,240	+47
East Anglia	1,382	1,470	1,669	1,872	2,075	2,210	+60
South West	3,229	3,411	3,781	4,349	4,702	5,030	+56
West Midlands	4,423	4,758	5,110	5,148	5,236	5,325	+20
South East	15,127	16,271	17,230	16,796	17,400	18,010	+19
Wales	2,599	2,644	2,731	2,792	2,910	2,980	+15
Northern Ireland	1,371	1,425	1,529	1,538	1,595	1,651	+20

Source: Mintel

Figure 1.6

The rise of teleworking

Technology is increasingly in place to work from home and employers are becoming more amenable to the concept of *teleworking*. Of course, it is easy to get carried away with predictions of how fast it will all happen. Conservatism and cultural barriers will certainly retard the process. However, it seems probable that there will be a major increase in full-time employees working from home by the year 2000.

As the number of freelance workers is also increasing at a rapid pace, and as working relationships become more flexible, such a shift could quickly gather pace in the 1990s.

A steady influx

The internal drift of people within the EU towards wealth creating centres will be complemented by a continued influx of hopeful immigrants from Eastern Europe and other under-developed areas. The European immigration and refugee problems are currently at serious levels, creating an expectation that further influxes will be severely curtailed. However, if and when the current recession in Europe recedes, and as the demographic shortfall becomes more of an economic problem, significant numbers of carefully selected workers can be expected to flow into the EU.

Exporting jobs

For those who do not get under the wire into the economic paradise of the EU the consolation prize could be a significant shift in economic activity out of the EU to low-cost producing countries in eastern Europe, north Africa, the Middle East and further afield. In the same way that US jobs have relentlessly migrated south into Mexico, and Japanese, Korean, Taiwanese and Hong Kong jobs are beginning to migrate to lower-cost Far Eastern countries, the same process can be reliably expected to occur in Europe.

EMERGING CONSUMER MARKETS

That this migration of jobs and wealth is already happening can clearly be seen in the emergence of new consumer markets worldwide.

The newly enriched workers of the developing world are flexing their muscles as consumers. Market growth in the developing world highlights the opportunities available to those companies currently slugging it out for minute market share gains in the mature markets of the developed world. So far, fear of the unknown has inhibited many smaller companies in established markets, from fully exploiting the opportunities available in emerging markets.

Traditional consumer markets in the developed world have become more competitive, with increased internal and external competition, static or very low rates of population increase, stagnant economic growth and increasingly powerful retailers and distributors. These factors, coupled with the ease of technology transfer, have all reduced volume and margin potential for many companies.

By contrast, less mature markets, with rising populations, rapidly growing GDPs, positive trade balances and large amounts of inward investment, offer huge scope for those companies willing to seize the opportunities. Southern Europe, south America and the Far East are particularly attractive, with increasing political stability and relatively open markets. In the next decade large parts of eastern Europe, Africa and the Orient will be in the same position (See Figure 1.7).

Branded manufacturers entering these markets are finding that aspirational brand preference is high but that short-term pricing and profit margins often need to be low to gain market share.

The need to react quickly to the opportunities available was highlighted by Michael Perry, Chairman of Unilever PLC, in *AdWeek*, on 14 December 1992.

'. . . the first question to be asked of any successful brand today anywhere is, will it travel? And how fast will it travel? Because you have no time to take this process slowly but surely. If you don't move that successful brand around the world rapidly you can be sure your competitor will take

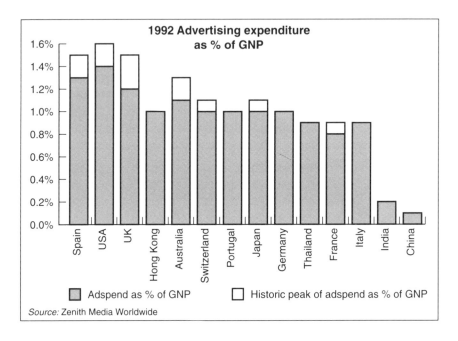

Figure 1.7

the idea, lift it and move it ahead of you. Speed to market is of the essence. But the point . . . central to all of this is a global brand is simply a local brand reproduced many times.'

The rush to benefit from global marketing applies right down to the very smallest organisations.

For example, Snell & Wilcox, a small British company which has projected itself into a world leadership position in the arcane and highly technical area of television standards conversion. In a narrow market niche, selling exclusively to television engineers and technicians, it has acquired an unassailable reputation for excellence. It won the Queen's Award for Export Achievement in 1990, exports 90 per cent of its production and dominates the world market in its product sector.

GROWTH IN GLOBAL MARKETS

There is no doubt that the scale and accessibility of world markets have both increased rapidly in the last decade and that the number of companies now looking at the world market rather than the domestic market is growing. Many have realised that as barriers between markets come down, if they do

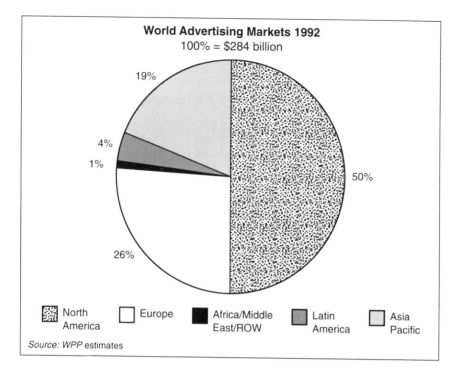

World Advertising Markets 1992
100% = $284 billion

19%

4%

1%

50%

26%

North America | Europe | Africa/Middle East/ROW | Latin America | Asia Pacific

Source: WPP estimates

Figure 1.8

not combat the competition from abroad it won't be long before the competition arrives on their own doorstep.

Economies of scale have been, and are increasingly being, used as a means of achieving competitive cost advantage to ease entry into new markets. The American multinationals were the first to pioneer world markets with world brands, and remain some of the most disciplined at doing so. However, the Japanese have taught the world a lesson in many markets, from zips to motorbikes and, most recently, cars.

The urge to look more widely in terms of markets is heightened by the fact that economic growth rates are significant in many developing markets, while many of the mature markets are either stagnant or displaying negative growth.

GROWTH IN GLOBAL MARKETING BUDGETS

Reflecting the size and importance of the US and European economies, total worldwide marketing budgets are still predominantly spent in those two geographical areas. For example, according to WPP estimates, (see Figures 1.8 and 1.9), the US accounts for approximately 50 per cent of all marketing

Worldwide marketing services expenditure 1992 ($bn)

	USA	UK	France	Germany	Japan	Rest of World	Total
Media Advertising	136.2	13.8	10.7	13.9	36.0	73.4	**283.9**
Public Relations	12.6	2.0	0.8	0.9	3.3	1.8	**21.4**
Market Research	2.8	1.1	0.7	0.8	0.7	2.1	**8.1**
Non-media advertising:							
Graphic & design	16.2	4.7	1.6	1.9	7.3	2.6	**34.3**
Incentive & motivation	2.7	0.7	0.3	0.5	0.9	1.5	**6.6**
Sales promotion	154.3	16.7	10.7	11.6	40.2	65.3	**298.7**
Audio visual communications	3.5	0.7	0.6	0.7	0.8	1.3	**7.7**
Specialist communications							
Real estate	1.1	0.2	0.1	0.3	0.7	0.5	**2.9**
Financial communications	1.4	0.5	0.1	0.3	0.8	0.2	**3.4**
Ethnic	1.6	0.2	0.1	0.1	0.1	0.3	**2.4**
Public affairs	5.8	1.4	0.5	0.6	1.4	0.6	**10.3**
Direct mail	26.4	4.9	2.5	3.3	8.0	11.0	**56.2**
Recruitment	4.0	0.5	0.2	0.7	0.9	1.5	**7.8**
Healthcare	4.5	0.8	0.5	0.7	1.3	1.1	**8.9**
TOTAL	**373.0**	**48.3**	**29.4**	**36.2**	**102.5**	**163.2**	**752.6**

Source: Industry Associations, government associations; WPP estimates

Figure 1.9

services expenditure worldwide. However, other markets are growing strongly and will continue to do so as both GDP and consumer sophistication increase.

In response to the growth of consumer markets around the world marketing budgets are growing inexorably.

REDUCTION OF PRODUCT LIFECYCLES

One of the major problems facing many companies, particularly in the big ticket consumer products markets, is the rate at which changes in consumer tastes and the development of new technologies are cutting product lifecycles.

A good example is the consumer electronics market where developments are happening at such a rate that the large consumer electronics companies are trying to manage the release of whole new technologies, like the Compact Disk (CD) and the interactive laser disc. Only when previous technology investments have been recovered through the market are new technologies being heavily marketed. Another is in the Personal Computer

(PC) hardware and software markets where launch timetables have been cut short to avoid early product obsolescence.

Better market information and flexible production systems, coupled with the inevitable march of technology, mean that marketeers will have to get used to recovering investments over much shorter time periods than ever before.

INCREASING PACE OF TECHNOLOGY TRANSFER

External technology

In an increasingly competitive world the rate at which production and IT development move from one company and country to another is breathtaking. If the technology is not *proprietary* to the company it will not take long for competitors to catch up with the latest state-of-the-art developments.

One of the more extreme manifestations of this process is the growth of the world counterfeit trade in branded goods. There are many examples of poor quality products being sold in developing markets which damage brand reputations. There are also many examples of almost identical products, using the latest technology, passing for the real thing. Even ignoring this shadowy trade there is no doubt that the speed of competitive response to new methods is gathering pace.

Internal technology

Perhaps more seriously, the cost and difficulty of establishing ownership of proprietary technology is also increasing. The battle by Glaxo over its Zantac patent in the US demonstrates the huge investments and sales revenues which can be at stake over fine details of patent, trademark and intellectual property rights law around the world.

Many companies with innovative technologies simply do not have the commercial muscle or the experience to ensure that their technology developments are properly protected worldwide. Consequently alliances or joint ventures are formed with local manufacturers which further speed the dissemination process around the world.

GROWTH IN POWER OF THE RETAILER

Villains or heroes?

During the 1980s UK retailers developed a tight grip over the business of many branded goods manufacturers. This remains an everyday problem for manufacturers and suppliers in the food sector, and in an increasing number of non-food categories. Non-traditional areas have progressively found themselves in the multiple retailers' sights, as they have searched for new volume and profit opportunities. Fresh foods, freezer products, baking, garden and home products, and most recently, pharmacy and petrol, have all been targeted.

The primary reason for this growth in power has been the commercial pressure towards retail concentration. The trend has been towards fewer, larger stores and fewer, more efficient retailing operators. A few names now dominate the national grocery retailing market; Marks & Spencer, Sainsbury, Tesco, Gateway, Safeway, Asda, while Waitrose, Morrisons and Lows have great strength in limited geographical areas. Other retailing sectors have seen similar patterns of concentration. Look at Iceland in freezer centres, Boots in pharmacy or MFI in flatpack furniture.

From the consumer's point of view this has been no bad thing. The efficiency and appearance of stores have improved out of all recognition. We now have some of the best retail outlets in Europe. Product reliability and quality control have moved rapidly forward. The choice of products has expanded, and in many cases prices have dropped in real terms.

It is for these reasons that retailers have been able to develop their own corporate brands as the emblems of quality, reliability and innovation. They have been the people's champions, and the people have rewarded the better retailers with loyalty above and beyond the call of duty. Many now have more confidence in, and aspirational empathy with, Sainsbury's own-label products than they do with traditional branded goods. The Marketing Society recognised this achievement in 1992 by awarding Sainsbury the 'Brand of the Year' award. In some cases own-label items from quality retailers sell at a premium to traditional branded products. In new products, own-label has even begun to lead branded manufacturers in certain areas like prepared meals.

Branded goods manufacturers have been hit by the 'double whammy' of constricted distribution and a gradual decline in the consumer's need to rely on individual product brands as the assurance of quality. The massive distribution and buying power of the major retailing chains means that they can often dictate purchasing and payment terms to their suppliers. Some retail buyers have clobbered their suppliers in the search for better terms, and consumers might conclude that this has worked to their benefit.

The cost to the consumer has been a rise in retailer net margins from somewhere between 2 and 5 per cent, to between 5 and 10 per cent. The change may imply huge returns on capital, it may be outside the norm in many other countries and it is certainly leading to calls for a stewards enquiry.

Number of Grocery Retail Outlets, 1979–1992

Year	Multiples	Co-operatives	Independents	Total G.B.
1979–1992	16.7	−53.5	−36.6	−36.3
1979	5,524	5,315	51,949	62,333
1980	4,994	4,919	51,494	61,407
1981	4,789	4,467	47,334	56,590
1982	4,594	4,096	47,334	56,024
1983	4,565	3,599	47,068	55,232
1984	4,473	3,279	47,068	54,820
1985	4,483	3,131	47,088	54,682
1986	4,418	2,969	47,068	54,455
1987	4,272	2,819	42,941	50,032
1988	4,261	2,704	42,941	49,896
1989	4,296	2,614	42,841	49,851
1990	4,439	2,545	41,223	48,207
1991	4,577	2,481	32,663	39,721
1992*	4,600	2,471	32,663	39,734

*Estimated

Source: Nielsen Marketing Research

Figure 1.10

The debate will continue over the next few years as referrals to the Office of Fair Trading, and battles over market entry for new retail outlets, grind on. During the debate, consumers will continue to share in the benefits of a highly sophisticated retail sector together with further price reductions. Archie Norman, the ex-McKinsey Chief Executive of Asda, recently predicted the start of a major price war.

Consumer-drive change

Consumers who benefit may not realise that, in fact, it was they who had a large part to play in the move to retail concentration in the first place. Changing consumer lifestyles had increased consumer expectations, of both products and service delivered through the retail channel. Inflation and rising input costs had created tight constraints on what consumers were prepared to pay. A relatively stable population and a static grocery market had created pressure for efficiency gains rather than organic growth. All of these factors created pressures on retailers to improve the range and quality of their products, while simultaneously putting margins under tight constraints. Under these pressures the independent sector wilted. The number of independent grocery outlets progressively declined throughout the 1980s. (See Figure 1.10).

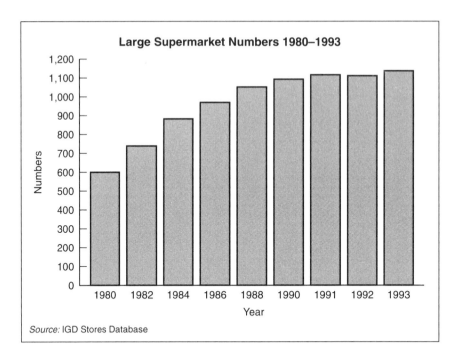

Figure 1.11

It is true that the number of multiple and Co-operative outlets also decreased. However, according to the Institute of Grocery Distribution (IGD), between 1980 and 1990, the average size of multiple-store outlets increased from approximately 7,000 square feet to just over 12,500 square feet, while the average size of new stores increased from 20,000 square feet to over 30,000 in the same period. What the multiples lost in number of outlets they recovered in floorspace and efficiency (see Figures 1.11 and 1.12).

For some time the co-operative sector remained reasonably resilient, but it has progressively suffered at the hands of the multiples. Their relative efficiency compared with co-operative stores can be seen from the growth in sales per square foot achieved by the multiples, which have powered ahead (see Figure 1.13).

Improvements in sales per square foot have stemmed from product innovation, efficient, high quality buying, well targeted marketing and state-of-the-art technology, in stocking, electronic point of sales, scanning and powerful new financial analysis systems. The increasing size, and well-planned design and siting of stores, economies of scale and the efficiency of the very latest technology have all played their parts.

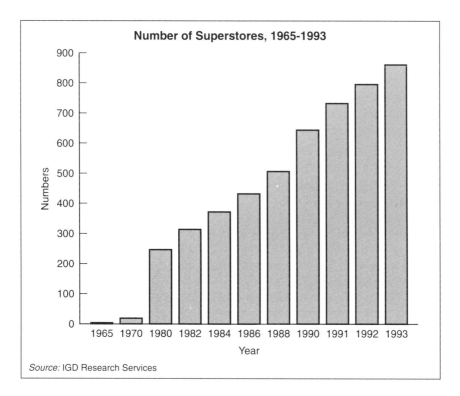

Figure 1.12

The push towards larger, better located stores and technically advanced operations, at every point in the delivery chain, ensured that the large multiples acquired an increasing share of the market (see Figure 1.14).

The last great price war

A crucial period in the recent history of multiple retailing occurred in 1977 when Tesco launched Operation Checkout, which was followed shortly afterwards by Sainsbury's Discount 78 Campaign. The price war which followed floored many of the two giant retailers' rivals and effectively allowed them to dominate the market, which they have done ever since.

Once the blood letting had ended, average UK retailer net margins strengthened. M&S enjoyed a net margin of nearly 11 per cent, Sainsbury achieved 8 per cent and Safeway and Tesco net margins were in excess of 7 per cent. The other players in the retail market aspired to these levels, which were far higher than is typical either in the US or the rest of Continental Europe.

High volume retailers like Sainsbury found themselves in the enviable position of consolidating their distribution base, extending the number and

Sales/sq.ft/week of multiples and co-ops 1977–1991

Year	Multiples		Co-ops	
	Current Prices	Constant (1980) Prices	Current Prices	Constant (1980) Prices
1977	2.90	3.90	2.35	3.16
1978	3.70	4.65	2.65	3.33
1979	4.45	4.99	2.90	3.25
1980	5.40	5.40	3.50	3.50
1981	6.20	5.71	3.65	3.36
1982	6.87	5.87	4.15	3.55
1983	7.17	5.94	4.46	3.70
1984	8.33	6.53	4.42	3.47
1985	8.85	6.73	4.83	3.67
1986	9.24	6.81	4.81	3.54
1987	9.98	7.11	4.95	3.53
1988	10.47	7.16	5.55	3.80
1989	10.84	7.00	5.67	3.66
1990	11.54	7.00	5.35	3.00
1991	12.72	8.06	6.85	4.34

Source: IGD Research Services

Figure 1.13

size of their outlets, increasing market share, and therefore volume off-take, and of pushing up margins by clever marketing to their customers.

Market share: Multiples, Co-ops, Independents

	1978	1980	1982	1984	1986	1988	1989	1990	1991	1992
Multiples	57.9	60.9	64.7	68.7	71.8	73.9	74.2	75.8	77.8	78.0
Co-operatives	15.3	14.2	13.1	11.9	11.1	10.9	10.8	10.3	10.4	10.4
Independents	26.8	24.9	22.2	19.4	17.1	15.2	15.0	13.9	11.8	11.6

Source: A C Nielsen/IGD Research Services

Figure 1.14

The mother of all battles?

However, the halcyon days of the 1980s have turned increasingly turbulent. The recession of the 1990s has caused a decline in disposable incomes and an acute price consciousness among consumers. The EC is opening up the opportunity for cross-border competition. One consequence has been the rise of the foreign discount store.

Growth of the Discount Outlets, 1989–1993

	1989		1990		1991		1992		1993*	
	Actual	Increase	Actual	Increase	Actual	Increase	Actual	Increase	Actual	Increase
Aldi	0	+0	15	+15	37	+22	63	+25	63	–
Netto	0	+0	1	+1	20	+19	43	+23	45	+2
Shoprite	0	+0	2	+2	11	+9	35	+24	35	–
Kwik Save	643	+76	661	+15	745	+84	768	+23	781	+13
Lo Cost	353	+65	320	–33	298	–22	285	–13	278	–7
Solo	0	–	0	–	0	–	47	+47	47	–
Food Giant	0	–	0	–	15	+15	20	+5	21	+1
Dales	0	–	0	–	0	–	4	+4	4	–
Discount Giant	0	–	0	–	1	+1	7	+6	7	–
Pioneer	0	–	0	–	7	+7	11	+4	77	–
Normans	22	+2	19	–3	19	–	21	+2	21	–
Discount Superstore	0	–	0	–	0	–	5	+5	5	–
Budgens Discount	0	–	0	–	0	–	1	+1	1	–
Ed	0	–	0	–	0	–	0	–	3	+3

*April 1993

Source: IGD Research Services

Figure 1.15

Aldi of Germany and Netto of Denmark have led the foreign charge. Low cost operations, minimal staffing, a small number of between 1,000 and 3,000 key lines, and aggressive pricing, as much as 20 to 25 per cent below the main grocery retailers, typify this sector of the market. This sector will grow, although in many cases it will not replace the conventional supermarket, but will simply provide a place to buy staple products cheaply.

Perhaps more worrying for the major companies are the discount warehouse clubs. Costco of the US, which has 100 huge stores and turnover of £23 billion in the US, has arrived in Europe and is trying to get a foothold in the UK market. The concept of bulk buying in exchange for huge discounts has certainly caught the attention of the press and will no doubt appeal to the public.

Not surprisingly the established players are using every trick in the book – most publicly, opposition to planning applications to impede progress. Asda and Tesco in particular have also begun to return to their roots as aggressive, low-cost retailers.

Future trends

The extent to which these new outlets will disrupt the status quo is subject to question, particularly if the major chains respond with price weapons in the short term. For example, some pundits believe that the 8 per cent market share currently taken by discounters might only rise to 16 per cent in the next 5 years. The discounters may well damage the weaker multiples and independents rather than the major chains.

It seems likely that the UK retail pattern will slowly gravitate towards the more fragmented pattern of the US and Continental Europe, with more competition between operators. However, there is some evidence to suggest that the integration of the European market could lead to greater concentration in the EU retailing sector rather than greater fragmentation. Competition and low margins are currently the norm in many parts of Europe, but those markets may, at least partially, follow the UK experience towards concentration and higher margins. For example, concentration is already growing in France and Germany and may spread elsewhere (see Figure 1.16).

The plight of the manufacturer

Whatever the long-term outcome, the short-term reality is a daunting one for many branded goods companies. It seems unlikely that the new players will have the scope to widen margins for manufacturers, although there may be some opportunity to regenerate brands and therefore long-term margins, because consumers may want more branded reassurance in the new outlets.

Major retailer expectations that manufacturers will finance new product development, working capital, branded promotional support, in-store activity, price and other promotions are unlikely to change. The expectation that there will be both strategic, branded advertising support and tactical, Co-operative retail advertising will continue.

Own-label won't go away

Nor will own-label go away. The tendency among retailers to utilise spare capacity in the manufacturing sector to produce low-price, own-label products will continue, creating further pressure on brands. Brands are not only competing against other brands in their own sectors but also against the corporate brand of the all-powerful retailers (see Figure 1.17).

The trend towards own-label continues and the IGD predicts that own-label will represent 37 per cent of packaged grocery sales by the year 2000. Own-label is currently lower in the rest of Europe, but is rising fast (see Figure 1.18).

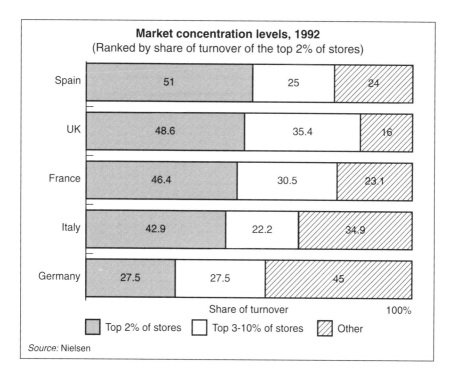

Market concentration levels, 1992
(Ranked by share of turnover of the top 2% of stores)

	Top 2% of stores	Top 3-10% of stores	Other
Spain	51	25	24
UK	48.6	35.4	16
France	46.4	30.5	23.1
Italy	42.9	22.2	34.9
Germany	27.5	27.5	45

Share of turnover   100%

Top 2% of stores   Top 3-10% of stores   Other

Source: Nielsen

Figure 1.16

Own-label share of multiple packaged grocery turnover

Year	% Own-label in Multiples
1978	23.0
1979	22.2
1980	21.9
1981	22.9
1982	24.8
1983	26.9
1984	29.0
1985	30.0
1990	33.0
1991	34.9

Source: AGB/TCA/Nielsen/Euromonitor/Superpanel

Figure 1.17

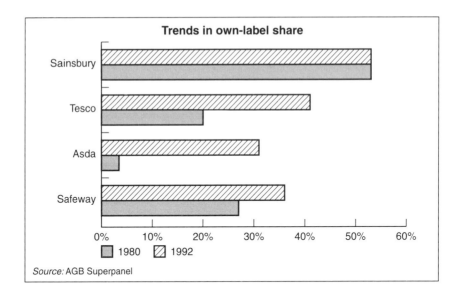

Figure 1.18

	Private label					
	1986	1987	1988	1989	1990	1991
16 weeks ending December	28.7%	29.4%	29.4%	29.9%	31.5%	31.4%

Private Label share by Value at December 1991

Canned foods	27.0%
Frozen foods	42.4%
Packet foods	23.5%
Dairy products	41.0%
Bakery products	35.0%
Sauces & ketchups	27.2%
Beverages	35.0%
Pet foods	8.0%
Toiletries	21.9%
Dentifrice	16.2%
Toilet soap	22.1%
Cleaners	22.8%
Paper goods	43.6%

Source: AGB Superpanel

Figure 1.19

Fortunately for some the penetration of own-label is far lower in certain product categories than in others (Figure 1.19).

Technology, limited manufacturing capacity and strong branding are the main barriers to own-label entry.

Marketing implications for manufacturers

As a result of these pressures there has been an enormous escalation in the cost of marketing for many FMCG companies, including above and below the line consumer marketing expenditure. Promotional expenditure, including price cuts, extra value offers and the cost of marketing to the trade have become particularly debilitating. The escalation in trade discounts, particularly to the major multiples, has maintained constant pressure on brands and manufacturer margins.

For many, this element of marketing expenditure has expanded year-by-year as a percentage of sales, forcing manufacturers either to put up prices to recover the extra costs, or to offer lower returns to their shareholders. In many cases the latter option has been the only possibility.

The food industry has been caught in a bind between increasingly powerful retailers, forcing up the cost of marketing to the trade, and consumers who are more value conscious because of the recession and declining levels of disposable income. Intense price competition, particularly from retailer own-label products, means that it often isn't possible to cover cost increases with equivalent price increases.

As a result, the control of marketing costs, as opposed to other environmental factors, has become a major strategic issue for all FMCG companies. In the US these pressures have led to much speculation about the 'death of the brand' as price premiums have been squeezed inexorably. To the over-stressed manufacturing executive it seems that he is caught in a spiral of competing on price then cutting back on marketing expenditure in an endlessly vicious circle.

Cold comfort farm

On the other hand branded manufacturers may take some cold comfort from the fact that the retailer stranglehold has reduced the number of viable brands on the shelves. In the past, many sectors might include three, four, or even more, brands. Now that many retailers manage categories more actively and aggressively it is unlikely there will be more than one main brand, a discounted 'fighting' brand and an own-label in any given sector.

The quality of the relationships between retailers and their suppliers also varies, some being much better partners than others. M&S, for example, is noted for the long-term partnerships it forges with suppliers. However, beware the manufacturer who gets too dependent on a single retailer. Should the chosen brands rejoice in the security and market share afforded by such an intimate relationship with the retailer, or cringe from the mortal embrace?

Will the pattern of the 1980s be reinforced in the new European market or will competition from abroad loosen the chains? Aldi, Netto and the discount clubs are nibbling at the edges of the retail market. The current adverse publicity and threats of a reference to the Office of Fair Trading may also suggest that the power of the large UK chains may be waning. However, it would be foolhardy to predict the early demise of such a powerful group or to assume that the concentration of retailing power in the UK will be rapidly reversed.

THE FUTURE OF THE BRAND

The announcement by Philip Morris in the spring of 1993 that it would significantly discount the price of its Marlboro brand in the US to counteract competitive threats, particularly from the own-label market, sent shock waves through the stockmarkets, with branded goods stocks experiencing significant mark downs. Similar actions by Procter & Gamble and other major manufacturers jangled nerves still further.

As a result, analysts have had a field day prognosticating about the future of brands. But just as reports of G K Chesterton's death were 'greatly exaggerated' the death of the brand is not imminent. However, the death of individual brands may be, if manufacturers are unable to balance the demands of the consumer, distributor and retailer, while retaining sufficient margins to build and maintain their brands and make a decent profit.

DEVELOPMENT OF NEW SALES CHANNELS

The retail environment is constantly changing and adapting. Superstores, discounters, warehouses, and convenience concepts are all being developed and altered to fit changing tastes. However, none of these concepts breaks the traditional need for the consumer to visit a store. In the next decade, as leisure time becomes more important, and as interactive phone, video and computer systems develop, there could be a major growth in new ways of marketing to the individual consumer.

Network marketing

Network marketing, with one-to-one selling in the home, has a particularly undesirable image at present. Some hardsell organisations have given the user-friendly concept – pioneered by Avon and Tupperware – a pushy, unpleasant reputation. But the individual demands of the future consumer, and the search for routes around conventional distribution channels, to profitable consumer niches, could result in a total reappraisal of this sales channel.

Teleshopping

As the price, reliability and communications quality of systems reduces, as cable penetration in the home increases, and as distribution logistics develop, the idea of interactive, screen-based shopping, with direct delivery of purchases to the home, comes closer to reality. Some retailers are already including this in their service for certain items.

Direct marketing

First Direct and The Co-operative Bank's 'armchair banking' services demonstrate the latent demand for 24-hour direct banking service to cut out time-wasting trips to the High Street. More convenient and cheaper to use, this style of marketing has been avidly adopted by other financial services operations, notably Royal Bank Of Scotland's Direct Line insurance service, which has made millions of customers and the operation's founder, Peter Wood, particularly happy. All the major composite insurers are rushing into the breech and are moving away from costly individual broker-based distribution systems, at least for simple, low value policies.

MEDIA FRAGMENTATION

Two simple statistics illustrate the rate of change in the media marketplace. Firstly, in 1980, there were only 29 commercial TV channels in Europe; by 1993 there were 114 and the number increases by the day. The increase in the number of channels offered by BSkyB demonstrates the speed of change. A whole new package of channels was launched in October 1993 and its £1.8 billion investment is finally returning a profit month-on-month. Secondly, in 1988, only 3,000 hours of TV fiction programming were produced in Europe, yet according to the Nomura Research Institute 250,000 hours were screened on all channels in 1993.

Against this background, the pressure for programmers and programming authorities to accept sponsorship is increasing. In the UK TV market the value of sponsorship is currently only £15 million, but Granada published a booklet on the subject suggesting that '. . . *the opportunity to move far beyond commercial breaks, allowing the advertising message to be an integral part of the television programmes themselves, has arrived.'* This kind of opinion does not go down well with the ITC, which has tried to restrict the growth of editorial involvement by TV sponsors. However, in the current environment it seems like Canute trying to hold back the tide. As long as sponsorship is done within effective guidelines it is hard not to see it becoming a part of everyday viewing.

There is no doubt viewing patterns are changing. In the UK 86 per cent of homes currently receive only four terrestrial TV channels, with 2 per cent receiving cable and 12 per cent satellite. The 14 per cent of homes receiving cable or satellite now have over 20 channels available to them. In the 1980s the growth of cable TV in the US increased the number of channels available to the average American household from single figures to over 30. This trend will be repeated in the UK. It is predicted that by the year 2000, 25 per cent of UK homes will have cable TV and 20 per cent will have satellite, and that they will be able to receive at least 30 channels. A fifth terrestrial channel is also likely to be launched. The number of homes with multi-channel capability will rise from 14 per cent to over 45 per cent in just seven years.

The share of audience that the different channels attract will admittedly depend more on the quality of programming than simply on the technology. Even in the US where cable has been around for ten years the network stations still achieve 60 per cent of audience share in prime-time and 50 per cent in non-prime time. In the UK the ITV companies have £500 million to spend on new programming and the BBC has huge reserves of talent to keep its programme saliency. There will be fragmentation but it will not be driven entirely by technology.

However, the technology becomes more and more awesome. The dramatic increase in potential viewing capability described so far ignores the effect of digital TV technology, which will allow ten times as many signals to be broadcast on the same bandwidth. So instead of receiving 30 channels the average multi-channel home could be receiving 300 channels in the year 2000. These will be used to broadcast a much wider range of specialist programmes, and to have sequential screening of programmes. For example, the same film could start every 10 minutes on six different connected channels, to give greater choice and flexibility to viewers.

In cable homes the interactive capability implicit in fibre optic technology means that there will be two-way communication traffic. Telephony, television and computing are converging, and many homes will soon have fax, computer feeds, voice messaging and entertainment piped into the one terminal. Teleshopping, teleworking, teleconferencing, interactive game shows, direct marketing and market research will soon become everyday features of life. The integration of these services threatens the duopoly in the UK telecommunications business, because one of the features of cable is that it provides an opening for other telecommunications companies to provide basic telephony. British Telecom has already linked up with BSkyB and other defensive moves can be expected.

Meanwhile QVC, the US home-shopping channel, which had sales of £1 billion in 1992, is set to sweep into the UK. The link between Bell Atlantic, one of the US regional telecommunications companies and QVC's parent company will give greater financial muscle to its development outside the US. Shoppers enter their purchases via the screen and in four or five days the goods arrive direct to the home. Macy's in the US has launched a 24-hour home-shopping channel and similar moves can be expected in the UK.

Not only will there be a change in the way we use the TV terminal there will almost certainly be a gradual decline in the mass TV medium, as high quality niche programming develops. There will be a growing need for specialised programming for niche audiences and the opportunity for precisely targeted messages. In the US, TV programme journals now include complex viewing matrices, and as channels proliferate in the UK programme selection will become a science! The key fact will be that small groups of consumers will be able to choose specific programmes to suit their own tastes.

Radio stations, magazines and papers also continue to proliferate as deregulation occurs and as production costs come down. The number of UK commercial radio stations increased from 29 in 1980 to 120 today, the number of UK consumer magazines increased from 1,500 to 2,000 between 1980 and 1992, magloids and regional supplements, all in colour, are increasing the segmentation of the national dailies. By the year 2000 we will be living in a world of selective viewing and reading rather than a world of mass communications. Furthermore, the decline of media inflation, associated with the proliferation of media, will strengthen clients' bargaining positions.

For the moment network television remains the single most effective consumer medium – but the declining network audience and the continued fragmentation of all media mean that other, more targeted, media will need to be rigorously assessed. At present (BARB) identifies 300 target audience subgroups, yet airtime is sold against only eight broad categories. This will change.

The need to buy media more intelligently and efficiently can only get greater. The need for media to be integrated in brand planning and the full range of communications, including sponsorship, PR and direct marketing media can only increase.

DEPENDENCE ON MARKETING SUCCESS

Many publicly quoted companies set profit improvement targets in the 5 to
10 per cent per annum range. For example, one major US corporation has
the simple but effective profit improvement principle of 'ten on ten', or a ten
per cent increase in net pre-tax profit on a ten percent increase in income,
year-on-year. This is a policy which it has achieved successfully for over 30
years. To meet targets of this kind in today's tough markets three options
present themselves:

- becoming the lowest cost producer
- acquisitive growth
- organic growth.

Becoming the lowest cost producer

By reducing costs and becoming the lowest cost producer. Many companies
have eliminated management layers and rationalised production facilities to
achieve this objective.

In Europe, for example, economies of scale in production and distribution
are increasingly being exploited as the single market becomes more of a
reality. If the US market, with 250 million people, can be efficiently served
by two or three plants it is rapidly becoming clear that Europe, with 350 million people, does not need one plant in each of its 12 member states. Plants
and companies are closing or merging as this lesson sinks in.

However, major reductions in cost are most easily achieved initially and
thereafter become primarily a matter of care and maintenance. There is, of
course, a limit to the reduction of costs beyond which performance, quality
and profitability become seriously affected.

Acquisitive growth

Alternatively, companies may grow through acquisition, either to increase
market share or to expand into new geographical or product areas. But,
despite a prolonged recession in the UK, and more recently in Continental
Europe, the cost of acquisitions remains high. Packaged goods companies,
in particular, have continued to command prices of up to 20 times earnings,
and the level of many stockmarkets remains historically high.

Organic growth

Finally, profit growth can be achieved by market share and margin gain,
domestically and internationally, through organic growth in traditional sectors, or through the development of new products and markets.

It is clear that the first two strategic options, while attractive in the short-run, rapidly reach the point of diminishing returns. As cost savings are squeezed out of the system and as acquisition opportunities decrease, for cost and rationalisation reasons, the only viable option remaining is to achieve real growth through new marketing initiatives and new marketing activity. It is this which puts marketing at the top of the corporate agenda as companies begin to anticipate a post-recessionary environment.

SHORT- AND LONG-TERM SIGNIFICANCE OF MARKETING FINANCE

In the current economic environment, established consumer markets are not generally in growth and costs are being driven out of many businesses by efficiency drives at the factory level. As a result there is more of a 'level playing field' than there ever has been in the past. The question is, how does a company grow against its competitors when they have also reduced costs and the total market is unlikely to grow in response to tactical initiatives? This is a question that many marketing oriented companies are asking themselves as they grapple with the problem of growth in static markets.

Corporate growth is unlikely to come from increased pricing, because no brand is strong enough to overcome a long-term disparity in price for parity technology. In developing consumer markets, opportunities are significant, but the first player into the market could either seize an unassailable lead or fall flat on its face.

If these problems are to be resolved, marketeers have got to use marketing innovation to create added value and successful market entry strategies. Active new product development is one way added value can be created to keep one step ahead of the competition. However, decreasing product development cycles mean that the speed with which low-cost competitors come into the market is constantly increasing. Another route is the presentation of existing products to consumers in more appealing and relevant ways.

In both contexts, innovative marketing communications will be crucial to creating and maintaining the next generation of brands. A multitude of marketing decisions face companies – all of which are costly and risky. A blunderbuss will not work any more and companies will have to develop their marksmanship.

At the heart of all these decisions and processes lies the issue of marketing finance. Balancing viable options demands a sophisticated financial response. In an increasingly demanding and competitive marketing environment, an understanding of key financial trends and developments could be crucial in keeping one step ahead of the competition.

Bibliography

'British Lifestyles' 1992, MINTEL Special Report

Planning for Social Change 92-93, The Henley Centre

The Demographic Revolution, Jane McLoughlin, Faber and Faber Limited, 1991, ISBN 0 571 16114 6

The Grocery Trade, The Institute of Grocery Distribution, 1992

Retailing, Verdict Research Limited, 1995

'Focus on Own Label', *The Grocer magazine*, May 1993

WPP Group PLC Annual Report and Accounts 1992.

2

IT'S A PEOPLE BUSINESS

'The wind and the waves are always on the side of the ablest navigators'
Edward Gibbon

INTRODUCTION

Sailing demands skill not brute force, teamwork not egotism, shared experience not individual knowledge. Companies are no different, and this is gradually being accepted and acted upon. The ablest sailors are not born with the ability to navigate, they learn their skills by working together.

If companies are to achieve everything which is expected of them in the nineties one of the key questions will be, 'How well do all people in the organisation work together?' The days of discrete functional disciplines, operating separately from one another, are over. Functional disciplines need to share their skills, and understand one another much better than they have done in the past. Corporate re-engineering and the need for more cost-efficient staffing, together with the integration of systems, are all breaking down functional barriers. The nineteenth-century hierarchical paradigms of management and departmental responsibility increasingly seem like quaint anachronisms.

Against this background it is likely that the concept of the *Learning Organisation* will proliferate. Managers will have to become coaches and motivators rather than authoritarians or doers. They will also need to practise the concept of *Empowerment*. Successful companies will have to let individual staff use their initiative, to achieve corporate goals within 'flatter' management structures.

At the same time an equally important question will be, 'How well equipped are the people involved to cope with the specific functional challenges which lie ahead?' Euripides' comment that 'the same man cannot be skilled in everything; each has his special excellence' has never been more true; while managers will work more closely together it is unrealistic to expect everyone to be equally good at all tasks. In fact, as the world becomes more technically demanding and complex it is likely that there will be more of a demand for specialist skills. For example, the traditional route into marketing, from sales, is gradually being replaced as both sales and marketing disciplines become more professional and separable. Recognising this, the UK Institute of Marketing took a deliberately academic turn in 1982, gained a Royal Charter in 1989, and now has 25,000 full-time members and 30,000 students. It repositioned itself away from an historical association with the sales function, to put itself in the mainstream of modern marketing. Meanwhile the UK Institute of Sales Management has developed its own quite separate constituency and skill base. Many marketing personnel now have specific vocational qualifications, and within the marketing discipline specialist skill-sets are fragmenting and developing; research, analysis, new product development, international, sector specific, general management.

However, as specialism proliferates there will be a growing need for individual managers to share common goals, understand other disciplines and to work effectively together. Specialism will pull in one direction, teamwork the other. Organisations which do not generate team spirit will never meet the corporate challenge of the 1990s.

In this spirit of co-operation and teamworking the need for organisations to adopt a *marketing culture* has become more important. Rather than simply having effective marketing people, running technically competent marketing departments, all personnel must share the same marketing vision. However, this principle is equally true in other areas of corporate activity. There will need to be a *finance culture*, an *innovation culture* and an *information technology culture* in many companies, as mutual respect for the aims, obectives and contributions of different disciplines increases. Marketing people may not become accountants, research technologists or IT boffins but they will need to embrace their concerns. They will need to speak the same language and strive for the same vision, and in far-sighted companies it is already happening.

The importance of personnel issues to marketing finance

It is clear that there is a huge change process in motion in terms of corporate structures and working methods. The selection, development and promotion of the right people is crucial to how well this process will work. They say, 'you can't teach old dogs new tricks' but some learn better than others, and as 'new dogs' arrive they need to be taught the right habits.

What many forget is that, in most companies, personnel is the most expensive resource, in both direct terms and in terms of what it can do for good or evil, depending on how well it is managed. It is therefore vital in a review of marketing finance to consider the question of human resources.

A growing management consensus

Management recognition of the changes taking place in the business world, and their impact on organisational and human resource strategies, is reflected in the results of a recent British Institute of Management Survey, which revealed the following percentages of respondents either strongly agreeing or agreeing with the following statements:

Human resource is a critical sucess factor	100%
Environmental and social pressures are increasing	98%
Customers are becoming more demanding	97%
Information can be processed and transferred more quickly	93%
The rate of change is speeding up	92%
More markets are becoming global	91%
Markets are becoming more open and competitive	87%
There is greater sensitivity to demographic trends	83%

There was also substantial agreement among respondents about how their organisations should adapt to meet these trends. The percentage of respondents who were undertaking organisational changes to meet the new challenges was remarkably high. Organisational changes were being undertaken by the following percentages:

Creating a slimmer and flatter organisation	88%
More work is being undertaken in teams	79%
Creating a more responsive network organisation	78%
Functions are becoming more interdependent	71%
Procedures and permanency are giving way to flexibility and temporary arrangements	67%
Organisations are becoming more interdependent	55%

(Material reproduced by kind permission of British Institute of Management)

Flattening the pyramid: shattering the monolith

The commonest trend in many organisations is the creation of management structures like flat pyramids with whole layers of management being either culled or redeployed. In other instances, the monolithic corporations of the past are becoming independent families of companies. As with IBM interrelated webs of subsidiaries, joint ventures, franchises and loose associations are becoming more and more popular. The process which has seen the world's great empires shatter into a myriad of independent states, bound together in commonwealths and groups of mutual interest, now has a corporate parallel. Both cost and efficiency gains will continue this trend.

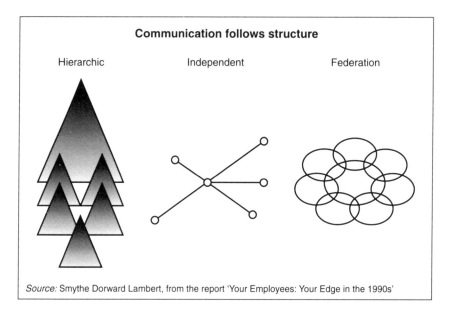

Figure 2.1

DEVELOPING PRECIOUS HUMAN RESOURCES

Unfortunately, not all companies have heard the message that change is on the way, or that flexibility is a prerequisite of future success. Many are not moving at a fast enough pace. In practice, there remain a number of structural and managerial problems to be resolved, before the full benefits of cross-functional cultures can be achieved in many organisations.

Taking human resource management seriously

To begin with, many organisations have yet to fully recognise that one of their most important assets is actually the talents of the people who work for them, rather than their fixed plant and tangible assets. This is a constant refrain of Tom Peters' *Liberation Management*, in which he argues that talented people, and the way they are set free to operate within corporate structures, will be one of the most significant management issues of the 1990s. Not only traditional *people* businesses, like management consultancy, but all types of business, will find that personnel motivation and imagination will be critical success factors.

Philip Sadler and Keith Milmer of the Ashridge management centre recently put forward a similar argument in their report, 'The Talent Intensive Organisation – Optimising your company's human resource strategies'.

Their report incorporated the results of detailed research among 50 organisations, primarily concentrated in the computer, electronics, high technology, software, financial services and pharmaceuticals sectors. They identified ten general human resource issues facing management. In summary these are as follows:

- defining a clear sense of corporate mission
- developing a flexible organisational framework
- nurturing personnel to respect and use each other's talents
- identifying required future skill-sets
- creating a pool of talented staff
- identifying people with high potential for the future
- building loyalty and commitment in non-financial ways
- setting clear objectives and ensuring they are achieved
- motivating and developing talented people
- evaluating human resource strategies in both non-financial and financial terms.

Outstandingly successful companies already owe much of their success to the seriousness with which they take these issues, looking at human resource management as a fundamental rather than as a cosmetic management exercise.

Issues specific to the marketing function

In a more parochial marketing context major personnel issues have affected, and continue to affect, the success of many organisations. These include:

The historical background of those entering the marketing function

The fact that many in marketing come from a sales background has often led to the accusation that marketing people think too short-term, and too much about executional results and sales figures, rather than long-term marketing strategies.

The analytical skills of many in marketing management

Partly because more emphasis has been placed on tangible campaigns, and target achievement, rather than on analysis of long-term trends and opportunities, financial and market analysis has been a traditional weak spot.

For example, Paul Baker, of the econometric modelling firm OHAL, which specialises in marketing models, admits that historically many of its customers either suppressed or ignored financial analysis, to concentrate on simple measures like market share and sales. In his words,

> *'Where costing and profitability data were input to marketing models they often did not take account of varying cost structures at different levels of demand. Many users simply ignored them.'*

The habit does persist but the situation is rapidly changing as marketing and finance teams work more closely together.

The adequacy of training given to marketing management

By contrast with many professions, the level of training across industry has always been poor, and this applies equally to marketing. However, the Institute of Marketing and various academic bodies are now actively attempting to redress the balance. The Government's DTI Enterprise Initiative and Investors in People programmes have also gone a long way to help the situation by raising awareness of marketing and training requirements.

The development of individuals with multidisciplinary skills

Unlike many Japanese firms, the concept of the company person moving from department to department, to learn more about all aspects of the business, has not been a common feature of UK corporate life. In fact, in the 'ghetto' world of many organisations, functional specialists often have more in common with peer groups outside the company than within it. This has tended to reinforce internal barriers, because the points of career reference and group loyalty are outside rather than inside the company.

Gradually this is changing as multidisciplinary teams, cross-functional secondments and interdepartmental promotions become more common. Corporate 'apartheid' by function is gradually giving way to a more multi-cultural ethos. This process is also being reinforced by cross-functional academic training fostered by bodies like the Chartered Institute of Management Accountants, which has promoted the concept of the marketing accountant.

The creation of multidisciplinary teams within organisations

It is now common in a growing number of companies for management accountants to be specifically attached to product groups or marketing departments. Understanding flows in both directions, facilitating both the finance and marketing processes.

Whitbread is a good example of this in action, and other organisations are adopting the idea. However, a large number of companies still retain rigid functional separation between departments.

The promotion of a marketing culture and understanding throughout organisations

Internal communications are crucial to this but internal communication and shared values remain inadequate in many firms. Many companies have yet to recognise or to act upon best management practice to resolve some of these issues.

At the leading edge of management practice things are changing fast but many organisations continue to operate much as they ever have. Whether they can be galvanised into action by emerging opportunities is open to question. In the words of Mike Hammer, the American management pundit, '. . . *an optimist is a pessimist with no job experience.*' An external threat is a much more potent stimulus than an external opportunity, and bitter experience suggests that radical change only seems to happen in times of crisis.

Will crisis be necessary before the average company takes action to shape itself for the new world of competition? Will crisis be necessary to change fundamental attitudes towards one of the most important corporate assets – the people who work in and make up the company? It may well be, but, if it persuades managers to invest in talent, it will have been a crisis worth suffering.

THE TALENT INTENSIVE ORGANISATION

In their report, Sadler and Milmer make the point that traditional management theorists like Frederick Winslow Taylor and Michael Porter underestimated the importance of individual talent to corporate success and profit, tending to look at management in a mechanistic way. For example, they point out that in the 500 pages of *Competitive Strategy* Michael Porter only devotes one page to human resource management. People are implicitly considered '*a factor of production*' rather than an essential ingredient of success.

They argue that many organisations already depend on identifying, nurturing and retaining talented people. However, the mind-set of senior management, who often feel threatened by this definition of competitive advantage, frequently stands in the way of progress. Strategies for managing talent must not be peripheral to business strategy but must become a central focus of it. Only when the very highest levels of management recognise this will organisations take full advantage of the benefits talented people can offer to their corporate development.

One of the problems for many managers is giving a tangible expression to the value of individuals within organisations. Paying staff the 'going rate' and checking the 'going rate' in the market, by reference to compensation consultancies, is one crude way of doing this, although very often it is only when individuals become consultants that organisations truly appreciate the marginal value they are prepared to pay for specific talents. As the practice of employing consultants becomes more prevalent the value of individuals to their employers will come more starkly into relief. For there is no doubt that *quasi-employment* will boom in the nineties.

The Shamrock Theory

Charles Handy in his book *The Age of Unreason*, (Business Books, 1991), has suggested the *shamrock* to best illustrate the corporation of the future; the first leaf representing a small core of key staff, the second representing a pool of regular subcontractors and the third, a moving pageant of free-lancers, consultants and temporary workers. The advent of reliable telecommunications and home-based computing are reinforcing this trend, as we approach the era of mass *teleworking*. The shamrock model will almost certainly spread in the 1990s as companies delayer, re-engineer and become more flexible. This will allow managers to acquire a better under-standing of the contribution talented people can make to their companies.

Human asset accounting

Another concept, which gives a tangible expression to the value of individuals within their organisations, is the academic concept of '*human asset accounting*'. It is quite clear that some organisations, with stable staff structures, robust selection, training and development programmes and enlightened personnel policies have a more valuable stock of human assets than those with high staff turnover rates and cheap skate approaches to personnel management. The idea of formal *human asset accounting* is an attractive one, but, like brand valuation, would almost certainly be swamped by arguments about technical definition and subjectivity. The problem is that human assets 'go up and down in the lift' every day and cannot be owned in the conventional sense. Some might argue that in practice this is not true for many Japanese and some paternal western companies. But formally adopting the concept is not likely in the near future.

This is a shame, because it is clear that stockmarkets implicitly value a company's human assets; look at the gyrations in share values when key players come and go. There are also isolated examples of personnel assets being valued in company accounts, most obviously in the case of transfer fees within football club accounts.

However, this particular area of intangible asset accounting is unlikely to feature in company accounts in the near future, other than as Notes to the Accounts, or as a commentary in the chairman's Statement or in the chief executive's Operational Review.

Unfortunately, cynics argue that when a Chairman's Statement suggests that, 'people are our greatest asset' massive redundancies will shortly follow. Many chairmen and CEOs continue to see personnel only as a cost, rather than as an investment for the future. Yet in the next decade *intellectual capital*, and the loyalty and motivation of that capital, will be one of the most significant contributors to corporate success. In the words of Christopher Lorenz of *The Financial Times*,

> *'Any chairman who has the courage and accounting dexterity to find a way of putting "his" people in the balance sheet will certainly be committed to taking them – and their continuing development and learning – as seriously as any of the company's other investments.'*

From 'maintenance' to 'design'

In the past, companies viewed 'personnel' primarily as an administrative, procedural and support activity. The personnel director was often not represented on the board and his department concentrated on such issues as contracts, salaries, personnel files, recruitment, training, union negotiation, welfare, pensions and appraisals – maintenance functions. In many companies the function was a 'cinderella' department, like internal audit and public relations. However, just as corporate governance and corporate communications have risen up the corporate agenda, the human resources debate has now reached the top of it in many companies. For example, *The ICL Way* states that, 'We are no longer mainly selling boxes of computer equipment. We are mainly selling solutions to business problems. If we are to be successful, to excel in all we do, to win rather than merely compete, then the full capabilities of all ICL people must be realised and released into action.' This sentiment will be reflected by many more companies in the years ahead.

Indeed, Merck, the US pharmaceutical giant and one of America's most admired companies, cites its criteria for evaluating operating companies as follows:

- ability to attract, develop and keep talented people
- innovation
- financial soundness
- quality of products
- use of corporate assets
- value as a long-term investment
- environmental responsibility.

In the words of Steven M Darien, Vice President of Merck's Human Health Resources Division, 'In evaluating Merck managers, we pay as much attention to the quality of people we recruit and develop as we do to their contribution to the bottom line'.

Gold collar workers

Sadler and Milmer go on to suggest that as employment philosophy shifts away from labour-intensive to talent-intensive organisations, and as intellect and innovation are put at a premium by more and more companies, the age of the *gold collar worker* will dawn. Rather than blue collar manual labour, or white collar managerial labour, companies will search out and cherish gold collar workers, those exceptional talents who genuinely add value to company performance.

They describe three varieties of gold collar worker; the *solo artists*, the *independent professionals*, and the *organisational people*. Traditionally, talented people have belonged to one of the first two varieties, but as the constraints within traditional organisations are relaxed, and as talented people come to be recognised and rewarded, they will feel more at home within companies.

Organisational structures

Organisational structures for managing talented people can be characterised as:

1 *Flat structures* – which are increasingly displacing traditional hierarchies. These generally appeal more to talented people, who have greater autonomy and decision-making responsibility, at all stages in their careers. They can be perceived to limit promotion but are generally the preferred option.

GE, the consumer white goods and electronics group, is a good example of a company which opted for a flat structure. It operates in markets with a demanding customer base and low-cost international competitors so it could not afford to ossify. To enhance innovation, decision-making and adaptation it drastically reduced management layers, removed group and sector management and created 14 core businesses reporting directly to the CEO. Staff functions were reoriented to add value rather than to merely control. As a result GE is number one or two in all its markets, is an open, fair organisation and the workforce has the motivation to succeed. In the words of Jack Welch, the CEO,

> 'For a large organisation to be effective, it must be simple. For a large organisation to be simple, its people must have self-confidence and intellectual self-assurance. Insecure managers create complexity . . . real leaders don't need clutter.'

2 *Networking structures* – represented by cohesive, autonomous groups which link cross-functional teams to specific market problems or issues. These decentralised units offer task orientation and the stimulus of intellectual peer groups.

British Petroleum Plc is a good example of a strong company buffeted by highly competitive and turbulent markets, the increasing pace of technical innovation and increasing environmental awareness. Over a long period of high profits and corporate success its management structure had become bureaucratic and unwieldy. To resolve these problems, BP reduced management layers, adopted a horizontal project approach and created ad hoc, cross-functional teams. Decision-making became more transparent and information was shared more systematically. Gradual cultural change, and a significant reduction of redundant management processes, have turned BP into a leaner, more responsive and more profitable company.

Management subcultures

Sadler and Milmer also identify three dominant subcultures in many organisations, *managerial, marketing* and *technical/professional*. They summarise the strengths and weaknesses of the three as follows:

Subculture	Strengths	Weaknesses
Managerial	1 Clear strategic direction	1 Inadequate understanding of core technology
	2 Focus on the bottom line	2 Slow to innovate
	3 Strong systems and procedures	3 Failure to attract/retain/ motivate top technical/ professional talent
Marketing	1 Focus on the market and the customer	1 Inadequate understanding of core technology
	2 Responsive to changes in demand	2 Failure to attract/retain/ motivate top technical/ professional talent
	3 Responsive to competitor behaviour	3 Sometimes weak financial controls
Technical/ Professional	1 Leadership in technical innovation	1 Lack of clear business strategy
	2 Strongly motivated technical/ professional employees	2 Failure to focus on market/customer needs
		3 Failure to focus on the bottom line
		4 Often poor man management

In the words of Sadler and Milmer, 'Each has strengths and weaknesses. In the talent intensive organisations studied there was a tendency for one subculture to dominate the others. In several cases there were deliberate attempts, past or present, to shift the dominant culture, usually from a scientific/technological one to a managerial or marketing one. The ideal would appear to be the development of a balanced culture in which all three subcultures can work in a truly complementary way.' For this process to work effectively the right people need to be recruited and trained throughout the organisation.

TRADITIONAL ROUTES INTO MARKETING

Historically, individuals have been chosen for what Professor Peter Doyle, Marketing Professor at Warwick University, describes as their 'right brain' capabilities; their creativity and flair. What is often understated is the 'left brain' characteristics of analysis and numerical ability. It also seems to be widely accepted that there is a promotional escalator which marketing managers step onto and don't get off until they reach marketing director. Most have an expectation that it will be a fast and fairly short escalator.

The problems created by these norms are that many marketing people have historically been excellent at the creative and executional aspects of marketing management but often shy away from the analytical or complex internal aspects of the task. There has conventionally been an aversion amongst marketing managers to the technical complexities of IT, production technology and the intricacies of finance.

As marketing management and direction becomes more central to the success of many organisations and as the need for greater integration with the rest of the business gathers pace there is an obvious danger that the lack of all-round individuals will stultify the process.

In the most professional marketing organisations, traditionally in the FMCG environment, like Procter & Gamble, Unilever and Mars, there is a tradition of recruiting and developing all-round skills. But many other organisations have lagged behind the leaders.

IDEAL CANDIDATES FOR THE MARKETING SUBCULTURE

There are many clichés about the background of sales and marketing managers, and the relationship between the sales and marketing functions.

One cliché is that recruits to the marketing function always come from the sales function. After a couple of years on the road as sales reps, the brighter, pushier sales people wind up in head office co-ordinating central functions, from analysis, market research, and new product development through to campaign planning and execution. Technical skills are learned on the job leaving holes in the knowledge of some marketing managers. The cynical sales team remembers the marketing some as a junior sales rep and mutual respect deteriorates. To get promotion the marketing manager moves on and the cycle begins again.

A variant on this is that successful salesmen, with well-organised zones, high commissions and generous perks, don't want to become bureaucrats at head office. The marketing recruits are therefore the less experienced and less successful sales people with a bent for intellectualising and organising. Trench warfare sets in between those 'who know how things really work on the ground' and the 'naive marketing prats at head office'. How many marketing managers have experienced the ignominy of having their ideas pilloried at the annual sales conference, before the frontline veterans retire to the bar?

Ignoring the clichés it is fair to say that the relationship between sales and marketing is often not a harmonious one. But as marketing people increasingly come from different backgrounds, and with more robust academic training, the situation is changing. The tendency to recruit more experienced people as brand managers, to pay them better, to give them more responsibility and to keep them for longer have all contributed to the change. Professional respect is increasing.

Where are they coming from? Some from MBA courses, many from specific marketing degree courses, others from market research, finance and technical backgrounds. One of the notable features of this new breed of marketing management is its *analytical skills* and *numeracy*, abilities which were often lacking in a previous generation of marketing people. The new recruits are also now in a position to develop such skills more thoroughly on the job, and to qualify for a chartered profession. These facts will become more and more important as marketing and finance people work hand in hand.

Rivalry and disdain are being exchanged for co-operation and respect. At the heart of this process is the recognition of technical competence and experience, together with the selection of the right people. Nowadays, the random selection methods adopted in the past are rapidly being replaced by sophisticated selection methods. Selection is no longer a lottery, it's a science.

OCCUPATIONAL PSYCHOLOGY

The leading exponents of the new science of selection and career development are Saville & Holdsworth, market leaders in the business of *'occupational psychology'*. Saville & Holdsworth is 'a world leader in the objective selection, assessment and development of people at work.' It is *'committed to helping organisations achieve higher productivity, by effectively matching people to jobs through fair, relevant and objective methods.'* Since it was formed in 1977, SHL has devised over 200 tests and worked for over 2,000 blue-chip companies. It currently has 50 occupational psychologists and human resource professionals in the field. A 1991 British market research bureau survey showed that 74 per cent of major UK companies now use occupational tests or personality questionnaires; a significant increase over the preceding decade. The occupational psychology business is booming and demand is growing exponentially.

The work that SHL does breaks into four distinct areas:

- diagnosis
- assessment
- development
- monitoring.

Diagnosis

- *Job analysis* – The fundamental prerequisite of understanding job demands.
- *Job evaluation* – Ensuring fairness and objectivity in job relativities for setting remuneration policies.
- *Attitude surveys* – Designing rigorous surveys of employee attitudes and behaviour, to facilitate organisational interventions.
- *Corporate culture questionnaires* – Measuring employee and management perceptions of the organisation's culture through a standardised questionnaire.

Assessment

- *Design of overall assessment procedures* – Combining fairness and objectivity with cost effectiveness in the design of any assessment procedure.
- *Test construction* – Creating tailored tests of maximum relevance to an organisation.
- *Application forms* – Designing valid application procedures that are time-efficient and boost an organisation's image.
- *Assessment centres* – Designing multiple assessment procedures with an emphasis on job simulations of high quality.

- *Individual assessment services* – Professional and managerial assessment on an individual basis.
- *Competence profiling* – Offering a reliable procedure for defining an individual's competence strengths and limitations, for any model.

Development

- *Management and personal development programmes* – Providing guidance on achieving the right balance of management and personal development action.
- *Development centres* – Developing assessment procedures at 'state-of-the-art' level for tailored staff development action.
- *Team building* – Analysing teams and developing courses of action to maximise team performance.
- *Performance appraisal* – Bringing fairness, objectivity and reliability into one of the most difficult assessment areas.

Monitoring

- *Validation studies* – Ensuring that assessment is working and delivering tangible productivity gains.
- *Equal opportunities* – Ensuring that all actions taken on the assessment or development of potential or current staff are relevant, objective and, above all, fair.
- *Attitude surveys* – Checking the outcome of interventions

Within this extensive menu of human resource management techniques the most important item for many companies is selection of the right people for the job. Of course, to some the idea of objective job matching is a threatening and expensive waste of time. They argue that it's all just mumbo jumbo, and that, like Scientology, its practitioners never let go. Selection is only the first stage in a process which the *'experts'* argue should occur *'from cradle to grave'*, as employees progress through the ranks.

In the case of SHL the process begins with a detailed job analysis and a *Work Profiling System – WPS*, followed by a variety of *psychometric* tests which gauge a person's suitability for a specific job, within a specific organisation. *Occupational Personality Questionnaires – OPQs* which are used to profile individual capabilities.

Within this process SHL consider 'Concept Model Personality Dimensions' – in *relationships with people,* is the subject assertive, gregarious, empathetic; in *thinking style,* is the person structured or abstract; in terms of *feelings and emotions,* is the individual anxious, controlled, energetic.

The OPQ methodology looks at *leadership styles* – directive, delegative, participative, consultative, negotiative; and at *subordinate styles* – receptive, self reliant, collaborative, informative, reciprocating. Above all the OPQ technique considers what *team role* an individual is likely to adopt. See the example below.

Team type	Attributes
Co-ordinator	Sets the team goals and defines roles. Co-ordinate team efforts and leads by eliciting respect
Shaper	The task leader who brings drive to the team. Makes things happen but may be thought abrasive
Plant	Imaginative, intelligent and the team's source of original ideas. Concerned with fundamentals
Monitor-Evaluator	Offers measured, dispassionate critical analysis. Keeps team from pursuing misguided objectives
Resource Investigator	Salesman, diplomat, resource seeker. Good improviser with many external contacts. May be easily diverted from task in hand
Completer	Worries about problems. Personally checks details. Intolerant of the casual and slapdash. Sees projects through
Team worker	Promotes team harmony. Good listener who builds on the ideas of others. Likeable and unassertive
Implementer	Turns decisions and strategies into manageable tasks. Brings logical, methodical pursuit of objective to the team

In balancing cross-functional teams this type of *psychometric* analysis demonstrates that companies need not only a mix of functional specialists. They also a mix of personality profiles if projects are to succeed.

In addition to personality profiling for job-matching SHL has a whole range of specific skill assessments, validation reviews and development techniques which can be brought into play. Tests are available for assessing the verbal, numerical, clerical, spatial, diagrammatic, mechanical and interest dimensions of individual employees. Undertaking these occupational psychology exercises is not cheap or simple. It involves total commitment from the top down, together with significant investment of time and money. Is it worth it?

To the sceptical and unconvinced manager working in a hard-pressed, competitive business it can seem like the band playing as the *Titanic* goes down. But SHL confounds its critics by pointing to numerous financial and performance indicators of how successful its techniques are. For example, one insurance company experienced an 11 per cent uplift in sales among those individuals selected with SHL involvement. A catering company cut early management wastage in half by using SHL 'psychometric' selection tests. A retailer improved individual store 'bottom-lines' by introducing a manager 'assessment centre'. Companies in these fields are not generally known for spending money without a clear return.

OPQ® is a registered trademark of Saville and Holdsworth Ltd.

COMPETENCY TESTING

At the heart of *occupational psychology* is the concept of testing individual 'competency' for specific tasks. What does *competency* actually mean?

In *Competence at Work*, Lyle and Signe Spencer define a 'competency' as an *underlying characteristic* of an individual that is *causally related* to *criterion-referenced effective and/or superior performance* in a job or situation.

By 'underlying characteristic' they mean a fairly deep and enduring part of a person's personality which allows prediction of behaviour in a wide variety of situations and tasks. By 'causally related' they mean that the competency causes or predicts behaviour and performance. By 'criterion-referenced' they mean something which can be measured against a specific criterion or standard.

They identify five types of competency characteristics:

- motives – what directs the individual?
- physical traits – what physical characteristics and consistent responses?
- self concepts – what attitudes, values and self image?
- knowledge – what information in specific areas?
- skills – what abilities with specific tasks?

They identify six steps in designing competency tests:

- define performance effectiveness criteria
- identify a criterion sample
- collect data
- analyse data and develop a competency model
- validate the competency model
- prepare application of the competency model.

In categorising available 'competencies' by which individuals can be judged the Spencers identify three to six *clusters* of distinguishable competencies. Each 'cluster' incorporates two to five individual 'competencies'. Each 'competency' then incorporates three to six *behavioural indicators*. The so called 'dictionary of competencies' apparently holds 350 generic behavioural indicators, by which individuals can be profiled. It's hard to imagine quite how complex *competency profiling* can be; it seems more like the search for DNA than interviewing candidates.

The Spencers go further by providing some generic *Competency Models* for different functions, based on a wide range of detailed empirical studies.

Apparently, 'Superior managers of all types and levels share a general profile of competencies. Managers of all types are also more like each other than they are like the individual contributors they manage.' As a result the analysis produces a generic profile which 'fits all managerial jobs reasonably well but, none precisely.' The models incorporate weightings for the relevant competencies based on empirical evidence. *Weight* refers to the relative frequency with which each competency distinguishes superior from average performers. For example, the generic model for sales looks like this:

Competency model for sales people

Competency	Weight
Impact and Influence	10
Achievement Orientation	5
Initiative	5
Interpersonal Understanding	3
Customer Service Orientation	3
Self Confidence	3
Relationship Building	2
Analytical Thinking	2
Conceptual Thinking	2
Information Seeking	2
Organisational Awareness	2

Model assumes Technical Expertise

By contrast the generic model for managers looks like this:

Competency model for managers

Competency	Weight
Impact and Influence	6
Achievement Orientation	6
Teamwork and Co-operation	4
Analytical Thinking	4
Initiative	4
Developing Others	3
Self Confidence	2
Directiveness/Assertiveness	2
Information Seeking	2
Team Leadership	2
Conceptual Thinking	2

Model assumes Organisational Awareness, Relationship Building, Technical Expertise and Specialised Knowledge.

The Spencers describe the skill-set for sales managers, pointing out that because their people represent their means of production they are heavily focused on people skills. Developing others, teamwork and co-operation all feature strongly, as does the helping and service cluster including, interpersonal understanding and customer service orientation. Sadly, 'Cognitive competencies are a much smaller portion of the distinguishing characteristics of sales managers than of most other managers.' Oh dear!

But while the Spencers' understated critique may have dented the average sales manager's ego they also have a few choice words for marketing managers, who apparently tend to function, '. . . more like individual contributors than like most managers . . . focusing more on pace setting for a small team than on leading and coaching their people.

'Although all these positions have titles of manager and have subordinates, the focus of the job seems to be more on the activities and functions of marketing than on the management of the subordinates.'

John Murphy, the Chairman of Interbrand, who has spent a lifetime consulting to FMCG companies, is more direct,

> *'The concept of the brand manager in most companies is that the manager isn't managing anything. The brand manager is merely a link between the company and the ad agency. A manager in this country is somebody who has been out of university for two or three years, joined the company as a trainee, did a couple of years repping, selling sanitary towels in Aberystwyth, and was considered to be quite bright and lively and was brought in and put in charge of a brand and given no data. He was given no seniority and no real ability to make decisions and in most companies he just ended up as a link person, not really managing a brand at all and in no way accountable for the financial performance of the brand. I've nothing against brand managers, I just think the brand management function should be doing a totally different and much more senior job than it is currently doing in this country. I think we need a fundamental reappraisal of the role of brand management in this country. It's happening in a few companies now, where the brand managers are being seen in a more senior and more potent role. But there is still a long way to go.'*

After politely calling marketing managers a bunch of individualist prima donnas the Spencers redeem themselves by pointing out that marketing managers display,

> *'Stamina and tolerance for stress and long hours; enthusiasm for the product and concern for the product's image; information seeking regarding the activities of competitors; focus on deadlines, sometimes making compromises to meet deadlines; and a concrete, hands-on learning style.'*

So even if they are prima donnas they are hard working, dynamic prima donnas. Perhaps fortunately, the Spencers spare the finance directors' blushes by overlooking the attributes of the typical financial manager.

One of the interesting things about competency testing is that a subject which many of us might consider to be a *soft* discipline is in fact incredibly *hard*. Its practitioners have elevated the subject into a science. Admittedly, some will call it a subjective pseudo-science, but then many dismissed Freud when he first started writing. It seems probable that as organisations become more complex, with cross-functional teams and heavy reliance on fewer but better individuals, in the 'flat' organisations of the future, more and more time and money will be spent on competency testing of this kind.

OBJECTIVE REMUNERATION COMPARISONS

One of the problems with competency testing is that to be accurate it must consider the individual circumstances of the company. The competencies required by a marketing or finance manager in one organisation will differ dramatically from another. I asked Saville & Holdsworth whether they could set down a grid of required competencies for the marketing and finance managers of the future, and how the competency profiles would differ from the past. They declined on the basis that each company is unique, and each company requires specific *work profiling* and *occupational profiling* analysis.

It is easy to understand SHL's point of view, although unfortunately it implies that defining what broad competencies are needed for the future is impossible, other than in very general terms. Also, if the noncomparability argument is actually true the assessment of remuneration patterns across the marketing industry as a whole must also be impossible. Does this make remuneration comparisons meaningless?

Hay Management Consultants remuneration research

Not all organisations share SHL's scepticism about the comparability of competencies. Hay, the world's leading personnel remuneration consultancy, with one of the largest continuous databases of comparative salary information, has developed a *job matching grid* using 40 years of empirical evidence. It brings consistent and comprehensive criteria to bear in establishing the relative worth of different jobs to an organisation.

In all types of organisation Hay has found that the relative value of jobs depends on a number of common elements.

Know how

- The depth and range of practical, technical, specialist, professional and general skills in the job.
- The degree of planning, organising, supervising, co-ordinating and managing involved.
- The extent of human relations skill required.

Problem solving

- The complexity and intensity of problems arising in the job and the nature and scope of the thinking required to solve them. How broad or detailed are the policies, procedures and precedents forming a job's thinking environment?
- The amount of analysis, judgement and innovation involved in analysing situations and making recommendations.

Accountability

- The degree of authority and discretion vested in the job and the answerability for the exercise of it.
- The scale of the areas of activity on which the job is expected to have an impact and the nature of that impact.

According to Hay certain relationships exist between these common elements. Different types of job need different combinations of the three. The shape and composition of jobs differ but the relative value to the organisation can still be explained and expressed through describing jobs in terms of *know how, problem solving* and *accountability*.

The relative worth of a job to one organisation must reflect the value standards of that organisation. Nevertheless, because jobs can be described in a common language, comparisons can be made between the organisations.

The comparison is achieved through using a series of guide charts to permit measurement for 'know how', 'problem solving' and 'accountability'. These charts are grids, each axis of which is a scale of increasing value. Jobs are located on the grid by selecting the definition in the scale which is most appropriate to the post under consideration. The numbering pattern, and hence the score, is then based on the concept of 'just perceivable difference'.

An example of how this grid system works is as follows (see Figures 2.2 and 2.3).

Hay job matching grids

Reference Level	Hay Job Unit Range			Most Typical Job Unit Total
13	228	–	268	252
14	269	–	313	291
15	314	–	370	342
16	371	–	438	406
17	439	–	518	479
18	519	–	613	571
19	614	–	734	677
20	735	–	879	805
21	880	–	1,055	954
22	1,056	–	1,260	1,142
23	1,261	–	1,507	1,372
24	1,508	–	1,800	1,628
25	1,801	–	2,140	1,960

Source: Hay Group

Figure 2.2

THE FUTURE OF CONVENTIONAL DISCIPLINES

The Hay system is a means of making objective comparisons between jobs, within organisations, as a means of ensuring that inter firm and interdepartmental remuneration levels are reasonable. It is effectively independent of specific disciplines, allowing the relative responsibility and importance of jobs in finance, marketing and sales to be objectively compared.

Some comparability will become an increasingly more important ability because, at least among general managers, there will be a fusion of disciplines. At the technical level there will be increasing specialism, often provided by outside specialists, but at the planning, co-ordination and management levels functional tiers will combine.

For example, in many food and drink sectors the concentration of buying points is reducing the need for sales reps and relationship managers. As the ordering, production, distribution and invoicing systems become more integrated and computerised the need for many sales functions will decline. Planning, analysis, pricing, new product development and promotions remain important, but these are primarily marketing responsibilities, and it is quite conceivable that in certain companies sales and marketing functions may be telescoped into one.

A similar elision of management roles can be imagined with finance managers if marketing accountants and numerate marketing analysts develop within companies. The arrival of such multi-skilled managers will inevitably

Job matching grid – marketing jobs

Reference Level/Job Unit Range	TITLE		
	FMCG/Consumer	Marketing Services	Financial Services
22+ 1056+	Marketing Director		Marketing Director
21 880–1055	Marketing Mgr II Marketing Director		Marketing Mgr II
20 735–879	Product Group Manager II or Marketing Mgr I		Marketing Manager I
19 614–734	Product Group Marketing Mgr I	Marketing Services Manager or Buying & Marketing Manager	Direct Marketing Manager
18 519–613	Senior Brand/ Product Mgr	Market Research Mgr Product Development Manager	Product Manager
17 439–518	Brand/Product Manager II Marketing Exec.	Business Development Officer	
16 371–438	Brand/Product Manager I	Promotions Asst. II	Research Asst. II Marketing Officer
15 314–370	Asst. Brand/ Product Mgr	Business Development Assistant	
14 269–313		Marketing Services Officer	
13 228–268		Promotions Asst. I	Research Asst. I
12 192–227		Marketing Statistician	

Source: Hay Group

Figure 2.3

ensure the development of a balanced culture, with disciplines and subcultures working together in a genuinely complementary way.

How many multi-skilled managers any organisation needs to train will probably become an issue, because for every multiskilled manager there will still need to be a team of single skill implementers. However, the arrival of cross-functional managers will enhance the attractions of marketing for more experienced individuals. John Murphy, the Chairman of Interbrand believes that, at present, 'Few MBAs would become senior brand managers

– they see themselves as completely different. The job is not seen as a particularly senior role in most companies. You do it before you go to business school, not afterwards.' As more rounded, entrepreneurial roles develop that perception may well change.

FINANCIAL BENEFITS OF MULTIDISCIPLINARY TEAMS

In the words of John Warren, Group Finance Director of United Biscuits,

> 'in the past you had a marketing group and a finance group and the only time they coincided was at budget time. They probably hated each other because one didn't understand the other. Why not actually have a finance department located in the marketing group?'

As the tendency subsides for one subculture or another to dominate company operations the incidence of projects owned by finance, sales, marketing or research will subside, helping to achieve the productive balance referred to by Sadler and Milmer.

The overhead benefits of multidisciplinary teams are obvious; less people producing better results in less time. However, beyond the simple benefits of lower headcounts, fewer meetings and so on, there are huge synergy benefits to be obtained by informing the whole marketing process with a clearer financial perspective. Paul Baker of OHAL testified to the fact that many marketing people have traditionally been indifferent to the financial measures available within OHAL systems.

John Murphy, the Chairman of Interbrand, points out that,

> 'The whole of accounting is about isolating costs and allocating cash-streams and overheads, and it is no more difficult to do that for a brand than it is for a factory or a production line or anything else. It's just that most marketing people don't ask for it to be done and don't have any interest in it being done. The finance department usually gives people the data they ask for – they don't see themselves as being particularly pro-active in the supply of information and they often don't know enough about brands to know how the data ought to be presented. So fundamentally the poor quality of brand profitability data is the fault of the marketing department.'

John Warren, the Group Finance Director of United Biscuits, puts in a word for the ability of finance people to contribute to the process,

> 'I think finance people understand marketing. Everybody in the boardroom tends to be an amateur marketeer, and the finance people are no different. Everybody has his own theory about the advertising, the products, the packaging design, but typically, the level of financial expertise

*is relatively low. It's often a depressing aspect of a British managers edu-
cation, but that is quite often the case and they are very reliant not just on
the financial director but the finance function for control and guidance.
In many cases, that financial expertise is not sufficiently disseminated
throughout the management culture and all the different functions.'*

He adds,

*'I think there should be a healthy balance. You don't want companies
which are run by marketing guys with really bright ideas, without someone acting as Devil's Advocate saying 'hold on, do you recognise the risks
we're taking? What proof have we got? How many can we afford to have
going at any one time?' You need to have those two perspectives.'*

Does it actually work anywhere else in the world and how can such a fundamental change be achieved?

INTERNATIONAL COMPARISONS

Because European, and particularly British, companies have been used to
particular styles of human resource management for much longer than their
US, Oriental and developing world competitors, there is an inherent inertia
which will take either crises or top-level management intervention to
change. The shocks of the Thatcher free-enterprise culture and the Single
European Market are tremors which have stimulated change in some companies, but traditions which go back to the Industrial Revolution and the
Empire die hard. Companies which until now have mainly traded in the
domestic market have further to go than the multinationals which have seen
how different human resources strategies can impact favourably on performance and profit.

Germany after the war, Japan in the fifties, sixties and seventies, the
'tiger' economies of the Far East, and 'sunrise' industries in the US have set
the pace, which we have reluctantly followed in the UK. It is a source of
great pride in some companies that the Directors' Dining Room has been
abolished, yet very often little else has changed; a token gesture to change
while inter-active management styles, open management, quality circles and
team-working are taken for granted elsewhere. The influx of Japanese firms
into the UK – Nissan, Honda and Sony, to name but a few – bring with them
assumptions about the way human resources should be managed as a critical
success factor. They and others are gradually evangelising the UK industrial
hinterland, but there is still a long way to go.

It is unlikely that we will adopt Japanese methods 'lock, stock and barrel'
because the underlying cultures, traditions and social hierarchies are so different. In fact, many international companies are beginning to recognise that
they need to adapt management styles to different markets. For example,

Professor John A. Quelch of the Harvard Business School makes the following point,

> '*Most multinationals are at varying stages of development around the world and they need more than one type of manager. A European consumer goods company might appoint 'cabinet members' as country managers in an increasingly integrated Europe, but put 'traders' into Asia, where markets are growing faster and national socio-economic differences are greater. Meanwhile, the 'potentates' who run the company's operations in Latin America, where tariff barriers still limit cross-border commerce, might still remain in place.*'

However, many companies work hard to create a consistent corporate culture side-by-side with different local traditions.

In both these processes there are two critical factors. One is *internal training programmes*, the other is *internal communications*; the two are inter-twined. How can values and information be communicated in both directions to improve employee understanding, technical skill, corporate vision, loyalty and, above all, commitment.

INTERNAL COMMUNICATIONS – THE CATALYST FOR CHANGE

In breaking down deep-seated, subcultural prejudices, and in ensuring that all personnel understand and are working effectively within the new, flexible corporate environment, 'internal communications' will be vital.

It is amazing how little companies spend in this area. How many companies have a simplified version of the annual report? How many produce simplified annual results? How many discuss future objectives with their staff, in the way that they court City analysts? How many have properly resourced corporate videos or publications for internal consumption? How many have structured seminars programmes for senior management to discuss strategy with their staff?

Unfortunately the answer is, 'not many'. The ridicule which greeted Jon Birt's attempt to meet and discuss his vision of the BBC's future with every member of the corporation, typifies the attitude of many in the UK. A genuine attempt to 'open up' the management of a dusty, traditional bureaucracy met with cynicism and resistance.

Some companies do spend a lot of money on the process; far more consider the whole exercise a mild embarrassment and an irritation. An interesting statistic, in the Public Relations Consultants Association (PRCA) 1992 Annual Report, reveals the scale of the problem. PRCA members account for a very large proportion of corporate expenditure on *public relations* in its widest sense, including corporate affairs, crisis management and

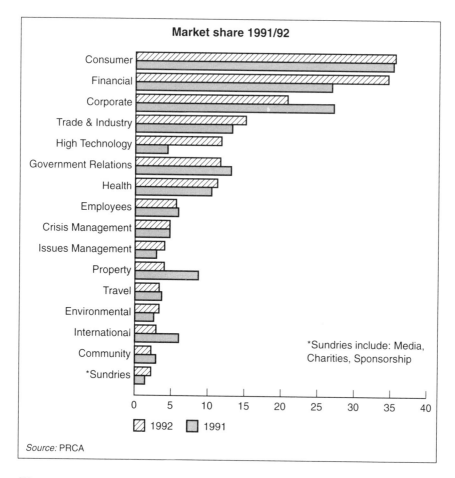

Figure 2.4

internal communications. According to the PRCA, of the £166 million fee income earned by its members in 1992, only 3.3 per cent of the total, or £5.5 million, was attributable to employee communication programmes. This represented a *drop* on the previous year, when 3.4 per cent of total PRCA revenues came from this source. In real terms revenues attributable to internal communications dropped by approximately 7 per cent in a period when companies were supposed to be taking their human resources more seriously! (See Figure 2.4.)

In some ways this is a false statistic because many expenditures find their way into other budget lines; marketing, finance, personnel, company secretarial. In addition, a large chunk of internal communications expenditure is spent internally and never passes through an external agency. However, the figures do give a very strong indication that the area is simply not taken seriously enough.

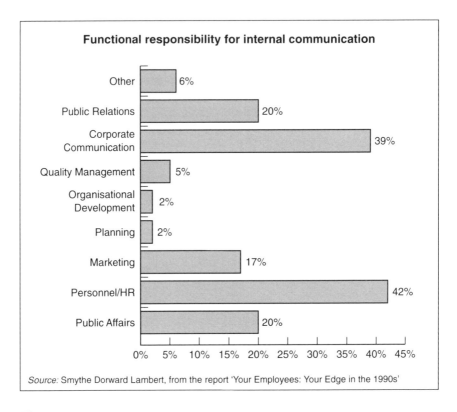

Figure 2.5

Smythe Dorward Lambert is a Communication Management Consultancy which specialises in this area. For several years it has been researching attitudes and internal communications programmes among a wide number of companies, and how internal communications contributes to the achievement of corporate strategies. Its research report 'Your Employees; Your Edge in the 1990s' provides a useful insight into how internal communications can become an instrument of change and an added value process, rather than an irritating and time-consuming overhead. Smythe Dorward Lambert researched the attitudes and practices of 90 UK companies, many of which were major blue-chips, and therefore one might assume at the leading edge of best practice.

Yet, even in this group there is extensive fragmentation of responsibility for this crucial task: (See Figure 2.5). The report also shows the most frequently used internal media: (see Figure 2.6).

The research also indicates the prevalence of gathering information in the opposite direction: (See Figure 2.7).

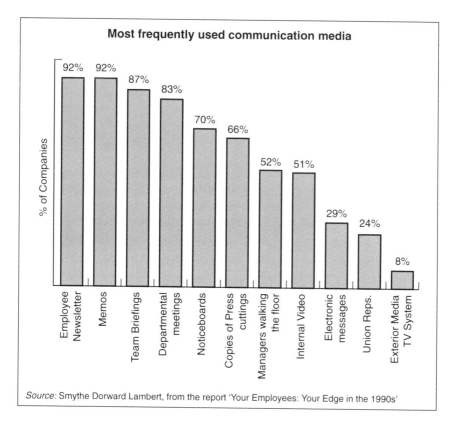

Figure 2.6

Fragmentation and a top-down communication style still tend to prevail. The practice of cascading information up and down organisations through regular team meetings is still only developing as a technique.

At the PRCA's 1993 Cambridge Summer School, John Smythe described the different styles of internal communication and the benefits to be obtained from taking the discipline seriously (see Figure 2.8).

He outlined three distinct cultures for managing change via internal communications; *top down/bottom up* by means of management communication and the passage of information up and down the organisation, listening to people via audits and engaging in direct conversations between management and staff; *team communication*, where people work every day in teams and engage in both team and intrateam meetings on a daily basis; and finally *human resource processes*, where communication is integral to the human resource function and involves the setting of goals, rewards for achievement and discipline for incorrect action.

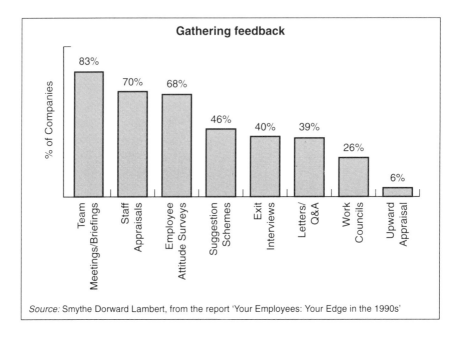

Gathering feedback

Source: Smythe Dorward Lambert, from the report 'Your Employees: Your Edge in the 1990s'

Figure 2.7

Firms need to define which basis they want to operate under; centrist, directive, uniform, and secretive, as many have in the past, or whether they intend to adopt a more collegiate, consensual and open style of management. The latter offers benefits through all levels of communication, including instruction, the provision of information, debates about information, understanding of individual and team roles, involvement of staff in day-to-day decision-making processes, and ultimately to participation in policy definition, strategy formulation and long range decision making.

If adequate resources and commitment are allocated the benefits to be gained include the ability to:

- inform
- involve
- change
- integrate.

THE FUTURE

These are the very attributes which will turn the theory of flat, multifunctional, team organisations into practice. To realise them there is a need to

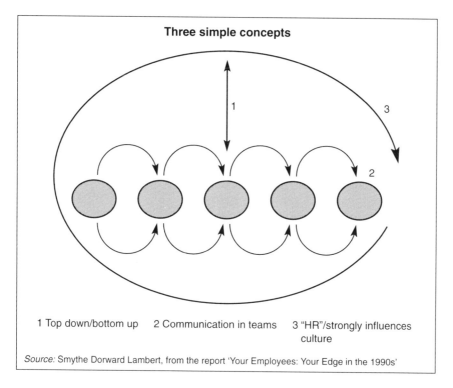

Figure 2.8

focus the internal communications function, to consider it as a core management process, and to resource it better. Organisations like M&S, John Lewis and Lloyds Bank have already gone a long way in this direction and have reaped the rewards. Many others will follow in the 1990s.

Bibliography

Liberation Management – Necessary Disorganisation for the Nanosecond Nineties, Tom Peters, Macmillan London, ISBN 0 333 53340 2

The Talent Intensive Organisation, Philip Sadler and Keith Milmer, The Economist Intelligence Unit, ISBN 0 85058 698 4

Organisational Trends – Who is doing what?, Colin Price and Alan Little, Price Waterhouse, 1993

Competence at Work – Models for superior performance, Lyle M. Spencer and Signe M. Spencer, John Wiley and Sons, ISBN 0-471-54809-X

Competency Based Human Resource Management, Edited by Alain Mitrani, Murray Dalziel and David Fitt, Hay Group, Kogan Page, ISBN 0 7494 0771 9

Rewarding the Advertising Profession, A report for the IPA, David Haigh, 1991

Your Employees; Your Edge in the 1990s, The Second Annual Survey, 1993
Smythe Dorward Lambert

The New Country Managers
Professor J.A. Quelch
McKinsey Quarterly, No. 4, 1992, pp. 155–165.

Extracts from Saville and Holdsworth Ltd are copyright, and reproduced with their kind permission.

3

THE IMPACT OF INFORMATION TECHNOLOGY

'Man is still the most extraordinary computer of all'
John F Kennedy

THE RISE OF COMPUTER SYSTEMS IN MARKETING

John Kennedy's remark is as true today as it was when he made it 30 years ago, but the computer industry is trying hard to prove him wrong.

Federal Express

Taking Federal Express as just one example, the advance in computer systems now means that every morning when the Chief Executive Officer starts work he has a detailed, sub-analysed report of the previous day's activities worldwide on his desktop PC. He can see sales by customer, by region. He can see turnover, volumes, and a wealth of other management data. This is a fully integrated, management information system, one large part of which is also the marketing information system.

But even the breath-taking power of this kind of integrated system will be overtaken. It is not an 'intelligent' system, just an information system designed to improve the decision-making ability of the the most extraordinary computer of them all – man. In Winston Churchill's words, 'This is not the end. It is not even the beginning of the end. But it is perhaps the end of the beginning.'

In the coming decade we will have not only powerful integrated data systems but, also, complex analytical and decision support systems at our disposal. Expert systems are currently in the development stage. They may not replace men, but they will speed up and simplify policy formulation and tactical execution.

Typical problems in today's market

Unfortunately, even the integrated systems which do currently exist are few and far between in many marketing departments. Competitive advantage is being lost every day in the marketing departments of the UK.

If you were to ask the average marketing director, 'What problems are you facing?' his response might be, 'Are we meeting customer needs?', 'How do I know which customers we should love to death so that we don't lose them?', 'Which customers contribute most to the bottom line?', 'Where are the real profits coming from?', 'Am I spending too much on marketing activities?', or, 'How can I reduce the cost of marketing activity?' The response might also be, 'How do I get the right information?' or, 'Why are the systems always so slow?'

Modern, computerised marketing information and management systems, go to the heart of these dilemmas. They help the business to operate and senior management to re-engineer their operations for lower cost and greater efficiency, while simultaneously responding more effectively to customers' needs. But all too often companies have not yet made the required investment and commitment.

Arriving late at the party

Unfortunately, marketing is one of the last major business functions to fully embrace computer technology and to make it an integral part of the process. The production, inventory, distribution and finance areas have been highly computerised for many years, and are becoming increasingly so, but marketing somehow seems to have been left behind. Sales responded first; perhaps because of the opportunities for recording and controlling large quantities of customer data, sales contact reports and buying patterns. It may also have been because IT offered a way of providing a better service, in the form of customer response and sales-call planning. Marketing is only just catching up, and it has been suggested that even now only one marketing department in ten actually uses IT as a genuinely integral part of its work.

Marketing wallflowers

One reason for the slow response may be the old clichés about the background and training of people in the different disciplines. One might expect numbers oriented, control freaks in the finance department to enjoy the intricacies and systematic approaches demanded by IT. Technical people in production are naturally inclined towards technological solutions. Sales people live and die by numbers and customer delivery so they have a vested interest in harnessing systems to help crunch the numbers. By contrast, it is said that marketing people are intuitive, inspirational types who need to synthesize information and produce subtle and innovative answers to creative problems. According to Kevin Morley the marketing people in Rover used to be referred to as 'the flower arranging department' for this very reason.

Mechanical systems first

However, a more likely answer is that the first corporate functions to be automated were the straightforward mechanical operations which lent themselves most to an automated approach, hence accounting, stock control, customer databases and so on. With a limit on investment funds, time constraints on IT departments and only a gradual development of software solutions 'bread and butter' systems were inevitably the first to be computerised. Even in these areas progress has not always been smooth. How many apochryphal stories have we all heard about public utilities cutting off their customers over a zero value invoice!

The problem with many Marketing Information Systems is that they require the storage, analysis and manipulation of vast amounts of data, from many different sources, and often need to include additional extraneous information to provide useful answers. Until many of the internal data sources had been reliably computerised the value of marketing information systems was limited. In addition, many of the more complex manipulative programmes require highly sophisticated and powerful processors to handle the data, and it is only relatively recently that these have become readily available and affordable.

As a result of their arrival, the situation is now rapidly changing and many marketing organisations are actively promoting IT as a way to save time, make better decisions, improve productivity and to achieve greater internal and external accountability

To date, most progress has been made in the more mechanical areas of sales and marketing, rather than in the interpretive and analytical areas. For example, IT systems are being increasingly used for straightforward tasks like sales analysis and reporting, key account management, customer service and campaign analysis. In the latter case, simple systems track leads to get a better idea of where to place advertisements and where to direct scarce marketing resources. Such systems are generally fairly crude, and in many ways are effectively just notation systems, for recording where advertisements were placed and what responses were attributable to them, rather than being more intelligent, interpretive or planning systems. Reliable systems of the latter sort are still being argued over and developed.

Computerising the creative progress

Even in mechanical areas, many organisations have nowhere near exploited the full potential of what is available. For example, at the creative production level it is now possible to install artwork systems in both client and agency premises and to transmit them via an Integrated Services Digital Network (ISDN). High definition colour output is often superior to the manual product conventionally produced by agencies. Finished creative work can be sent for publication or printing without the need for conventional production processes, in half the time of traditional methods. Once such systems are set up, costs and times are a fraction of the old methods and changes can be made very rapidly. Yet, to date, only a small number of marketing departments, largely in the retail and blue-chip FMCG environments, have installed such systems. However, simple systems which interface with finance, production and sales are being automated inexorably.

Impetus from finance

In fact, there is no doubt that in many companies the *marketing function* is being persuaded to go further by the *finance function*. As basic finance systems have matured many finance directors have begun looking at the decision support systems which feed into the corporate and financial planning function. Marketing is clearly one of the most important areas and is being evangelised by the finance people. As they are both the source of capital budgets and the fulcrum for corporate accountability this trend is perhaps not surprising.

For example, John Warren, the Group Finance Director of United Biscuits, prompted McVitie's to become one of the first companies in the UK to buy METAPHOR EIS, a marketing data interpretation system.

> *'We tried to steer it away from being a system for a central group of finance people, who held the information and disseminated it, to being a common database available to anybody. We believed it was essential that the marketing and sales people, the people who made the decisions, had access to the information, so they didn't have to come and ask an accountant. The system covered all data available; shipping invoices as well as market research data.'*

Poor quality of brand related financial data

Marketing information and decision support systems are not new, nor do they necessarily have to be fully computerised to be effective. The key is having the right information to make decisions. Without the right information managers are effectively making decisions in a vacuum.

John Murphy, the Chairman of Interbrand, an organisation which spends much of its time tracking product revenue and cost streams, for brand valution purposes, takes the view that,

'. . . a lot of decisions made in regard to expenditure on brands are made extremely badly. People don't collect accurate sales and financial data relating to their brands and they often fail to split out the information they do have, brand-by-brand. Many don't split out own-label from branded production either. So strategic, brand-by-brand decisions are often made extremely badly. That leads to all sorts of other expenditures being inappropriately applied. For example, companies often just adopt religious views about how much advertising they will spend on given brands. They don't rationalise why.

"We spoke to the marketing director of one of Britain's biggest brand-owning companies trying to get information on its brands, and he replied, 'Don't bother me with that, just go and speak to the ad agency.' If people don't use the right data when they make decisions they are going to come unstuck. We found their biggest, strongest brand was one they were almost ashamed of. They had an idiosyncratic, cash-cow brand which was producing an absolute fortune and it was given to their most junior brand managers. The brand everyone loved to death, and which they all thought was wondrous, was losing them a fortune. It had been for years, and they didn't even know it. The brand they despised was the one brand holding the whole thing together, but they'd never actually looked at the figures properly.

"I have been enormously impressed by some leading branded goods companies, Nestlé, for example. Their financial data is on a brand-by-brand basis, and they have the ability to produce it quickly and in a form which is comparable, and they can make decisions on it. Most companies are not like that. For example, some of the breweries don't gather any brand-related data at all. They aggregate all their data, which is collected at brewery level. If you say 'how is Brand X performing against Brand Y?' people don't know.

"A lot of food companies produce both branded and own-label on the same production line. In case after case, they haven't got the slightest idea that the branded production is heavily subsidising own-label, because they aggregate the data.'

However, more and more companies are learning the error of their ways and the issue is finally being addressed.

Developing analytical systems

Graham Turton, a partner with the marketing division of Price Waterhouse Management Consultants also believes that to date the quality of computer analysis for marketing purposes has been poor. Inadequate computerised information systems are,

> '. . . a very common problem, which up until now companies have not been able to effectively address. Not necessarily from any lack of desire on their part, but just because the systems to address them haven't existed in packaged form, and they haven't had the resources to develop them from scratch.'

Manual systems, pulling in data from a whole range of sources, can be effective, of course, and this is how many marketing departments continue to function. But as the building blocks of corporate computer systems have been developed, both internally and externally, marketing information systems have gradually grown and become more integrated and ambitious.

At present more and more companies are becoming convinced that the elements are in place to create really effective integrated systems. The basic data sources are becoming more robust, systems more frequently 'talk' to one another, information is being processed much more quickly, analytical software is becoming more sophisticated and new, low-cost hardware is capable of supporting complex systems. The emphasis has moved from hardware to software and the hunt is on for software that really works.

At present there is only a limited range of prepackaged software and many companies are being forced by circumstance to build systems from scratch. But as the pendulum begins to swing from bespoke to off-the-peg there will be an explosion in demand for marketing systems.

Defining needs

Before embarking on the computerisation process marketing organisations need to clearly define which functions they wish to automate. For many, the need to manage customer files remains the main incentive for investing in IT. Despite new developments the most important sales and marketing packages remain applications which are based on the extracting of customer data from a database and turning it into useful information. Ian Guthrie, a partner in the Price Waterhouse Marketing Information Group believes that the main problem facing marketing people is translating sales and marketing information into 'actionable intelligence'.

For example, when Price Waterhouse recently surveyed 200 senior corporate executives on the subject of customer management, it found that the question of how to retain customers was the single most important problem facing them. Ninety per cent of respondents felt that this was a prime concern. More than 60 per cent of those questioned had no idea what proportion of customers their organisations were actually retaining.

Graham Turton makes the point that even when companies do have information on customer retention rates, they are often unsure which customers are buying which products, in what volumes and at what contribution levels. For many FMCG companies the problem is not simply one of tracking overall brand profitability but also individual customer and stock keeping unit (SKU) profitability. To adapt an old saying, many companies know that half of their client list isn't making a profit, but they don't know which half.

For example, if a company like Heinz had baked beans in ten different can sizes, sold through 50 different outlets, all with different prices, how would the management know what profit it was making in the absence of a highly sophisticated marketing information system? By creating marketing information systems to track such complex relationships companies can start to target marketing effort much more accurately in terms of salesforce activity, including promotions and the mix of deals they cut with individual supermarkets.

Among other things these powerful new systems are finally enhancing the quality of strategic sales management.

THE IMPACT OF LOW COST COMPUTING

The main driver behind the whole process of change is the rapid decrease in cost and increase in power of available computer technology.

A few simple facts illustrate the rapid pace of change. In 1980 computers were able to execute 330,000 calculations per second. By 1994 it is anticipated that they will be able to execute 6.5 trillion calculations per second. In the early 1980s 75 per cent of all computing power was on mainframes; the equivalent figure today is no more thn 5 per cent. During the 1980s the PC market grew from almost nothing into a $100 billion business.

Above all, the power and low cost of new technology has made it worthwhile to put fast, user-friendly systems on every executive's desk. Open systems and windows software have effectively allowed the average executive to forget about hardware hassles and to concentrate on applications which can really help.

WHAT SYSTEMS ARE AVAILABLE?

The following overview summarises the main system functions which have been or are being automated:

Overview of Sales and Marketing Systems

Market Analysis	Data Management	Campaign Management
– Segmentation – Statistical analysis – Modelling – GIS – Forecasting – Research and competitor analysis	– De-duplication – Data quality reporting – Data enrichment – Propensity modelling – Data maintenance – Scoring	– Define campaign parameters e.g. audience, message, objectives and media – Record and analyse campaign results – Define and analyse test cells – Plan and monitor tasks and budgets – Report on progress and costs

Direct Mailing	Customer/Marketing database	Performance Analysis/ Reporting
– List selections – Record mailing history – Merge, purge and personalisation – Create print file – Letter file maintenance	– Customer and prospect database • name • address • history of relationship • contacts • sales and orders – Marketing database • products • campaigns • market data • competitor information • market research	– Product performance – Segment performance – Sales channel performance – Campaign performance – Staff performance

Sales Management	Telemarketing	Interfaces
– Sales administration – Contact management – Diary management – Lead management – Sales planning – Capture of marketing intelligence	– Call list management – Scripting – Contact management – Auto-dialling – Order entry	– Internal systems • finance (invoicing) • production • distribution – External systems • 3rd party data providers • list brokers – EIS – Remote user access

Source: The Price Waterhouse Sales & Marketing Software Handbook, Pitman

Figure 3.1

Developing the customer database

At the heart of all marketing systems is the customer database. High quality customer database systems should have the ability to:

- record full customer histories
- deduplicate and verify names and addresses
- accommodate file imports
- record and facilitate direct marketing activities
- segment data in several dimensions
- perform scoring and propensity modelling
- report flexibly.

Getting different applications to share information is one of the hardest problems to overcome with customer databases. For example, one large insurance organisation found that because its motor and general insurance portfolios were kept on different mainframes, which didn't communicate with one another, brokers were continuing to do business with the motor side despite being blacklisted for nonpayment on the general side.

The problems of integrating data are significant when operational systems like sales order processing are already well-established. Unfortunately, far too many organis- ations find their information on customers is split across different systems so that they are unable to produce a consolidated picture of their activities with each customer.

As a result of this there is a trend towards the development of core cus- tomer databases with direct links into operational and financial systems. In other words the customer database is at the heart of the whole system rather than at the margins of several subsystems.

The application becomes the core reference point for all customer data and, provided an adequate toolset is available, it will satisfy many of the information needs of sales and marketing departments. Such systems demand the use of the latest, large-scale relational database systems, which, along with the underlying hardware, have the power to handle huge volumes of transactions and enquiries. In many cases this implies a bespoke solution. Bespoke systems represent a significant investment for both business-to-business and consumer organisations and need to be very carefully planned. However, the potential benefits of improved accuracy and timeliness of information for decision support are enormous.

Emphasis on practical applications

Because the more interpretive and projective areas of marketing activity are not easily computerised, most sales and marketing software packages devel- oped to date have concentrated on the practical aspects; particularly of the sales function. The more judgemental side of marketing, including campaign design, is less well-represented with systems.

For example, the few packages which do exist in the campaign planning area tend to be isolated from, rather than integrated with, customer tracking and sales analysis systems. The fact is that the market is still very young. More than half the suppliers are less than two-years-old and there is overlap and confusion.

Through the software maze

To find a way through the maze of software available Price Waterhouse has spent three years building-up a marketing information systems group, within its consultancy practice, which has developed tailor-made systems and created an internal database of packaged software products for sales and marketing applications. *The Price Waterhouse Sales and Marketing Software Handbook* (Pitman) identifies and evaluates all major packages available in Europe and the UK.

According to Price Waterhouse there are over 30 different applications specific to the marketing sector currently available in the UK, and many more in the US and Europe. Looking at the marketing process in terms of phases, the key functionalities fit into the following framework: (see Figure 3.2).

1 Market Information and Analysis

A company's ability to analyse its customers and markets is crucial to its success. As customers become more expensive to reach, it becomes more important for businesses to identify their target audiences, using both internal and external market data. Historically, many companies have simply examined the latest reports from their market research agencies, scanned the sales data and drawn their own conclusions. Often, companies only analyse their markets thoroughly during product launches or on an ad-hoc basis.

The sort of questions which need to be answered on a regular basis are, 'Which are the primary target groups?', 'What are the characteristics of each group?', 'What factors effect buying behaviour – price, performance or image?', 'What are the keys to shifting brand loyalty from the competition?', 'What effect does the distribution and sales channel have?' A whole range of questions need to be answered about the brand preferences, buying behaviour and profit contributions of different consumers. Similarly, many detailed questions about competitive action need to be mapped and evaluated.

A good market information and analysis system should provide a full range of data analysis functions, including segmentation, market penetration modelling, statistical analysis, regression analysis, price modelling and forecasting. A well designed system will enable better informed decisions to be made at

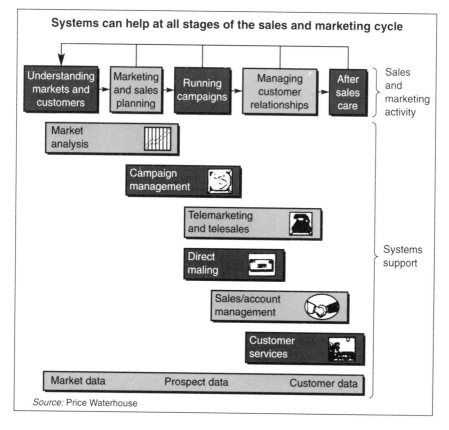

Figure 3.2

the planning stage, which will ensure better use of the marketing budget. It will provide a clearer understanding of competitive positioning and market share, and will improve the ability to spot opportunities and market trends. Most significantly, it will enable a company to identify who its customers are and what they are likely to want to buy.

2 Campaign Planning and Management

Some of the key questions which need to be answered are, 'What communications are most appropriate for the chosen target audiences?', 'What mix of media and techniques are most cost-effective?', 'What messages and formats motivate consumers most effectively?', 'How can marketing communications be co-ordinated with salesforce activity?', 'Is the weight of communications activity optimal?', 'Did campaigns meet their objectives and why?', 'Are the agencies doing their jobs effectively?'

Companies invest tens of millions of pounds in their promotional campaigns. Yet, the business of planning the mix of media, timing of activity and nature of the messages remains a remarkably subjective affair. In later chapters we look at some attempts to systematise this planning process, which so far remains largely impervious to automation.

However, even at a more prosaic level surprisingly few companies seem able or willing to monitor the effects of campaigns, or to control the costs. By simply using a campaign management system, a company can ensure that realistic and measurable objectives are set. Quantifiable objectives and targets can be defined at the outset, then systematically tracked.

The more effective systems link each campaign to its budget and monitor its success against a financial measure, for example cost-per-response. It is also possible to measure the effectiveness of particular test cells and interpret the relative success of different elements of the communication, for example the format, creative tone and sales proposition. Systems should be able to accommodate data from external agencies and should allow managers to plan the detailed tasks necessary for a campaign's success. They should also be able to identify those tasks or agencies that are over-budget or late in delivering. The key element of a good system is its ability to relate consumer or customer responses back to the original campaign targets.

It should be possible to measure the actual performance of a promotion in terms of number, value and quality of responses and to compare the results with original estimates. By having a greater understanding of what works and why, a company should then be able to run more effective campaigns. Future campaigns benefit from better planning and more informed decision-making. Marketing managers are able to identify which promotions deliver real benefits, and to determine the reasons why. Most importantly, managers can use such systems to help justify marketing communications expenditure, particularly in the current climate when marketing budgets are under constant pressure.

3 Direct Marketing and Mailing

Direct marketing software is becoming increasingly sophisticated, particularly in terms of the analysis, segmentation and selection of target audiences. Many organisations create databases from existing customer name and address files, prospect list-building initiatives and from specialist brokers. These sources are merged then interrogated. In the case of large, consumer databases this involves a huge amount of cleaning and de duplication activity, for which a wide range of software is available.

Before prospects can be mailed a number of important checks need to be performed. Post Office Address File (PAF) comparisons need to be made to ensure that the addresses are all in the correct postal address format. Names and addresses must be compared so that duplicates can be eliminated. This ensures that there is only one customer record. Deduplication is in fact easier said than done because many files include the same individual more than once, with minor differences in name or address spelling, arising from incompatible data entry on different lists which have been merged. Nothing looks less professional than two letters arriving at the same address, for the same person, with minor differences in spelling.

Several systems help to maintain databases from which to select specific targets. Such systems maintain customer and prospect data, based on responses to mailing campaigns and as a result of other interaction with customers, for example through customer service systems. The primary objective of list-building and maintenance programmes is to increase the response rate to individual mailshots and to reduce the costs of wasted postage and literature. It is also to minimise damage to the corporate reputation arising from nonsensical errors creeping into mailing programmes.

The effectiveness of individual mailshots clearly depends on many variables, including the offer, the audience, the message and the creative element of the communication. It is therefore important that direct mailing systems should interact with campaign management systems in order to manage and measure direct mail activity more effectively.

4 Telemarketing and Telesales

Telephone-based sales staff have always been seen as an inexpensive but highly effective sales channel. The value and scope of products sold through this sales channel is increasing all the time. As more organisations adopt telephone sales, so the need for a smarter, more responsive approach increases. This can only be achieved through the implementation of sophisticated telemarketing/telesales software which provides all the information the operator needs at the touch of a button.

Such systems incorporate the ability to recover not only information from the main customer database but also to recall the history of the telesales dialogue with individual customers and different message prompts for operators. The ability to predefine telesales messages, by recording scripts for operators, significantly improves the professionalism and success rate of the system. The interaction with electronic diary systems means that when a customer is told he or she will get a follow-up call in a week, a month or a year it actually happens on the day.

Some of the key functionalities are as follows:

- contact management
- call list management
- scripting
- call management
- fulfilment
- reporting.

5 Account and Salesforce Management

There is nothing more frustrating or embarrassing for a sales rep than not having all relevant information to hand. It makes all the difference when servicing existing clients, and building customer loyalty, or pitching to new prospects. It is also well known that administration and sales disciplines mix about as well as oil and water; sales people like to sell not to fill in forms. Any system which cuts the time needed to produce a quotation, write a proposal or take orders is a godsend. On the one hand it means that the rep can be more efficient and cover more ground. On the other it means more time on the golf course. In a nutshell making each of these tasks easier is what account and salesforce management systems are all about.

A good software package should allow key account and sales-force management staff to have all relevant data at their finger tips on a timely basis. Systems should ensure that all the activities of the front-line team are totally co-ordinated. This should eliminate any embarrassment, or worse, loss of credibility, caused by unco-ordinated contacts with a customer or prospect. It also allows the management team to set a clear direction for front-line activity and to measure the performance of team members against achievable objectives.

Effective systems enable staff to identify potential customers according to their propensity to spend. Salesforce activity can then be planned to ensure sufficient prospects are identified, and that prospects are turned into good customers. The chosen system should allow all the activities and events which take place between a company and its individual customers to be recorded. Members of the salesforce should be able to see at any time the entire history of contact with a particular customer, including order details, contracts signed, products bought, enquiries, phone calls, letters and meeting reports. An effective key account and salesforce management system helps ensure that all front-line staff communicate effectively and in a co-ordinated manner. By using these systems, staff become better informed about their accounts and the activities of their colleagues. They are also relieved of many tedious administration tasks.

For example, Price Waterhouse recently found that one company's sales force was spending less than 30 per cent of its time dealing with customers, with the rest taken up on administration and travel. By reducing the administrative burden and more effectively targeting the core list, a new system allowed the salesforce to increase its effectiveness by 35 per cent. Customers now receive a more responsive and co-ordinated service, which is an important step on the road to achieving customer loyalty. Requests for help or information are less likely to be forgotten and more likely to be carried out on time. Managers receive better information about sales activity, and can plan for the future more effectively. If the right information is gathered, it also allows companies to effectively monitor the activities of the competition. Once in place, the system can grow over time, as further, relevant information is added. By co-ordinating its front-line activities in this way, a salesforce can very quickly shift up a gear in its effectiveness, as customer loyalty increases and key staff are better equipped to respond to their demands.

6 Customer Service

With a powerful and flexible customer database available it should be possible to more effectively handle the critical matter of customer relations. Many organisations have a range of individuals who can answer customer queries using a shared database. Many other organisations, particularly those in business-to-business, high value or long-term repeat product and service markets, have adopted the *service point provider* concept. Instead of passing customer enquiries from person-to-person around an organisation, a single individual is empowered to deal with any enquiry.

In both cases the contact person should have all relevant information to hand. In the case of a specific service point provider, the system's function is similar to that of a telemarketing system except that the operator needs to be much more conversant with the company's business. Unlike the telesales system it is the operator who decides the next question or course of action. Consequently, the customer service system needs to provide rapid access to the appropriate information. These systems are particularly relevant for companies whose customer base is made up of long-term, repeat customers. In particular, a number of large utility companies are developing such systems as part of their drive to improve service.

A good system will allow the caller to be identified very quickly, typically by account number or by name and postcode. If it is a first-time call, for example someone who wants a telephone connected, the system should be able to deal with the addition of a new account. Subsequently the system should be able to access all information relevant to the caller: contact history, payment history, service history. It should also be possible to answer queries or assign an action. This might involve on-line access to another system. For example, assigning a service engineer to a call-out.

A customer service system enables a company to understand the types and volumes of enquiries that it receives. It can identify the areas of most concern and feed the results back into the planning process for the future. As markets fragment and competition increases, companies will be judged much more harshly on the type and quality of the service they provide. The company with the ability to respond quickly and effectively to enquiries, of whatever kind, is more likely to maintain and build its customers base.

WHAT ARE THE BENEFITS?

Historically, information has been available to the marketing function but it hasn't been integrated and it hasn't been possible to manipulate the data to plan the business or to plan and control budgets. Control of actual performance against budget has been quite a way post-event. In future powerful new marketing information systems will enable managers to understand the dynamics of their business much more quickly and accurately, and plan ways of responding to changes in the marketplace more effectively.

Quantifying the benefits of IT can be hard, although most users agree that sales have increased since installing a system, either directly, through a sharper customer focus or indirectly, by being more efficient and having more time to spend on value-added tasks. For example, if a travel agent with a powerful prospect database management system wants to fill ten seats on a plane, it will cost nothing to target ten more people who might be interested in taking the unfilled flight.

Similarly, in the financial services sector, thousands of pounds of fixed cost and marketing expenditure are recovered with each life policy or pension scheme sold. Targeting prospects quickly and easily can result in significant incrememental sales. Meanwhile mass market FMCG companies will probably consider broad-scale, branded consumer marketing more important than one-to-one sales activity. Executive information systems for reporting on market trends, point-of-sale information-gathering tools and campaign management systems may be more appropriate for such companies.

Although the technology is still in its infancy, the benefits far outweigh the shortcomings. The ability to cross-reference the history of each client relationship, the details of every sale made, and every advertisement placed, and the ability to analyse all relevant information to target future prospects and customers is invaluable.

WHAT ARE THE COSTS?

What companies spend on IT is not an easy number to assess. So to help answer the question Price Waterhouse conducts an annual computing survey, among 1,000 IT executives of companies with five or more staff in the data processing function. They are asked to predict IT budgets for the forthcoming year. The resultant budgets are split into companies with up to 500 staff, between 500 and 5,000 staff and over 5,000 staff. For 1993 the professionals predicted the following (see Figure 5.3).

The average spend is shown in Figure 3.4.

The analysis is also split by industry (see Figure 3.5).

Analysis by corporate size

IT budgets by total number of employees (£000s per installation)

Employees		1992 actual	1993 forecast
up to 500	Hardware	348	349
	Software	135	132
	Telecommunications	68	66
	Staff	329	311
	Outsourcing	96	105
	User spend	173	170
	Total	**1,149**	**1,133**
500 to 1,000	Hardware	855	835
	Software	302	286
	Telecommunications	176	167
	Staff	955	883
	Outsourcing	249	295
	User spend	450	510
	Total	**2,987**	**2,976**
over 5,000	Hardware	2,703	2,593
	Software	750	720
	Telecommunications	751	721
	Staff	2,628	2,521
	Outsourcing	653	712
	User spend	3,018	3,392
	Total	**10,503**	**10,659**

Source: Price Waterhouse, IT Review 1993

Figure 3.3

Despite the recession IT budgets have continued to grow in real terms. Now while there are no firm statistics on companies with less than five data processing staff, observation suggests that IT remains a major investment even for small companies, as powerful new systems come on the market.

Perhaps inevitably certain industries spend far more than others. According to Glen Peters, partner in charge of the Price Waterhouse Marketing and Customer Management Consultancy, wholesale banking companies dedicate anything up to 20 per cent of total costs to IT, while in retail banking IT represents 4 to 5 per cent of costs. IT spends are more conventionally compared with turnover. In Glen Peters' view telecommunications companies spend in the order of 5 per cent while petrochemicals, manufacturing and retailing operations spend as little as 1 per cent.

The Average IT spend

IT expenditure (£000s per installation)

Employees		1992 actual	1993 forecast
IT Hardware	Mainframe/midrange	517	502
	PC/Workstations	375	370
	Maintenance	309	302
	Total	**1,201**	**1,174**
IT Software	Application	206	202
	System	206	200
	Total	**412**	**402**
Telecommunications	(Networks and usage)	275	268
Staff		1,236	1,208
Outsourcing (FM, consultancy, etc)		339	373
Total average dp department budget	(A)	3,463	3,425
Corporate IT spend outside dp department	(B)	773	818
Total IT expenditure	**(A+B)**	**4,326**	**4,243**

Source: Price Waterhouse, IT Review 1993

Figure 3.4

Within these total commitments different business areas currently command widely different slices of the cake. Again in Glen Peters' view, among the top 200 companies in the UK, less than 10 per cent of the total IT spend is allocated to marketing systems.

'Some companies spend as little as 3 per cent of their total IT budget on marketing systems.

'Over the next few years I believe the proportion will jump as high as 30 per cent. The prime reason for this increase will be the desire of companies to build fully-integrated, customer database systems, from which all other systems will hang. This will not only give them powerful planning opportunities but also the ability to know sales patterns in detail on a timely basis. It may seem shocking but in my opinion less than 10 per cent of UK companies know what they sold yesterday. But the retailers do!

'If the platform for the other marketing systems is not accurate none of the other marketing information or decision support systems will have

Categorised IT budget forecasts by industry

(1993, £000s per installation, totals also related to turnover)

	Hardware (%)	Software (%)	Telecomms (%)	Staff (%)	Outsourcing (%)	User spend (%)	Total (= 100%)	Total (% of turnover)
Manufacturing	767 (28)	293 (10)	181 (6)	745 (27)	251 (9)	551 (20)	2,788	0.7
Process industry	1,232 (31)	493 (12)	211 (5)	1,373 (34)	147 (4)	548 (14)	4,004	1.1
Retail Distribution	957 (30)	328 (10)	246 (8)	930 (29)	373 (12)	346 (11)	3,180	1.6
Utilities	1,706 (20)	628 (8)	409 (5)	2,524 (30)	211 (3)	2,873 (34)	8,405	2.3
Finance	2,415 (29)	783 (10)	587 (7)	2,284 (28)	646 (8)	1,469 (18)	8,184	2.9
Education/ Research	313 (21)	89 (6)	54 (4)	383 (25)	196 (13)	467 (31)	1,502	2.3
Public administration	948 (26)	363 (10)	195 (5)	1,059 (29)	380 (10)	743 (20)	3,688	1.7
Computer Services	2,762 (45)	608 (10)	276 (5)	1,713 (28)	480 (8)	250 (4)	6,089	4.3
Other industry	436 (22)	218 (11)	218 (11)	721 (37)	166 (9)	182 (9)	1,941	1.1
UK average	**1,174 (27)**	**402 (10)**	**268 (6)**	**1,208 (29)**	**373 (9)**	**818 (19)**	**4,243**	**1.6**

Source: Price Waterhouse, IT Review 1993

Figure 3.5

any value. This is partly a question of getting all the various sub-systems talking to one another, and partly systems design. For example, many garage forecourt retailing systems fail to provide sales data on a line-by-line basis. What's the point in building a sophisticated analytical marketing model if the system doesn't deliver a basic sales split. For this reason I believe at least half of all IT expenditure for marketing will be spent in this area for the next few years.'

According to Bob Shaw, former Chairman of the Association for Information Systems in Marketing and Sales (AIMS), companies could be spending between 10 and 20 per cent of their overall IT budgets on technology for sales and marketing, working out at roughly 0.25 per cent, or 0.5 per cent of a company's revenue. Unfortunately, he acknowledges that to date it has been '. . . a real problem getting the management to set aside an IT budget for the marketing department.'

What the cost of systems implementation will be for individual companies is impossible to generalise about, because each client requirement is unique. However, in both percentage and in absolute terms the amounts will be high.

In Graham Turton's words,

'Obviously it is a leap of faith for many companies to make such huge investments. Even for large organisations it's a very large commitment to install these systems, but the pay-back is very good.'

IMPLEMENTING SYSTEMS

Because modern systems cost such large amounts of money to install and maintain a lot of time needs to be spent by marketing people with IT specialists, to fully understand what is required from the systems and what options are available. It is vital that the business case for any development has been thoroughly proven before the system goes ahead. It is also vital to implement systems in phases. A pilot version should be built to enable marketing users to understand what they can get out of the system. Involvement generates commitment and the enthusiasm to run the system. Someone arriving one day with a bunch of keys saying 'here's your new system!' seldom works in practice.

Key issues in the planning process

Understanding

Sales, marketing and IT staff all have to know what is going on and what the system is for.

Commitment

Support has to be sought from key board members.

Common goals

Sales, marketing and IT staff have to have the same goals in mind.

Skills

Sales, marketing and IT teams need to be thoroughly trained in what the system will and will not do. Members of the team also need to demonstrate cross-functional skills.

Communication

IT staff need to work closely with sales and marketing staff.

Market intelligence

Management needs to review what others in the market are doing and how new systems would create an advantage.

Running the project

Use a proven methodology and a comprehensive plan so that no tasks are omitted or half completed.

Key issues in choosing a system supplier

1 Develop a statement of system requirements.
2 Issue invitations to tender.
3 Review responses from suppliers against system requirements.
4 Build a shortlist of between three and five suppliers.
5 Have comprehensive demonstrations showing each aspect of the systems.
6 Give scores to suppliers' offerings and develop objective comparisons.
7 Evaluate whether the supplier teams are compatible with your own.
8 Review the financial stability of the different suppliers.
9 Assess whether each supplier can be trusted to deliver to the brief.
10 Consider whether this will be an important or marginal contract for each supplier.

OPERATIONAL PROBLEMS

A number of problems frequently raise their heads and can be summarised under the following:

- data conversion
- business dislocation
- retraining
- garbage in garbage out syndrome

- access security
- inadequate initial brief.

A survey of suppliers found that the most common problems were as follows;

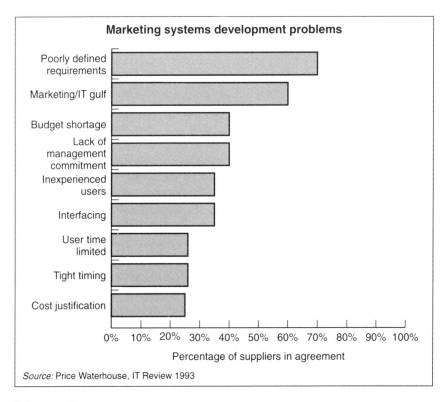

Figure 3.6

The two keys to avoiding such problem areas, and to wrapping up any problems if they arise, are the existence of a systematic planning process at the outset and a post implemention review process at the end of the project.

ANALYSIS PARALYSIS

One of the more important side-effects of the information explosion is the almost impossible task of reducing and manipulating available data. Very few marketing people are either trained or capable of dealing with it all. One of the difficulties is actually finding the time to specify tabulations, analyse data and interpret results. The availability of infinite analyses and sub-analyses could result in the time honoured mental complaint of 'analysis paralysis'. It's always easier to analyse available facts in ten different ways than to make a decision.

An alternative reaction to the data overload could simply be to ignore it all. In the words of Tony Ayers, the Chief Executive of advertising consultancy Media Audits,

> 'I see so many clients with such vast amounts of data available to them, which they are not using. Client companies have got themselves into such a state of reduced numbers and tight budgets that they are pulling in data they don't use. We are aware of one or two companies where there is direct point-of-sale data available daily, but it is not being analysed, or linked with the input data from advertising and promotion. It scares me! In FMCG markets it puts more and more power in the retailers' hands because they have the data and are analysing it, and the branded-goods advertisers are not.'

Or, in the words of Roger Scarlett-Smith, Vice President of Marketing in the Consumer Division of SmithKline Beecham Inc,

> 'All the data we need is available, internally and externally, but being able to analyse it in a meaningful way is by no means a trivial problem.'

The result will be a significant increase in market research and market analysis spending by many companies. The function of the market analyst will grow and become more distinct from the role of the generalist marketing manager, who will increasingly take decisions based on predigested information.

Because of the shortage of qualified individuals to fulfil this analytical function and because of its massively increased importance it is quite possible that companies will subcontract large elements of the data reduction and analysis function to specialists. In the words of Phil Barnard, the Chief Executive Officer of Research International,

> 'Data overload and "information anxiety" caused by vastly increased computer power, will result in a plethora of data reduction consultants'

AHEAD OF THE GAME

More and more examples are emerging of how the new marketing systems are delivering real benefits. The new technology is already providing added value and competitive advantages to a number of far-sighted companies. For example, systems implemented in recent years include:

In early 1992 *Prudential Assurance* put together a sales and marketing system based on a set of integrated front end tools supported by relational and multi-dimensional databases. The system incorporated a marketing customer database, a demographic profiling tool and a product management application. The system was designed to give clues about the company's market penetration in specific product and demographic areas, something which it is usually hard to do accurately in the financial services sector. However, by using the system to analyse customer behaviour and buying patterns the company has been able to direct marketing and sales effort towards more promising areas. The total investment was in the order of £250,000 but David Wilson, the General Marketing Manager, believes that the system has already paid for itself, doing away with the need for some bought in services and helping focus sales activities.

In mid-1991 *Sun Alliance*, one of the UK's leading general insurance companies, experienced huge productivity improvements in its broker division, exceeding 30 per cent within three months, by giving its broker fieldforce lap-top computers with detailed customer management software.

As a result of the new system, quotations, policies and broker administration and commission payments can be handled more efficiently. Service responses have become faster, fewer complaints have resulted and customers have been retained. In practice, benefits can often be hard to measure. For instance, it is difficult to quantify the benefits of 'improved management information' or to prove incremental sales are achieved as a direct result of the system. However, observational evidence is compelling.

In late 1992 *First Direct*, the direct banking subsidiary of the Midland Bank Group, introduced a marketing database which was specifically designed to target and segment customers within its customer database. Although the bank now has 1 per cent of the UK ABC1 market, and is adding 10,000 customers per month, over 80 per cent of account holders have accounts with other, conventional branch banks. The objective of the database was to increase customer loyalty and business volumes, and therefore revenues, from its customer base. The system works by modelling individual customer profiles on propensity-to-buy criteria, using information on previous purchasing behaviour and by using multiple regression analysis to identify the next most likely product purchase. The system has been highly successful at targeting and supporting a direct product dialogue with customers.

At the end of 1992 *Guinness Brewing* introduced OSCAR, a telephone based customer management and sales systems for publicans. The new operation included an extensive review of the company's outlet system as a result of switching from a mainframe based system. The new system was developed from an off-the-shelf package and incorporated full customer service records and sales information. It not only provides a more responsive service for publicans but will incorporate reporting terminals for area managers and mobile terminals for sales staff.

EFFECT ON CORPORATE STRATEGY

As discussed in the next chapter, the impact of the information revolution on corporate strategy is significant. The main issue is that while companies may have wanted to integrate teams of functional specialists in the past the simple mechanics of business operations, reinforced by available systems, made this impossible. The power and flexibility which will be available in the future will change all that, broadening the possible horizons for corporate structure change.

CONCLUSIONS

According to Ian Angell, Professor of Information Systems at the London School of Economics, artificial intelligence is nonsense. *'Every technology has its myths. Mud technology had Adam and Eve, clockwork technology had Coppelia, electricity had Frankenstein; the technology of our particular age, computing, has Artificial Intelligence . . . It's about time we hammered a stake through its heart.'*

Whether we ever develop systems that will make marketing decisions for us the fact is that over the next ten years computers will make it possible for much better informed and analysed marketing decisions to be made. Those companies which shrink from the investment and the effort will be the losers.

Bibliography

The Price Waterhouse Sales and Marketing Software Handbook 1993, Debbie Gorski & Jonathan Ingram, Pitman Publishing, ISBN 0 273 60184 9

The Price Waterhouse Information Technology Review 1993/94

The Information Edge, N. Dean Meyer & Mary Boone, McGraw Hill Book Company, ISBN 0 07 041 1782 2

Liberation Management, Tom Peters, Macmillan London, ISBN 0 333 53340 2

Creative Accounting, Ian Griffiths, Routledge, ISBN 041 508 4652

4

CORPORATE AND MARKETING STRATEGY

'Fashion is made to become unfashionable'
Coco Chanel

THE CORPORATE COUTURIERS

How would designers, dressmakers, fashion houses, supermodels and the style press make a living without it; fashion, that great despot whom the wise ridicule and obey. Nothing is more hideous than obsolete fashion, and an industry has been created to find ways of keeping monied women one step ahead of the crowd.

Ironically, while billionaire women pay fortunes for flimsy designer dresses, their menfolk are equally avidly putting on and taking off fashion garments from the corporate catwalk; down-sizing, right-sizing, integrating, divesting and quality circling as the seasons pass.

An industry has grown up to meet their needs; academic prima donnas, strategy boutiques, designer label consultancies, power dressing MBAs and the management press. They busily put together the latest collections, touting them about at inflated prices, filling thousands of column inches and finally spawning a host of *pret à porter* management techniques. Some are robust and have a classic appeal, others are completely off-the-wall; the difference between Calvin Klein and Vivienne Westwood. However, when they have been accepted by the common herd, they are all just last year's fashions, and the industry moves on to the next great trend.

So what are this year's fashions? Should they be taken seriously and are they worth investing in? Will any of them survive the test of time? One interesting new management theory recently appeared in the leader pages of *The McKinsey Quarterly*, that Vogue of the strategy consulting *demi-monde*. John Brady and Ian Davis, both partners with McKinsey in London, argue that new challenges and a new competitive environment mean that the marketing function must reinvent itself. Are they right? Is there a fundamental crisis in so-called 'marketing oriented' companies? Will there be a major shake-up in the way marketing operates in many companies, as a result of

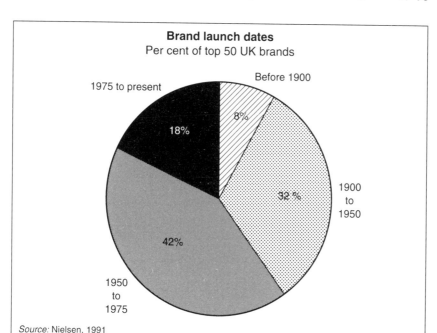

Brand launch dates
Per cent of top 50 UK brands

Before 1900 — 8%

1900 to 1950 — 32%

1950 to 1975 — 42%

1975 to present — 18%

Source: Nielsen, 1991

Figure 4.1

their insight? Or is it just more hype to sell the corporate emperor his new season's clothes?

MARKETING'S MID-LIFE CRISIS

Brady and Davis argue that after decades of rapidly rising marketing costs, and despite the much vaunted contribution of marketing culture to corporate success, the marketing function, with its inflated budgets, salaries and perks, is finally coming in for attention and even criticism.

> '. . . doubts are surfacing about the very basis of contemporary marketing: the value of ever more costly brand advertising, which often dwells on seemingly irrelevant points of difference; of promotions, which are often just a fancy name for price cutting; and of large marketing departments, which, far from being an asset, are often a millstone around an organisation's neck.'

They acknowledge that marketing departments have executed necessary structural changes, caused by globalisation, information and communication technology, strategic planning and organisational design. But, in the last two

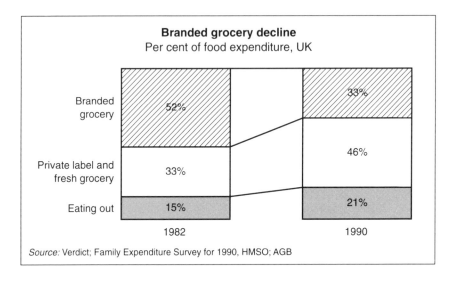

Figure 4.2

decades they suggest marketing has failed to come up with any new ideas, either to reverse declining consumer loyalty to manufacturer brands, or to prevent the shift in power from manufacturers to retailers. Line extensions have masqueraded as genuine new products and the opportunities presented by technology have been missed. New marketing frameworks, and fresh approaches, which might help build long-term trade and consumer relationships, are few and far between.

They point to the fact that between the 1950s and 1970s product innovation, and investment in building consumer relationships, propelled manufacturer brands into a dominant position, supporting rapid corporate profits growth. New products like the fridge, washing machine and freezer, coupled with powerful new media, like commercial television, helped create powerful brands. Nearly half of the top 50 UK brands originate from this period (see Figure 4.1).

But now marketeers are failing to read the right market signals. They are failing to navigate their companies through a changed, and more hostile, environment. Powerful retailers have reduced the scope for consumer contact; trade purchasing and distribution channels have become narrower and more challenging. Retailers have dictated product design, development, manufacture, quality control, stock holding, delivery and payment terms. Own-label has become a major threat (Figure 4.2).

Real-time sales data, captured by modern EPOS systems, has massively increased the required response times. Manufacturer margins have also been squeezed, helping to fund a 20 per cent per annum increase in retailer profits

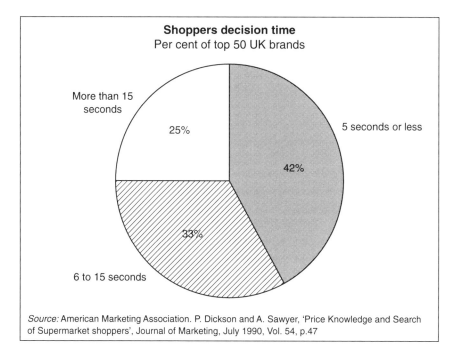

Shoppers decision time
Per cent of top 50 UK brands

More than 15 seconds — 25%

5 seconds or less — 42%

6 to 15 seconds — 33%

Source: American Marketing Association. P. Dickson and A. Sawyer, 'Price Knowledge and Search of Supermarket shoppers', Journal of Marketing, July 1990, Vol. 54, p.47

Figure 4.3

thoughout the 1980s. Manufacturers did manage to increase their own profits – by 10 to 15 per cent per annum between 1975 and 1990 – but this growth largely came from other functions than marketing.

Production delivered, with manufacturing resource planning, benchmarking and just-in-time delivery. Distribution delivered, with simplified logistics, warehousing systems and new delivery methods. Sales delivered, with greater use of shelf-space planning, product profitability analysis, and the adoption of customer servicing software. But, while their colleagues concentrated on reducing costs and improving efficiency, all marketing managed to deliver in the eighties was price rises ahead of inflation.

This created the strategic opportunity for cut price own-label, which recently prompted the draconian slashing of prices by Philip Morris, on its Marlboro cigarette brand, by Procter & Gamble on many of its brands, and by a number of other major branded goods manufacturers. Product attributes simply did not warrant the price premiums many brands had awarded themselves.

The reason is that marketing departments have become risk averse. In many categories innovation has come more from packaging manufacturers and retailers than from branded manufacturers. Monotonous line extensions have diverted attention and resources away from the development of genuine new products, which might keep own-label at bay, out-manoeuvre the competition and create new markets for the future.

In addition, promotions are too often aimed at the trade rather than at the consumer, and many traditional marketing communications techniques defy accurate analysis as to their effectiveness. As a result, some companies are focusing more on the marketing department's ability to innovate.

Brady and Davis conclude that marketing is no longer delivering and will have to establish a new role for itself. Marketeers will need to focus more on consumer wants and needs, and on how products can be matched to them. This will involve far greater use of EPOS data and new consumer market research techniques, like product attribute trade-off analysis. Manufacturers will need to invest far more in understanding consumer behaviour at the point of purchase and during consumption. For example, it has been shown that three quarters of consumer buying decisions are made in under 15 seconds (see Figure 4.3).

Serious marketing organisations like Mars are already investing heavily in understanding the purchasing process better and in applying their knowledge in-store.

The same argument applies to understanding the psychological processes which drive consumers; for example, do they eat snacks to satisfy hunger or to take a break from work; if the latter then a decrease in smoking might boost the snack sector. Understanding these processes would make a huge difference in the search for genuinely new approaches to satisfying consumer demand with new products. It would also help in defining mass market and niche market opportunities.

Marketers will need to innovate in their use of the retail channel and will have to develop other, newer sales channels. For example, Brady and Davis cite the opportunity for a 'total system' for home-delivered, chilled foods, using modern delivery technology, and removing the chance of such foods being spoiled between chiller cabinet and fridge. A similar service has already been tried successfully in the German frozen food market.

Within the established retailer environment marketers will need to think creatively about how to fit their products and services profitably within retailer strategies. It would appear that companies are already breaking down the disciplinary barriers, and emphasising the ability to innovate, rather than simply to promote products according to out-of-date formulas. For example, Elida Gibbs is apparently reformulating the marketing director role and redefining it as brand development director. More emphasis is being placed on innovation and product development than on advertising, sales and promotions.

Another solution will be to treat marketing as a process rather than as a department. Rather than splitting the organisation into marketing, sales and production, core processes like brand development and delivery will be handled without functional barriers. Brady and Davis end with the comment,

> 'In order to emerge from its mid-life crisis, marketing will need to take the lead in engineering its own future.'

PROCESS RE-ENGINEERING

The key word is 'engineering', although perhaps it should have been 're-engineering'. While marketers may take the lead they will no doubt need outside help; and, as we all know, strategy consulting firms specialise in re-engineering the future.

They do not accept assignments unless there is a very clear commitment to change, and like supermodels they 'do not get out of bed for less than $10,000 a day'. Not that this is necessarily a bad thing; strategic change is an expensive process and designer label consultancy, however pricey, is only one small part of the total cost. The main costs are internal. If there is insufficient commitment from the chief executive to pay the required fees, and to implement the resulting recommendations, it is better not to get involved in the first place.

However, there are many who believe that process re-engineering is worthwhile, and they are jumping in with both feet. Sometimes referred to as *Business Process Re-engineering*, or *BPR*, and sometimes as *Core Process Redesign*, or *CPR*, the idea is to implement radical change rather than to pursue a process of incremental improvement. Such exercises represent a move from separate performance improvement projects, to an integrated programme of improved corporate efficiency. Entrenched business systems and existing corporate structures have to be thrown into the melting pot and fundamentally redesigned.

Grinding out the fat

Some messiahs of the re-engineering movement are more colourful in their rhetoric than others. Mike Hammer, a highly articulate US management guru, recently commented, 'Re-engineering is not about cutting fat. The fat is not lying around, it is marbled in. You have to grind it up and fry it out.'

In fact, Mike Hammer takes the credit for popularising the term 're-engineering'. In *Director Magazine* he recently defined the technique as, 'the fundamental rethinking and radical redesign of business processes, to achieve dramatic improvements in critical contemporary measures of performance, such as cost, quality, service and speed.' He also credits the new technique with, 'reversing the Industrial Revolution' because it breaks free from the principles of labour division that go back to Adam Smith and the 'pin factory'.

Hammer packaged a concept which had started in 1983 at the Massachusetts Institute of Technology (MIT), with a research project which looked at the likely impact of IT on organisations in the 1990s. MIT identified the importance of business processes, '. . . sequences of interdependent tasks and functions which together produce outcomes that contribute to the success of an organisation.' IT provided new ways of performing many of these basic functions.

A much quoted example of process re-engineering in action comes from Ford's accounts payable function. Its managers thought they had done well to reduce their workforce by 20 per cent to 400 until they found that Mazda ran its accounts payable department with just five people.

After analysing the various steps and stages in processing an invoice, Ford managers concluded that the bulk of wastage and delay was caused by invoice mismatches – when purchase orders, receiving documents or invoices disagreed with one another. They therefore instituted 'invoiceless processing', with immediate order, delivery, billing and payment confirmation, eventually cutting their staff from 400 to 100.

Systematic approach to business processes

Corporate re-engineering is currently the hottest technique for organisations seeking to maximise their personnel and material resources. The technique seeks to restructure business processes and eliminate duplication, delay and obsolescence, often using improved IT systems. It looks at organisations in a systematic way rather than focusing on discrete departments or divisions.

According to Dr Eddie Obeng, a Programme Director at the Ashridge Management Centre, businesses historically ran into trouble because they failed to think in terms of a single 'dynamic entity'.

> *'Businesses have been thought about in terms of functions and departments, but in reality the way you make money cuts across departments. It's actually a sequence of activities that goes from one skill area to another until you produce something for which somebody will part with money.*

> *'When organisations started to delayer they disrupted most of their chains of activities and their service level went to pot. People were working flat out and nothing was coming out of the business.'*

By contrast, corporate re-engineering looks at the total flow of materials and information involved in the production process, and suggests ways of restructuring in order to maximise that process.

In his book *Building a Chain of Customers*, published by Century Business, Richard J Schonberger, the US authority on manufacturing and production, suggests that:

'Each of the four main business functions – design, operations, account-ing and marketing – is a "customer" for the others, and the links between and within the departments form a continuous "chain of customers" that extends to those who buy the products or service'. Reprinted with kind permission of The Free Press, a division of MacMillan Inc.

The linkages in the chain need to be strengthened, and that is what re-engineering is all about. Fortunately for the re-engineers circumstances are currently just right for change.

The role of the personnel function

At the personnel level the recession and the decline in collective bargaining have made radical change a realistic possibility. Forced confrontations with the unions during the Thatcher and Reagan years softened-up working prac-tices to the extent that it is now possible to implement radical restructuring, without public comment and often without causing major industrial relations problems. Personnel people have had a tremendous cutting edge in the last few years, as they have tackled union and motivational issues, to improve corporate performance.

The key to successful re-engineering is managing the personnel involved in it. In fact, part of the reason corporate re-engineering is currently in favour is that it fits in with and exploits several personnel management trends, which have evolved as part of the holistic approach to business man-agement. For example, once an organisation accepts that the whole process needs to be integrated, *networking* and *cross-functional teamworking* be-come inevitable. Managing people during this change process can be the hardest part of the whole exercise.

Core process redesign inevitably demands collective learning, which fits in with the increasingly popular concept of the *learning organisation*. When organisations re-examine and streamline production and business processes they discover that they also need to reconfigure personnel policies. Team leadership and coaching skills come to the fore, rather than authoritative leadership skills. This is particularly true in the flatter, leaner organisations of the 1990s as they cut out bureaucratic hierarchies and replace them with effective, cross-functional teams, often made up of relatively junior staff.

In this situation *empowerment* of the individual also becomes crucial. Empowerment requires senior managers to transform themselves into coaches and to pass responsibility for action and decision-making down the line.

In Dr Obeng's words 'When you take a process view you discover that the process can access and leave at any level in an organisation. So very often processes will go from somebody who is senior to someone who is junior in the organisation. With empowerment what you are actually saying is stop interfering with the process and let it happen.'

Of course, empowerment is a fashion which, like psychedelic clothing, has been seen before. In the 1960s it was called *worker participation*, but got lost in the industrial strife of the time. However, empowerment has a far better chance of succeeding because personnel and corporate conditions are now quite different, and the concept is integral to making core process redesign work.

IT acting as the catalyst

As discussed in the last chapter, IT systems are increasingly available to provide the kind of information flows between managers which allow functional barriers to come down.

Just one small example of this is the fact that high-powered, personal computers costing less than £1,000 can be networked, to create a seamless flow of management information between departments, factories, offices, regions and nations. In many large organisations managers can be anywhere in the world and still plug into the corporate main-frame, to communicate with one another and to get all the information they need.

As IT specialists are brought in, to systematically automate and integrate management structures and practices, they are inevitably asking awkwardly logical questions, and prompting a debate about the way companies operate. If they do not prompt an up-front review of the whole management process there is an obvious danger that companies will end up with a computerised mess.

However, although technology makes process re-engineering possible, and although IT systems analysts may prompt a logical review of workflows, the IT function should not drive the process. Rohit Talwar, an independent consultant and Chairman of the re-engineering study group of the Strategic Planning Society, questions the IT orientation of the re-engineering debate. Most consultancy teams in the field are 'schooled in IT, not in business' and IT has failed to deliver its promises in the past. Many re-engineering exercises are unfortunately just seen as IT department initiatives. They should actually be driven strategically, top-down, starting with two questions, 'Where do we want to get to as a business and how do we get there?', and 'What role do we want IT to play on that journey?'

Some key considerations

When considering a core process redesign initiative companies should consider;

1 What are the core processes?

By process is meant the flow and transformation of materials and informa-tion, incorporating logistics, operations, communication, co-ordination, synthesis and decision making; something which pulls together everything necessary to deliver one important component of strategic value. Few com-panies have more than a handful of core processes. Unfortunately, they are often unable to define them other than in functional terms. The starting point is to define the company's value proposition – its unique selling proposition to the consumer.

For example, a fast food business might only have three core processes: *logistics* – supplying, preparing and serving the food; *theming* – researching, branding and communicating restaurant formats; *property management* – finding, developing and managing the network. Everything else is a service function to the core processes.

When companies start talking about their 57 core processes stand back and start again.

2 What are the required performance targets?

Care needs to be taken in defining performance improvement targets. If a company operates in a price-sensitive sector it is more likely the required performance enhancement should be price reduction rather than service improvement.

Performance targets also need to be understood and agreed upon. For example, in one mortgage lending operation senior management was con-cerned about the time it took to process applications through to offer. Strangely, the mortgage department manager was unconcerned, because the speed of processing was fast once applications reached his team. Unfortu-nately, twice as much time was being wasted getting the mortgage application to and from the branches than was taken processing the applica-tions once they were received. Once this had been understood the whole process could be redesigned, and turn-around times decreased dramatically.

Most importantly there must also be a time-frame for delivering benefits. It is said that as a rule of thumb one third to a half of total performance improvements must be delivered within a year, if commitment is to remain high. Complex gant charts and talk of three to five year time horizons may not have the desired effect.

3 How far should re-engineering be taken?

Given the costs, risks and time involved it is necessary to carefully consider how far process re-engineering should be taken. It can be restricted to a single process or it can cascade down the organisation into multiple, inte-grated business model changes.

Levels of process redesign				
Increasing radicalism →				
	Single process redesign	Multiple process redesign	Single major business model change	Multiple, integrated business model changes
Level of ambition for change	Quick hits	Continuous incremental improvement	Major investment to be world class in one element of business system	Total commitment to becoming a world leader
Type of programme needed	Project-oriented improvement	Bottom-up initiatives (e.g. TQM)	Major process-specific investment	Total commitment to permanent change

Source: McKinsey

Figure 4.4

At the more complex end, a company may find itself in perpetual motion as it alters the way it does business. Whether this is ultimately good or bad for the organisation depends on levels of commitment, realised financial gains and the need for change prompted by the competition.

The potential benefits of business process re-engineering

One problem with finding examples of how well business process re-engineering works is that those companies which have fundamentally changed their business methods tend, for obvious competitive reasons, to be secretive about exactly how the change process was carried out, and what it achieved. In those cases where it has not worked corporate modesty forbids disclosure.

However, it has been suggested that when it works, business process re-engineering can deliver tenfold improvements in performance. The length of time the concept has been around in the US inevitably means that there are strong US examples of what the technique can achieve. For example:

IBM Credit, apparently cut the time needed to prepare a quote for buying or leasing a computer from seven days to one day, while achieving a tenfold increase in the number of quotes prepared.

Federal Mogul, a billion dollar auto-parts manufacturer, reduced the time needed to develop a new part prototype from 20 weeks to 20 days.

Bell Atlantic, cut delivery times from 15 days to just one.

Walmart, the hugely successful US supermarket chain, decided to improve its inventory management in one particular area – Pampers baby products. It drastically cut the supply chain from Procter and Gamble, eventually giving P&G responsibility for the entire process of inventory management, and for keeping Walmart's shelves stocked.

By doing this Walmart off-loaded a large part of its inventory costs, freed warehouse space and working capital, and found its stock replenishment system working more smoothly. Inventory management is now so streamlined that stock reaches the customer and is paid for before Walmart has to pay P&G. In return P&G gets 'preferred supplier' status with the chain and spin-off benefits including prime display positions.

In the UK a number of important examples of re-engineering are to be found, notably *First Direct* in banking and *Direct Line Insurance* in general insurance. The latter, a subsidiary of The Royal Bank of Scotland, has produced record earnings for Britain's highest paid executive, Peter Wood, who last year picked up £1 million and stands to make £10 million in 1993.

Lucas Industries, which also pioneered industrial benchmarking techniques in the mid 1980s, *National & Provincial Building Society, British Telecom (BT), Rank Xerox UK, Reuters, Baxi Partnership* and *Rolls Royce* have all undertaken process re-engineering exercises.

For example, BT cut the time to repair private circuits from five days to five hours as part of its drive to become more customer focused. Baxi mobilised its workforce to reorganise its manufacturing process, by using multiskilled teams to improve quality and productivity. Directors surrendered their conventional functions to take responsibility for 'portfolios of business areas and specialist functions'. The staff identified more closely with the customer, the product and the process from order to delivery.

Re-engineering sales, marketing and finance

A common phenomenon in many companies is that sales, marketing and finance departments are not on speaking terms with one another, let alone working together in one integrated process. They fight like cat and dog, while production and distribution departments innocently watch the inter-departmental scrap. Moving towards a customer focus means that companies will now have to remove cultural barriers and rivalries. Warring factions will need to work together to identify the processes which actually satisfy the customer, and gets the product or service out at the correct price.

Some of the questions which will have to be addressed as a team are 'Have we processed all the orders we might have taken?', 'Are we sure that we have incurred minimum costs in processing orders?', 'Is the customer getting what he or she wants, in a timely and efficient way?', 'Is customer information feeding into the marketing information system?' 'Which processes can be eliminated and how can we speed up the time between them?', 'Do we need five separate functions or can we coalesce them into three?', 'Could manufacturing, sales forecasting, warehousing, order entry, credit control, distribution, accounts be organised more seamlessly?', 'Is it sensible to have different people heading up all those different areas, a manufacturing director, a transport manager, an accounts manager, or is there some simpler way of putting everything together?'

In many ways companies with a crisis are the lucky ones. They are forced to work together to resolve these and other questions or they may go out of business. The hardest challenge is for those companies which are doing acceptably but could do so much better. In practice the majority of companies which have undertaken Business Process Re-engineering exercises have been forced to by some market cataclysm rather than by the vision of the CEO or the Board. This may change in future.

Caveat Emptor

But while there are enormous gains to be made there are also major corporate risks. Inter-disciplinary feuding and politics can proliferate as directors lose control of their fiefdoms. Staff can become panic stricken as they realise the potential threat to their jobs. For the impact on middle-ranking executives could be stunning. It has been suggested that up to 25 million middle ranking jobs could disappear by the end of the 1990s as companies across America shed functions and departments. 40 per cent staff reductions are expected to be typical, although they may go to 80 per cent. Employee to manager ratios are anticipated to move from 7:1 to 30:1. Even more startling figures could apply in Europe with its fragmented and over-manned industries.

While all this is going on customer service may suffer, and if the period of change is particularly difficult the consequences could be disastrous. For example, it has been estimated that 75 to 80 per cent of companies fail in their attempts at business process re-engineering because they do not think changes through properly. It is vital that functions are simplified before new work patterns or new IT applications are introduced. Above all, organisations must succeed in winning over the hearts and minds of the staff, and senior management must be seen to be involved. If these factors can be brought to bear the financial benefits could be staggering.

STRENGTHENING BUSINESS 'VALUE CHAINS'

Business process re-engineering is closely related to a rigorously financial way of maximising company profits, *Value chain analysis*. Taking a financial, rather than a functional or process, overview of the organisation one can identify a series of value chains, which, when connected together, result in the creation of shareholder value. In many companies the linkages between value chains are often broken or obscured by operational practice. In many the detailed information is not available to illuminate the process. The job of financial and marketing strategists is to lay bare and maximise those linkages in order to increase corporate value.

The key is to identify where in the whole chain real value is added and to increase it. Different companies naturally take different approaches to the way they wish to manage their value chains. For example, while Benetton has vertically integrated its operations in one company-owned value chain, from factory through to shop floor, M&S has avoided manufacture, by including supplier partners in its value chain. There is more than one way of skinning a cat and M&S has chosen to maximise value by managing its supplier relationships.

Many companies do not fully understand the process of value added through the chain. Nor do they understand how costs and revenues are related to one another. They are therefore unable to make strategic decisions about how far to vertically integrate their operations. By looking at the business as a series of discrete added value chains management can clearly focus on re-engineering the business for the future.

A natural development of this rigorously financial approach is the concept of shareholder value, propounded by academics who suggest that management should look at their companies as generators of cashflow, rather than at traditional accounting profits. By applying discounted cash flow analysis to sustainable cashflows management can estimate current and future shareholder value.

THE FUTURE OF TOTAL QUALITY MANAGEMENT

Total quality management is a recent example of an apparently sensible and enduring fashion damaged by over-enthusiastic consultants, excessive jargon, paperwork and over-exposure. The idea that organisations should dedicate themselves whole-heartedly to high quality standards throughout their operations sounds like common sense; apple pie and motherhood. However, in many cases the systematic application of TQM, and the demands TQM practitioners have made on everyday working routines, have pushed a simple and laudable principle into the realms of bureaucracy.

A similar fate seems to have overtaken BS 5750, the extremely onerous procedural quality standard set by the British Standards Institution. BS 5750 is intended as a quality standard for management. It requires that companies listen to what their customers want, ensure they have mechanisms for assessing product quality, and that they apply whatever lessons are learned in the process. Consultants write manuals and ultimately get a certificate is received from the BSI. Standards administrators love it; BS 5750 has gone on to glory in Europe as *EN 29000* and around the world as *ISO 9000*. An army of consultants make large amounts implementing the standard, and the BSI makes a tidy sum in certification fees. But many companies continue to puzzle over how it helps their competitive position. In fact, the extra costs it causes can lose customers for companies in tight margin businesses.

Like codliver oil, it is one of those things which matronly figures insist you swallow in large quantities, but can't quite explain why it's good for you. Many small businesses and service companies have wearied of the medicine and are refusing to take it.

Similarly, a recent study indicated that around 85 per cent of the organisations using TQM are disappointed with the results. Unfortunately, many companies find it too bureaucratic and have lost interest. The reality is that almost nobody has seen any money come back from it. Management 'experts' are rapidly moving on from TQM to process re-engineering.

ANALYTICAL APPROACHES TO STRATEGY FORMULATION

Until the eighties the analytical approach to business strategy formulation was considered the norm by academics, particularly in the great US business schools. *Hard* analytical values were rated more highly than *soft* interpretive ones. The result was that business schools turned out MBAs who many businessmen criticised for being dry, detached and dogmatic about business processes. Many behaved as though every business process was reducible to some form of logical analysis and resolution. There came a point at which many CEOs were apparently questioning the employability of intelligent but other-worldly graduates from the business school Ivy League.

In all probability the academics who taught them analytical skills had the understanding and sense to use structured, rational approaches in a subtle and responsive way. However, during the 1980s there was something of a crisis of confidence in the callow youths who passed through their seminar rooms.

The hard analytical school of thinking had been helped along by Frederick Winslow Taylor. In his book *Scientific Management*, published in 1947, he suggested that business processes could be analysed into specific elements and programmed for maximum efficiency. The idea that managers are more intelligent than their workers, and that spontaneity and initiative are best kept under control, militated in favour of a bureaucratic and hierarchical approach to both management and strategy formulation. This belief in analysis, measurement and rigid process led to a style of academic business research, writing and teaching which endured for decades.

Perhaps it was the influence of the Second World War, in which the application of rational science and a huge, hierarchical war machine had defeated the Axis. Certainly, as the decades have passed, blind faith in the infallibility of human logic and the rightness of hierarchies have both waned.

Michael Porter's book *Competitive Strategy* has been cited as the highwater mark of the analytical and rational approach to business strategy formulation. When published in 1980 the style of management it represented was at its zenith. Porter, an economist by training, perpetuated a somewhat detached view of business, as an economic process apparently separate from the real world of people at work. To a large extent the criticism of its detachment has been over-blown, and it remains extremely relevant today. Unfortunately, as we have seen, there is nothing more ridiculous than an out-of-date fashion. Porter had chosen to wear a tweed jacket when he should have been wearing a kaftan.

In the book, Porter defines and analyses five competitive forces to be considered when determining corporate strategy. These are:

- threat of entry
- intensity of rivalry among existing competitors
- presssure from substitute products
- bargaining power of buyers
- bargaining power of suppliers.

In assessing the threat of competitive entry into a market he logically analyses the various barriers to entry; *economies of scale, product differentiation, capital requirements, switching costs, access to distribution channels, cost disadvantages independent of scale* and *government policy*. The same rigour is adopted for each of the five competitive forces. He then advises that,

> *'Once the forces affecting competition in an industry, and their underlying causes, have been diagnosed, the firm is in a position to identify its strengths and weaknesses relative to the industry.'*

He goes on to argue that there are three ways to compete in the marketplace:

1 Overall cost leadership

Become the lowest cost producer.

2 Differentiation

Differentiate in order to command a premium price.

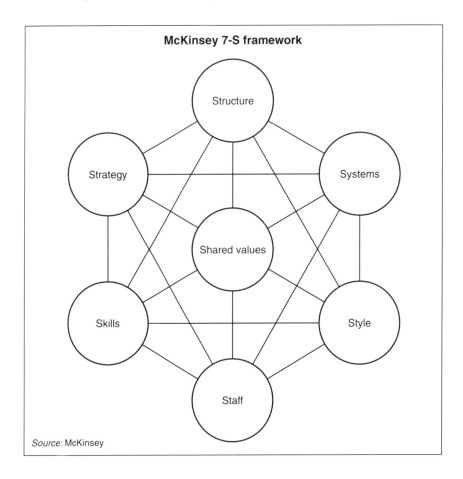

McKinsey 7-S framework

Source: McKinsey

Figure 4.5

3 Focus

Occupy a niche position.

The book then looks at the means of assessing markets and competitors, and how to achieve the three alternative strategies in different industries and under different market conditions. It outlines the obstacles as well as the opportunities.

Competitive Strategy is a classic, setting out clearly and succinctly a methodology for approaching strategy formulation. Unfortunately, for those like Michael Porter who find themselves in the fashion world, *classic* can sometimes be a polite epithet for dowdy.

THE RISE OF THE FLEXIBLE APPROACH

Someone who is most certainly not dowdy is the style guru of the moment, Tom Peters. Through a sequence of highly popular books he has argued for more emphasis on people and their skills, leading to a much more liberated view of the way business should operate.

When he was at McKinsey he was part of the team which developed the *McKinsey 7-S Framework* (see Figure 4.5).

This approach recognised the importance of *soft* as well as *hard* values as determinants of corporate success.

In his first book *In Search of Excellence*, which appeared in 1982, Peters, and his co-author, Waterman, outline what they had observed as the key attributes which characterise excellent, innovative companies. These were summarised as:

1 A bias for action

The best companies are both analytical and action oriented.

2 Close to the customer

Companies thrive only if they understand and intercommunicate with their customers.

3 Autonomy and entrepreneurship

Scientific management principles should give way to participation and involvement.

4 Productivity through people

People are not just a factor of production. Motivation is a critical success factor.

5 Hands on, value driven

A clear corporate philosophy and involved management are prerequisites of success.

6 Stick to the knitting

Don't get involved in businesses you don't know how to manage.

7 Simple form, lean staff

Corporate structures need to be simple, elegant and tightly staffed.

8 Simultaneous loose-tight properties

Great companies are both centralised in key decision-making areas and decentralised in day-to-day management.

The ideas in the book influenced a generation of businessmen and strategists who had become disillusioned with the mechanistic and dehumanised approach of the past. These ideas represented a much looser and more flexible way for companies to respond to the challenges of future markets.

In *A Passion for Excellence* and *Thriving on Chaos*, Peters' views on the need for more responsive, flexible and people-oriented companies continued to develop, and in his latest book, *Liberation Management – Necessary Disorganisation for the Nanosecond Nineties*, he describes the extreme flexibility companies will have to demonstrate if they are to meet future business challenges. The importance of the entrepreneurial individual, globalisation of markets and IT are leading to fragmentation of dinosaur organisations like IBM.

In *Organisational Ecology*, Michael Hannan and John Freeman refer to two fundamentally different types of biological propagation strategies. The *r-strategy* is the one adopted by the likes of flies and mosquitos; many reproductive events and low survival rates. The *k-strategy* is the one adopted by the likes of whales and humans; few reproductive events but high survival rates. The analogy in the current fast moving world is that fashions and technology are changing so fast that in many markets the flies have it over the whales. The k-strategists like IBM are being forced to move as far as they can towards an r-strategy to capitalise on fast moving IT markets.

That smaller companies are eroding the position of the conglomerates is illustrated by the share of GNP taken by Fortune 500 companies.

The Flow and Ebb of the Fortune 500

Year	Employment (Millions)	Per cent of GNP
1954*	8	37
1959	9	40
1969	15	46
1979	16	58
1989	12.5	42
1991**	11.9	40

Source: Fortune/Tom Peters Analysis
*First year of published rankings, taken from *Liberation Management*, p.555.
** Most recent rankings

Figure 4.6

Large organisations will become more decentralised and will progressively inject competition into the internal processes and service delivery mechanisms. The need for companies to be imaginative, flexible and to rely on people's intellectual skills are recurring themes in *Liberation Management*.

The Shamrock Theory

That flexibility is becoming the order of the day is reflected in Charles Handy's Shamrock theory of management described in *Age of Unreason* (Business Books 1991). He argues that, in future, organisations will have three *leaves* to their management resources. The first leaf will represent '. . . professional core workers who own the organisational knowledge which distinguishes the organisation from its counterparts.' This first leaf will be supported by a second leaf of subcontract workers and a third of part-time and temporary workers.

The joint venture generation

One manifestation of increasing flexibility and a more open-minded approach to business structures is the growth of joint ventures worldwide.

For example, the international plane makers are sinking their differences to design and build the superjet of the next century. Car makers are also coming together in joint ventures which cut the cost of model development and production.

The trend has also directly affected the marketing services business. The 1992 WPP Annual Report and Accounts comments on the complications the trend has created,

> '*As the major multinational marketing companies venture into new geographical markets and new product sectors, they inevitably invade each other's territory. Given the limited number of international agency networks the issue of conflict has come to the fore – an issue made even more complicated by the growth, over the last few years, of strategic alliances. Pepsi Cola is working with Unilever in tea, Coca Cola with Nestlé in coffee, Nestlé with General Mills in cereals, Unilever with BSN in yoghurts; and all have chosen to make agency appointments which have caused previous conflict arrangements to be redrawn. This development, together with the emergence of third networks within agency groups, suggests that traditional, hard and fast conflict policies may soon be modified.*'

Not only will marketing companies need to find new ways of working with competitors in joint ventures but their agencies which serve them will also need to adapt.

THE USE OF COMPETITIVE INTELLIGENCE

Internal focus putting companies on the defensive

One of the problems of the last few years has been that, in the search for survival, many companies have shrunk back into themselves, looking for cost savings and other efficiencies. They have become cautious, introverted and narrow minded. They have adopted defensive attitudes to both customers and competitors. They have spent so long knocking infrastructure and business practices into shape that many do not look carefully enough at what is going on in the marketplace. Lessons from the market are either not spotted or are not acted on fast enough. As a result, huge financial opportunities go begging.

Many companies have become reactive, both in the exploitation of new technology, in the way their businesses are structured and in the way products are distributed and sold.

Part of the problem is an ingrained cultural inertia. For example, in Britain academic disciplines are strong, yet somehow we don't seem to have the ability to turn technical or scientific breakthroughs to marketing advantage. Eyes are closed to innovations within touching distance. The first thing we know, a competitor, often foreign, has adopted new British technology and fundamentally altered market dynamics to our detriment. It is often to do with funding and marketing abilities, but also to a lack of imagination and entrepreneurship. Very often it comes down to simple myopia.

This extends to everyday operations. If companies only kept their eyes open for activity and potential activity in the market they would be in far better shape. Far too often major competitor breakthroughs or initiatives come as a complete surprise; look at the surprise with which Mars' arrival in the ice cream market was greeted. Yet there are always clear signs that something is going on.

The strategy formulation process

A simple summary of the steps in business strategy formulation is as follows:

1 Vision statement
2 Industry and environmental analysis
3 Competitor analysis
4 Sources of competitive advantage
5 Proposed strategies to achieve the corporate vision
6 External and internal initiatives
7 Discarded options
8 Financial strategy to match business strategy.

This process calls for detailed review of competitor activity, but very often companies either fail to follow the process or do not review it frequently enough. The arrival of new competitors in the market, contested bids, new owners of existing companies, fundamental changes in the marketplace, regulatory reviews, tightening of the supply of qualified staff or the review of major business processes all demand that competitor activity is minutely studied and fed back into the model.

The role of the finance function

Many would argue that of all the myopic disciplines finance is the worst. Yet the finance function is in a strong position to act as the competitive eyes and ears of the business, feeding crucial competitive intelligence back to the marketing and general management teams. It is also well placed to analyse the data. But all too often it is not employed in this way.

In a research report produced by the GAH Group Ltd, a strategy consulting boutique based in London, the benefits of *competitive intelligence* are clearly spelled out. In the report Mark O'Hare, the Managing Partner of the GAH Group Ltd, gives the example of 'Powertech', a large player in the industrial tools market. Although it had high market share, it never seemed to make an adequate profit. Prices charged by 'Sunrise', its main competitor, were too keen. A careful analysis of the product line-up of the two companies revealed that, on a like-for-like basis, 'Sunrise' products had 10 per cent fewer parts, and that the 'Powertech' range was three times as wide as the 'Sunrise' range.

'Powertech' re-engineered its products, cut its range and revised its pricing policy on low volume items. Its profits more than doubled within two years.

Some of the sources of competitive intelligence indicate the scope for a cross-functional approach, with significant financial involvement.

Published data

- annual Report and Accounts
- financial, business and trade press coverage
- advertising and competitor literature
- patent filings
- property planning and development applications
- trade conferences and speeches
- government and industry statistics
- market research reports
- stockbroking analysts reports
- directories.

Observation

- product comparisons
- service comparisons
- passive observation.

Internal sources

- staff knowledge
- informal contacts
- customer records.

External sources

- interviews with key groups
- credit analysis and ratings.

When gathered the data can be constantly used to analyse the company's marketing and business plans, its product launch programme and its own cost base. The information can be used to isolate key variables and to model competitive cost and price strategies.

Have you been Krolled?

All companies should be aware that, whether they are active in competitor analysis or not, the competition probably is. Some even go to the lengths of appointing corporate investigation agencies.

The most impressive of these is Kroll Associates, which was set up by a larger than life ex-lawyer from New York, the cigar smoking Jules Kroll. It boomed in the heady, take-over days of the eighties, when it was hired by Wall Street firms to provide defensive information on acquisitive companies and to complete 'due diligence' on potential bid targets. At times its methods have been questioned, most publicly by Sir James Goldsmith, when BAT hired the firm to help in its defence against Hoylake, Goldsmith's company. Mutterings were heard about phone tapping and rubbish sifting and questions were asked in Parliament.

Many financial institutions now use firms like Kroll as a matter of course and it has moved on into other high profile assignments like asset search, fraud investigation and crisis management. It also undertakes the more mundane business of general commercial intelligence. The unnerving thing about firms like Kroll is that the target company often knows nothing about the research study until the results are felt.

As companies define their corporate strategies the importance of competitive intelligence cannot be exaggerated, and, as the old saying goes, 'it's always better to get your retaliation in first'.

COST OF CAPITAL AND REQUIRED RETURNS

One of the hottest contemporary fashions in the area of corporate finance strategy is the concept of *Economic Value Added* or *EVA*. In the US, trendy CEOs have been getting their multicoloured braces in a twist with excitement over this new development. Like designer drugs and steroids it is being used to revive and rebuild flabby corporate bodies.

Stern Stewart & Co, a New York City based consultancy, has popularised the concept, which is said to have transformed the financial performance and stock market valuation of many large US companies. Coca-Cola, AT&T and the Quaker Oats Company, to name but a few, have benefited from the discipline of EVA. For example, the Coca-Cola share price has shot from under $10 to over $40 a share in just over ten years, during which time EVA has been applied to the company's operations.

Apparently, AT&T has adopted EVA as the *primary* performance measure for its business units. And according to the Quaker Oats Company CEO, William Smithburg, 'EVA makes managers act like shareholders. It's the true corporate faith for the 1990s.'

So what is this wonder drug? Essentially, EVA is a way of looking at corporate profitability after taking into account the real cost of capital, including shareholder capital. EVA is simply after tax profits less the total cost of capital. If the resulting figure is positive the prognosis is good, if negative the prognosis is dire.

The need for a new measure stems from the fact that many corporate managers seem to have forgotten that shareholder capital has a cost too. Far too many corporate executives have come to regard equity capital as a free meal ticket. In fact, it is both expensive and demanding. If it is not being properly rewarded it migrates to companies where it will be. All costs, including the cost of capital, must be covered, and additional value must also be created, if a company is to be considered a long-term proposition.

In the case of Coca-Cola, EVA focused the corporate mind on the allocation of capital resources to the highest yielding business units. Since 1987 the capital allocation emphasis has been on the higher EVAs available in the soft drinks concentrate market, the company's core business area. Other areas like pasta, instant tea, and wine have had capital severely rationed and have been divested. While the former earns nearly 30 per cent on capital the latter areas returned only 7 or 8 per cent, below the true cost of capital. EVA also created the impetus to find less costly ways of manufacturing and distributing concentrate, to minimise capital employed. In addition, EVA made corporate management look closely at the capital mix, to see whether debt gearing might not further enhance EVA. As a result of these measures Coke's EVA has increased 27 per cent per annum for five years, and its share price has shot up from $3 to $43 in 12 years.

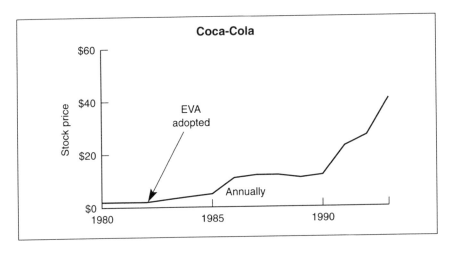

Figure 4.7

AT&T used the EVA methodology to allocate capital to individual business segments. In the capital intensive telecommunications business the ability to isolate real capital employed, and its costs, has been invaluable.

At Quaker Oats, EVA has been used to end a working capital nightmare caused by the fact that its operations were rewarded on bottom-line profit targets, without any internal charge for stockholding costs. This led to 'trade loading', which boosted period-end profits but massively inflated warehouse stocks, until EVA was introduced.

Basically EVA makes management run harder and capital sweat more to produce a higher return. Because the focus is on rewarding shareholder capital, instead of looking at just a theoretical accounting profit figure, the impact on share prices can be dramatic.

Of course, some practical problems do hamper EVA. For example: How should appreciating balance sheet assets be treated? Should related costs and amortisation be adjusted out? How does the company arrive at an appropriate weighted average cost of capital? What should the percentage return on equity be in the short-, medium- and long-term? How can capital costs be allocated to individual business units? Should they be marginal or average? However, while the answers may be subjective the task in resolving them is not insurmountable. And the payback is high.

At the end of the day, what it really shows is that which seems obvious to the average accountant is an amazing revelation to many marketing and operational people. Simple ideas, expressed strongly and clearly, are often the best ways of dramatically improving financial performance. Financial strategies which are too complex or arcane for the average manager to understand are doomed to failure. EVA has the simplicity and power to succeed.

RELATIONSHIP BETWEEN CORPORATE AND MARKETING STRATEGIES

Having done the shows and seen what is on offer corporate management must choose its wardrobe. The difficulty is, even with the new techniques to hand, that a number of perennial issues still need to be resolved in many companies.

Where have all the visionaries gone?

Every process of strategic change needs a visionary leader to define the parameters and see it through. The CEO must be able to motivate and lead all disciplines. But above all there must be a vision of the future.

The apochryphal story about the CEOs of Pan Am and Boeing conceiving the idea of the Jumbo jet while fishing off Alaska rings true with the far-sighted ambitions of the 1960s, when the US was conquering space and anything seemed possible. Visionary decisions need strong and decisive leadership. No amount of new techniques will achieve competitive advantage or corporate profit improvement without such leadership and vision.

When the founder of Sony, Akio Morita, decided to create the Walkman® he did it because he had a vision of the future and of a market need, and no one was going to get in his way.

The chicken or the egg?

Is it possible to define a marketing strategy without knowing exactly what that corporate vision is? There are many companies where marketing and finance people go off into corners to develop 'strategies'. But the only strategies which ultimately work are the ones which start at the top and cascade down the organisation.

Long- or short-term perspective?

The ability of any organisation to plan for the future depends on the current state of the short-term market and the depth of its investors' pockets. Studies have shown that the best position to plan for the long-term is a stable, profitable home market with far-sighted, patient investors. Unfortunately, many companies do not have these luxuries and have to cut their strategic coat to fit the environmental cloth.

Mass market or niche?

Which of Porter's strategies a company goes for is often not a matter of choice but of history. Analysis is all very well but the decision to go for low cost and volume, or differentiation and focus, is often not at the discretion of the management. It may be determined by the shape of the market.

National or international?

MARS' recent marketing initiative in the ice-cream sector was technology-related and involved production facilities spread across Europe. Many of the companies that are functioning effectively in the UK are subsidiaries of foreign-owned companies.

The fact is that the ability of companies to opt for a single country marketing strategy are rapidly disappearing.

> 'Many products have components from many parts of the globe. Increasingly, services too will have components from abroad and ultimately "foreign" will become less meaningful'. Charles M Perrottet, The Futures Group.

Convergence of international strategies?

And just as the opportunity to hide in a single country market is disappearing, market differences and investor expectations are rapidly being arbitraged. For example, German, Japanese and US car companies are increasingly playing in a world market where cost and technology determine success. As a result large players' strategies are rapidly converging on one another.

CONCLUSIONS

One thing which the new strategic techniques have in common is the integration of different disciplines and skills to arrive at a common solution. Whether it be in the recreation of the marketing function, the effort to re-engineer processes, the search for EVA or the acquisition of competitive intelligence, there is a growing need for greater co-operation and exchange of information and skill-sets.

If only one fashion endures it should be the fashion for greater co-operation between management disciplines in achieving strategic change.

Bibliography

WPP Group PLC, Annual Report and Accounts 1992

Competitive Strategy, Michael E. Porter, Macmillan, ISBN o o2 925360 8

In Search of Excellence, Tom Peters and Robert Waterman Jr., Harper & Rowe, ISBN 0-06-015042-4

Liberation Management, Tom Peters, Macmillan, ISBN o 333 53340 2

'*Competitive Intelligence*', Research Report, 1993, Mark O'Hare, The GAH Group

The McKinsey Quarterly 1993, Number 1 – Core Process Redesign, Number 2 – Marketing in Transition

The Director Magazine, August 1993, 'Reinventing the Company', Stuart Rock and Carol Kennedy

Accountancy Magazine, August 1993, 'Buzz Words: learning the language of business', David Oates

Fortune Magazine, September 1993, Number 19, 'The Real Key to Creating Wealth', Shawn Tully

Organisational Ecology, Hannan and Freeman, Harvard University Press, ISBN 0674 643 496

5

COSTING AND PRICING DILEMMAS

'Theory helps us to bear our ignorance of facts'
George Santayana

INTRODUCTION

Costing and *pricing* are intimately connected disciplines. Externally, one person's price is another person's cost. Internally, the starting point for the marketing department's pricing structure is the finance department's cost structure. But some suggest that there are major differences in emphasis between the two disciplines. Costing seems to be a hard factual subject, while pricing has more to do with conjecture and theory. Costing is the preserve of pedantic management accountants while pricing is more to do with free-thinking econometricians and academics. One is all fact, the other all theory.

It is true that costing is more concerned with the tough business of finding new sources of supply, of producing at lower unit costs, of beating down suppliers, and of finding more effective internal control and reporting systems. By contrast, pricing is more involved with consumer and customer behaviour, uncertain research findings, elasticities of demand, and a host of intangible variables.

According to this line of argument costing is more tangible and verifiable, and is therefore more of an applied science. Pricing, on the other hand, attracts theorists and theologians, laymen and women of the marketing congregation stand by for the white smoke to rise over their deliberations, in the quest for answers which might help them in their day-to-day lives. Pricing is more like a pure science, or an open-ended theological debate.

But in practice the uncertainties of both costing and pricing constantly create major problems for marketing and general managers.

For example, a common marketing blindspot is the belief that the product unit cost *is* the product unit cost. It is a fixed and immutable fact of life, and assumptions used in arriving at it cannot be questioned. That product costs vary with output, that they differ according to the cost allocation methods used, and that all costing exercises are incredibly subjective exercises, are frequently overlooked by marketing managers. When asked to discuss marketing plans there is often a blind faith in the 'standard cost' of production, which is used in all sorts of 'back-of-the-envelope' calculations. Yet basing a niche marketing strategy on unit costs which assume high volume, or a volume growth strategy based on low volume unit costs, can be fatal to the brand. If only marketeers had a more subtle appreciation of the subjectivity implicit in costing systems many wrong marketing decisions would be avoided.

Similarly, while there is a lot of argument between academics and commercial econometicians about the validity of price modelling strategies, empirical evidence seems to suggest that price modelling can be helpful. The results may not be academically perfect, but in an imperfect world they can be helpful in decision-making.

Before looking at the academic pricing debate it is worth considering one very practical costing development which has hit the headlines recently. It is an example of Michael Porter's advice in *Competitive Strategy* – that the lowest cost producer will win – taken to an absurd extreme.

DRIVING OUT COST TO BEAT THE COMPETITION

The Volkswagen saga played to full houses in a Hamburg courtroom, starring the ice-cool Dr Ferdinand Piech, Chairman of Volkswagen AG, and his messianic, cost-cutting head of manufacturing and purchasing, Jose Ignacio Lopez de Arriortua.

The Wagnerian Epic began when hard-pressed Volkswagen, Europe's largest carmaker and the fourth largest carmaker in the world, recruited Lopez de Arriortua from General Motors, one of its arch rivals. VW had been suffering from high labour costs, low productivity, a strong Deutschmark, a severe European recession and tough Japanese competition, particularly from Japanese assembly plants in Europe. According to Nick Snee of Investment Bank S.G. Warburg it costs VW 21 per cent more to produce a car than Renault and Peugeot, and the difference is even wider compared with its aggressive Japanese competitors. Until recently VW plants needed to operate at over 100 per cent of normal capacity to break even, compared with an industry average of 70 to 80 per cent. In 1992 VW made less than $50 million, on turnover of more than $56 billion, and in the first three months of 1993 it lost over $750 million. Piech, whose background is in development engineering, had set out a recovery plan including model rationalisation, production efficiency improvements, closer involvement with supplier production processes, and a cost saving plan which implied cutting 30,000 of VW's 274,000 staff, all of which offered savings of $5 billion a year.

Arriortua was a key element in this process. He had a reputation as a hard man and an interventionist with suppliers, extracting efficiency gains of up to 65 per cent. He was said to consider the struggle in the car market as a 'war', and had been credited with giving General Motors a huge cost advantage over its competitors, through better procurement and production. VW recruited Arriortua to work his magic on its own manufacturing process.

Unfortunately for Piech and Arriortua, GM took legal action to prove that the 'sorcerer' had taken his 'books' with him. GM executives testified in court that he took a hundred page specification of the cost profile for a new, small, GM model. They accused him of inciting GM colleagues to copy documents of super-efficient assembly lines, cost-saving techniques and information on other GM models. He was also accused of poaching seven GM staff and offering jobs to 40 others.

The consequences of losing the courtroom battle are immense. The charges are both criminal and civil and involve huge fines and imprisonment for any convicted executives. The scandal has even affected the VW brand. Gerd Burmann, VW's Head of Strategic Marketing, was recently quoted in *Fortune* Magazine as saying, 'In the ratings of our brands with customers, we have lost some points.'

The VW battle is an extreme version of a struggle which is going on in many sectors, as companies seek to minimise costs, reduce prices and thereby gain market share and extra profitability. In the words of Roger Scarlett-Smith, Vice President of Marketing for SmithKline Beecham Consumer Healthcare,

> '. . . there is a general recognition that low cost production is critical because it enables a higher margin to be generated to support publicity and other initiatives. It's not just financial directors who think this way; there is a general recognition throughout business that low cost production is a strategic weapon.'

The question for many companies after the challenges of the late eighties and early nineties is 'Can costs be cut any further?' United Biscuits is a company which has moved mountains to cut costs without sacrificing quality, and yet John Warren, the group finance director, believes further cost savings are achievable,

> 'It's said every year that we can't take any more costs out of the business, but every year we do. In the 1980s we closed three biscuit factories, going from eight to five. £30 million has been cut since then, all of which has been reinvested to pay for increased marketing. Within that marketing spend, less has been spent above-the-line. Because of market conditions

we have been forced to invest in either price-based promotions or incentives for the retail trade. Over the next five years we plan to drive further significant costs out of the business. But they are becoming increasingly difficult to achieve, and it requires further capital expenditure to drive them down. In effect, returns on capital are being eroded to reinvest in the marketing sphere.'

In fact, unless companies can continue to drive down costs they face the choice of either cutting marketing budgets or reducing shareholder returns, either of which could have severe repercussions; the former by debilitating brands, the latter by laying companies open to takeover. Again, in John Warren's words,

'All the environmental pressures we face are reflected in what is happening to the overall marketing budget. We are very good, as an industry, at driving costs down; achieving more efficient production, optimising delivery systems and driving costs out of the supply chain. But eventually, unless we can be very clever in controlling production costs still further, or cutting marketing expenditure, we are going to end up with a severe squeeze on margins. It's a fundamental problem.'

If companies can add value from a low-cost base, they can make more profit. Unilever and Procter & Gamble are busy doing it by fundamentally reappraising their product ranges and delivery channels, managing unnecessary activities and people, and shortening their supply chains; adding more value with lower costs. Driving down the cost base to reinvest in brands.

The crucial task for companies in the competitive 1990s is to cut out costs and thereby bring down the operating break-even point. This will create room for both increased marketing and better returns for shareholders.

SUBJECTIVITY AND VARIABILITY IN COST ALLOCATION

We are all familiar with traditional, economic break-even analysis. The vertical y axis shows the costs and revenues, and the horizontal x axis shows the volume of sales. The sales revenue line usually shoots up as a steep, straight line from left to right, finding the break-even point where it meets the total cost line. Some charts show relatively low fixed and high variable cost components; this would be true of many low-tech, food production processes, where ingredients are more significant than the mixing or cooking equipment. Others show high fixed costs and low variable costs; this would be true in the pharmaceutical industry, where original research and plant investment are far larger cost components than raw materials. Most show revenue

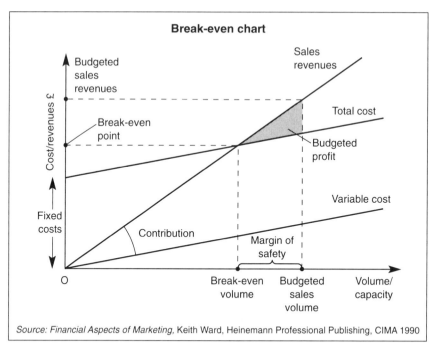

Figure 5.1 (a)

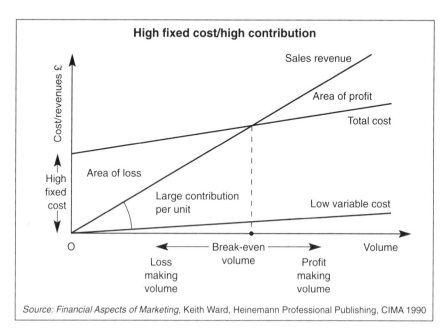

Figure 5.1 (b)

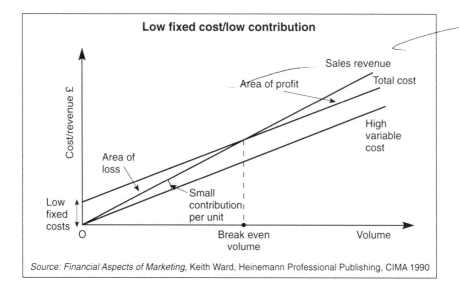

Source: *Financial Aspects of Marketing*, Keith Ward, Heinemann Professional Publishing, CIMA 1990

Figure 5.2

gradients reassuringly steeper than cost gradients. In all cases the lines are all nice and straight, and easy to follow (see Figures 5.1(a) and (b) and 5.2).

The trouble is that this gives a totally false picture, which is often not rectified in the minds of many managers. Simple cost and revenue relationships are not what real life costing and pricing are all about. The definition of fixed and variable costs is not straightforward. It can be extremely hard to separate fixed from variable costs. Where for example should the accountants put 'overheads', which may or may not vary with different activity levels? Where should financing costs go, either of the whole operation or of specific product lines?

Dividing lines are hazy and cost profiles are more commonly 'sawtoothed', with unit costs moving up in steps through different volumes of production. Revenues are equally hard to simplify, with volume discounts and overproduction affecting income. The relative gradients of costs and revenues are never as clear as theory suggests, and quite often intersect one another as volume moves out to the right.

In addition, there is an inevitable debate as to whether the data should be presented in aggregate or split by product, individual customer, market sector, plant location, distribution channel or even by operating region. Is the data available to do all, or any, of these analyses? Can the analysis be relied upon where it is available? Has it been checked by marketing people for reasonableness?

Example: Product line profitability and cost analysis

	PL1 (£)	PL2 (£)	Total (£)
Sales	369,444	551,820	921,264
Variable costs	199,538	298,036	497,574
Gross contribution margin	169,906	253,784	423,690
Less:			
Variable marketing expenses			
Selling	18,426	27,636	46,062
Warehousing	12,534	18,792	31,326
Transport	7,374	11,052	18,426
Advertising	18,426	27,636	46,062
Credit and collection	11,058	16,584	27,642
General accounting	5,898	8,838	14,736
Variable marketing expenses	73,716	110,538	184,254
Contribution margin	96,190	143,246	239,436
Product controllable margin			
to sales (%)	(16.29)	(12.91)	(14.27)
Less:			
Product line fixed expenses	36,000	72,000	108,000
Margin available for common			
fixed expenses and profit	60,190	71,246	131,436
Common fixed expenses			77,982
Net profit before tax			53,454

Source: Strategic Planning & Marketing – Patrick McNamee

Figure 5.3

An example of a detailed costing and profit and loss analysis by product line as shown in Figure 5.3.

The same analysis could be re-expressed with distribution channels as the focus (see in Figure 5.4).

The same data could also be analysed in several other ways to assist in marketing planning. The only limiting factors are the power of the computer systems, the availability of relevant data and the time of the financial people. As systems become more powerful cross-analysis of this sort will be automatic. Marketing managers will need to absorb the information coming through. Marketing people will need to understand the principles and the areas where subjectivity could arise. They may need to interpret different reports according to the situation.

Example: Channel of distribution profitability and cost analysis

	CH1 (£)	CH2 (£)	Total (£)
Sales	737,010	184,254	921,264
Variable costs	398,058	99,516	497,574
Gross contribution margin	338,952	84,738	423,690
Less:			
Variable marketing expenses			
Selling	32,244	13,818	46,062
Warehousing	21,930	9,396	31,326
Transport	12,894	5,532	18,426
Advertising	32,244	13,818	46,062
Credit and collection	19,350	8,292	27,642
General accounting	10,314	4,422	14,736
Variable marketing expenses	128,976	55,278	184,254
Contribution margin	209,976	29,460	239,436
Controllable contribution by channel (%)	(16.77)	(4.26)	(14.27)
Less:			
Channel fixed expenses	86,400	21,600	108,000
Margin available for common fixed expenses and profit	123,576	7,860	131,436
Common fixed expenses			77,982
Net profit before tax			53,454

Source: Strategic Planning & Marketing – Patrick McNamee

Figure 5.4

Another reporting format, this time oriented around a specific customer is shown in Figure 5.5.

Unfortunately, many marketing managers are either unaware of, or uninterested in, the boring details, and are happy to accept one crude unit cost figure. When marketing managers abdicate responsibility for costing analysis the chances of producing nonsensical marketing strategies are greatly increased. An example of the danger is implicit in the own-label decision, which depends on a very clear and subtle understanding of costing structures, and the relative impact of different levels of production on them. These need to be understood and checked on a regular basis, not just by finance people but by marketing people.

Example: Segmental Reporting Format

SEGMENT: CUSTOMER:- TESCO

SUB-SEGMENT: PRODUCT:-

	A	B	C	Total
	(£)	(£)	(£)	(£)
Sales Price	48.00	60.00	29.00	
Direct Production costs p.u.	(25.00)	(35.00)	(25.00)	
PRODUCTION CONTRIBUTION p.u.	23.00	25.00	4.00	
Variable non-production costs p.u.	(3.00)	(2.00)	(1.00)	
(e.g. off-invoice payments)				
Contribution per unit	20.00	23.00	3.00	
Total Sales (in units)	18,000	7,000	8,000	
PRODUCTION CONTRIBUTION	360,000	161,000	24,000	545,000

Less: Other Variable costs (that do not vary
      solely with the number of units)

1. Transportation	55,000	
2. Debtors Costs	35,000	
3. Order Processing Costs	3,900	
4. Trade Promotions (e.g. Case-Off/Co-op Adv.)	74,350	(168,250)
		376,750

NET CONTRIBUTION

Less: Short-run controllable fixed costs

1. District Office	22,000	
2. Advertising	47,000	
3. Administrative Salaries	25,000	
4. Salesforce Salary and Travel	31,000	(125,000)

SEGMENT CONTROLLABLE MARGIN	251,750
Less: Long-run non-controllable costs	(10,000)
NET SEGMENT MARGIN	241,750
Less: Charge for fixed corporate investment	(150,000)
RESIDUAL SEGMENT MARGIN	91,750

Source: Accounting for Competitive Marketing – J. Ratnatunga, published by CIMA, 1988

Figure 5.5

Some companies find themselves in the position of having spare capacity
simply because marketing management has demanded increases in productive capacity, to meet marginal demand. The existence of under utilised
capacity immediately creates the opportunity and the necessity for own-
label, to soak up spare volume. So, inadvertently, in the search for extra

volume the marketing manager has created a strategic weakness which the own-label buyer can exploit. Some companies have even been forced into supplying own-label products at prices closer to marginal cost than the mainstream brand. If the marketing planner works to a simple definition of unit costs there is no intellectual constraint on requesting extra volume, even though this might create unabsorbed extra capacity.

The reverse of this is the company where management accountants spread the total fixed costs of plant and equipment over the production of a line running at half capacity. If the unit cost given to marketing managers recovers full costs over a small run it is unlikely the product will ever be priced competitively. Potentially winning products may never see the light of day because of such vagaries in the costing system.

Both these situations happen in companies where understanding between management accountants and marketing people is poor. It is not a hypothetical situation; it happens every day. On one apochryphal occasion it is said that Winston Churchill was given the controls of a plane as it came in to land, but because of engine noise he didn't realise he had control of the plane. One heavy landing later the pilot asked why he had been so careless. He is reputed to have laughed and said, 'That was less a case of falling between two stools; more of stalling between two fools.'

The fault-line between finance and marketing in the area of product costing creates identical conditions in many companies.

COMMON COSTING BASES

Take your pick of costing methods

Some common concepts used in deriving unit costs for marketing purposes include:

Marginal costing

The simple, direct variable costs associated with one extra unit of production, or whatever extra volume is under consideration.

Differential costing

An extension of direct variable costs, but where an increase in volume demands a step increase in fixed costs. These then have to be recovered against incremental production.

Average costing

This can be contrasted with differential costing in that it seeks to average direct variable costs across the whole production volume.

Absorption costing

When assessing the value of stock and work-in-progress, for balance sheet purposes, a decision has to be made on whether certain costs should be 'absorbed' into the stock valuation or written-off as operating costs.

Standard costing

Standard costing is particularly relevant in complex and continous manufacturing processes where assumed, or 'standard', input costs are used to calculate unit costs. Variances between assumed and actual costs are usually self-balancing if monitored on a regular basis, and the existence of a 'standard cost' makes both marketing planning and financial accounting a great deal easier.

What do we do with the variances?

The problem with standard costing systems is that they are subject to the same questions of definition as we have already considered. What costs should be recovered? Should they be direct, semidirect, indirect? What happens to unforeseen or major variances? Is the organisation flexible and fast enough to spot problems and take account of them?

What do we do at stock valuation time?

At the year-end it may be necessary to write down stock based on market value criteria. Is the marketing department working to the same agenda or basing its decisions on an anachronistic costing structure?

This is not intended to be a text on cost accounting. The important point is that the area is highly subjective. Data vary dramatically from period to period, key strategic decisions are directly connected to the costing process and yet many marketing managers remain ill-informed about the process. The advent of computers, with many levels of data analysis, potentially opens up this area to greater scrutiny. However, this assumes that there is an understanding of costing theory and an appreciation of how important subjective cost allocation decisions are to brands marketing.

The number of marketing people going on courses for 'finance for nonfinancial people' is a hopeful sign. Unfortunately, many eyes glaze over with incomprehension when costing appears on the agenda. Courses tend to be short, with a huge amount to take in. Many cross themselves and thank God they don't have to work in the finance department. A much more sensible route is the continuous, in-house approach adopted by some companies, with the allocation of marketing accountants to product and brand marketing teams.

PROCESS COST ALLOCATION

If the general area of costing methodology is a 'black hole' for many marketing people the area of multiproduct cost apportionment is its darkest pit. Many companies simply do not gather accurate data on products coming out of the same production process.

Chocolate production is just one example where a whole range of products rolls out of the same integrated process. A chocolate factory can produce as many as 20 or 30 different product formulations using different blends of cocoa butter, cocoa powder, carob, vegetable fat, milk, milk powder, sugar, glucose, and malt among other ingredients. How does it separate cost streams as the products come out of the process? In fact, the problem is not that great where batch processing is in operation, because ingredients can be weighed-in and costed, for matching with the final product. But what happens if there are concurrent runs, split processes, by-products? What if the factory is opened and cranked up for just one batch? How are the operating costs attributed? What happens if the standard costing system is out of kilter? What if the standard costing system is simply not sophisticated enough?

These are very real problems and are a constant refrain of John Murphy, the Chairman of Interbrand, who needs to gather accurate revenue and cost streams by product and brand for brand valuation and brand management consultancy work.

> '. . . costing systems, margins and brand profitability are seen by marketing people as nothing to do with them. Most have no idea what costing systems do or why the information produced is relevant to marketing.'

MARGINAL OR FULL COSTING

One of the perennial problems facing marketing people is whether, and to what extent, marginal pricing should be used as a strategic weapon. Some of the more important situations where it could be appropriate are:

Maintaining market share

In stable, low-growth markets many companies, either overtly or tacitly, marginally price to maintain share, usually in periods of soft demand or intense competition. For example, discounting has been prevalent in the car market at one extreme, and in the biscuit market at the other, throughout the recession.

Blocking new competitors

Marginal costing is often used to justify marginal pricing as a spoiling move directed at new market entrants. This may be directed at completely new market players, or new products from existing players. It may be national or regional, channel specific or global.

New sector penetration

The reverse of the previous example is the use of marginal costing and pricing to ease market entry into new sectors or into existing sectors with new products. This technique has been used extensively by food suppliers from other EU countries seeking to gain market entry into the UK, notably in the dairy business.

Maximising volume; minimising unit fixed costs

The higher the volume the larger the production run over which fixed costs can be spread. This should result in higher overall profits, unless replacement or extension of fixed plant becomes necessary.

Own-label activity

Maximising volume to minimise fixed unit costs is often the primary justification for own-label activity. Another reason may be to squeeze other branded competitors. The combination of the company's own market share and the incremental own-label share is often greater than pre-own-label share, and has the effect of severely pressurising other branded competitors.

International diversification

There are many examples of international companies cross-subsidising markets by marginally costing and pricing products, to gain entry. In the post war period Japanese companies are alleged to have done this, to build international market share in the zips and motor cycle markets. Anti-competitive restraints now exist in many countries to prevent domestic manufacturers being slaughtered by foreign competition effectively dumping their products. However, such cases take a long time to be adjudicated and are exceptionally hard to prove.

Where does marginal costing end?

The difficulty with using marginal costing and marginal pricing as strategic weapons is that they are hard, if not impossible, to selectively apply. Once the market is entered, the new product launched, the competition seen off, the extra volume obtained, the own-label line created or the short-term profits maximised, a long-term problem remains. Like drugs it's hard to give up the habit, and after a brief high cold turkey sets in.

They may be used for short periods or in clearly defined areas, in specific sectors or to target certain groups of customers. If the market audiences can be ring-fenced the policy may also be sustainable. But very often the word travels and the whole price structure comes under pressure. Unless they can be used to permanently change the competitive structure of the industry, resulting in less competition and much higher prices in the future, the policy is ultimately self-defeating. A fragmented and competitive market, with few barriers to entry, is not the place to maximise long-run profits using marginal costing and pricing strategies.

THE STAMPEDE TO CUT PRICE

Death of the brand?

The Friday in April 1993 when Philip Morris decided to cut the domestic US price of its Marlboro cigarette brand by 40 cents a pack, to combat the effect of cheaper brands and own-label products, is now referred to on Wall Street as *Marlboro Friday*. In the following six months, 25 of the leading, branded-products companies lost nearly $50 billion from their stock market capitalisations, as analysts became convinced that premium brands were dead.

In London, the same worries affected many branded companies stock market ratings. For example, a recent analyst's report by Chris Wickham and John Wakely, of Lehman Brothers, entitled 'The end of the brand?', considered the price pressure on brands, particularly in the confectionery, soft drinks, super-premium distilled spirits and instant coffee markets. The authors made the point that,

'*Increasing price competition seems to have set into the consumer goods sector. This is particularly true in the middle market where consumers are trading down. But it is trading down in price, not quality, that is occurring. Furthermore, where a super-premium category exists, most sectors are also experiencing trading up from the middle market. This middle market is getting squeezed.'*

However, some sectors are more affected than others. In identifying those which are most at risk some of the relevant issues that need to be addressed are: how significant the price premium is compared with private label; whether competitive products are available at lower prices but equivalent quality; whether a significant proportion of sales are in supermarkets; whether a significant proportion of sales are in the developed world; whether a super-premium segment exists in this category; whether proprietary technology exists in the production process; whether advertising expenditure is less than 10 per cent of sales; and whether the real price of the product has increased over the last 5 to 10 years.

If the answer to more than four of these issues is *Yes,* competition is likely to be or become even more intense. Companies where large portions of their product lines fit this category – for example, UK food and beer, and much of continental European food may be vulnerable to own lable competition.'

They use the chocolate and biscuit markets by way of contrast. Although a large part of the chocolate market is in the developed world a large proportion of sales are outside the supermarket channel, marketing support is significant and technology is rapidly developing. Biscuits, on the other hand, score badly on virtually all counts; admittedly there is a super-premium sector but it has suffered of late, and while real prices have remained competitive advertising support has collapsed, way below 10 per cent of sales for many brands.

Brands on the run

In the US, own-label products sell at 15 to 40 per cent below their branded equivalents and own-label now takes 18 per cent of total supermarket sales. Admittedly this per centage looks low by UK standards; UK companies have lived with increasing own-label penetration for at least a decade. But the US own-label per centage is rapidly rising and US branded goods companies are only just waking up to the real challenge of own-label activity. 'Also ran' brands will not survive and manufacturers are reacting with vigour.

For example, Procter & Gamble has responded to the threat by cutting the price of Pampers three times in the last year, to compete better with own-label nappies. The Pampers brand had acquired a 35 per cent premium to almost identical own-label nappies; as a result its market share had dropped 10 points to 39 per cent by early 1993, equivalent to $440 million of lost sales. In the cost-cutting spree to reclaim market share P&G dropped Pampers prices by 17 per cent, regained 3 per cent share, and is now set to drop its prices by another 5 per cent. In the words of Edwin Artz , P&G's CEO,

> '*Brand loyalty is very much like an onion. It has layers and a core. The core is the user who will stick with you until the very end . . . we lost the outer layer of our users.*'

P&G has also recognised that up to 25 per cent of its brand's Stock Keeping Units (SKUs) will not survive in a market where only the number one brand, the number two brand and an own-label will get shelf-space in the future. Weak P&G brands have therefore been culled, and 20 per cent of P&G's factories, together with 13,000 staff, representing 12 per cent of the workforce, are scheduled for the axe. Edwin Artz comments, 'We're not banking on *things* getting better. We're banking on *us* getting better.'

In the opinion of Warren Buffett, the legendary US investment guru, 'Your premium brand had better be delivering something special or it's not going to get the business.'

Kellogg's, Heinz, Coca-Cola and Pepsi Cola are just a few of the brands currently on the defensive from an onslaught of own-label products. Their refusal to manufacture own-label products themselves only holds up as long as their brands have clear product advantages, better marketing support and acceptable pricing. These are all being probed and challenged in the market.

Every day low pricing

Every day low pricing, or EDLP to its admirers, is a cornerstone of the P&G competitive strategy to fight back against the challenge to its brands. In P&G the concept is expressed as the *value pricing programme*. The price is held low by cutting out a portion of promotional funds and putting those savings back into lower list prices. Instead of highly priced brands which are periodically subject to discount or special offer, the core price is held permanently low by cutting out large chunks of the cost base. As far as possible the extra margins generated by cost savings are then ploughed back into product quality, product innovation and marketing support for the brands.

EDLP has also hit the UK with manufacturers aspiring to give traditional branded product quality together with permanently low prices. The pace is being forced by retailers like Sainsbury at the more up-market end, and Tesco at the down-market end. For example, in August 1993 Tesco launched *Tesco Value* a basic, cheap, tertiary own-label line. This line of 70 'white-label' products, with packaging like something out of the former Soviet bloc, provides reasonable quality, basic products at discounts of up to 50 per cent off many branded goods. The launch of *Asda Price* and the general move by retailers to outdo one another on value, for both branded and own-label products, makes the EDLP concept increasingly important.

Even the Gillette Company, with a commanding position in the blade and razors market, has striven to keep its products reasonably priced. For only a couple of pounds the shaving public can have the 'Sensor' system, a technically superior product to commodity disposable razors. By investing in research, by designing and building its own advanced manufacturing equipment, and by refusing to contemplate own-label production, Gillette has taken command of a sector which was suffering 'death by a thousand cuts' in the mid-eighties. By developing reasonably priced but high quality, innovative products, 65 per cent of US blade and razor sales are now accounted for by Gillette. The position is very similar in Europe. This strategy has made a significant contribution to Gillette's overall profit of $500 million on sales of just over $5 billion in 1992.

The company has committed itself to investing in 'growth drivers' – research and development, plant and equipment and advertising. New product developments come off-the-line faster than the competition can keep pace with them, and pricing is competitive to boot. The new 'Sensor Excel', which is due for its European roll-out in 1994, has five small rubber fins around the blade to stretch the skin for a smoother shave. It sells at a 15 to 20 per cent premium to Sensor and looks set to be a blockbuster.

Companies like Gillette, Compaq, Wrigleys, Campbell Soups and Swatch all seem to have acquired the knack of keeping brand prices at acceptable levels, rapidly developing new products while providing heavy marketing support. The virtuous circle.

Advertising as a defence against price cutting

As cost and price reduction become the norms, unless companies are investing heavily in new products, advertising and marketing become the most significant variables between brands. In the words of Gordon Brown, of Milward Brown International,

> 'Price cutting works immediately, and because the effects are so transient, they're easy to see. Creativity roots ideas in the brain so that they influence how people decide about brands in their own good time, so it has a smoother effect. When I fertilize my rose bushes, they don't grow six inches as the fertiliser hits the ground – but I'd be a fool to stop!'

Advertising and marketing generally are also critical in averting the price squeeze. Alan Gottesman, of Paine Webber, the stockbroking firm, makes the following point,

> 'As companies move to diminish the price spreads, the competition will have to hinge on something else. There isn't much else besides brand awareness. We will probably see a move towards non-price-based product

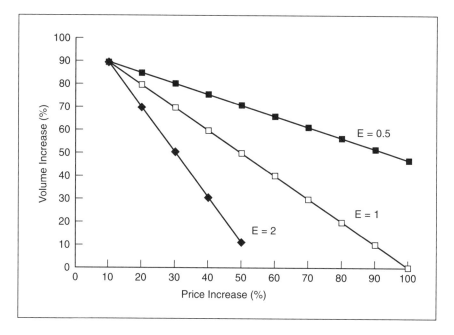

Figure 5.6

differentiation, heralding, if not quite a Golden Age, at least better times ahead for advertising.'

Although brands remain under pressure, the need for brands to differentiate themselves through their communications, and maintain a direct relationship with their ultimate consumers, signals a growing demand for marketing services – certainly advertising but also public relations, direct marketing and sales promotion. The final word goes to WPP,

'The recent decision of Philip Morris in the United States to make significant price cuts on its Marlboro brand has prompted trade press speculation that battles between brands may soon be a thing of the past and that future market competition will be based on the single dimension of price. It should be remembered, however, that tobacco manufacturers have for some time been denied access to many traditional advertising media and that heavily discounted products (some from Philip Morris itself) have been rapidly gaining market share. Marlboro continues to enjoy a price premium, the envy of most of its competitors and remains a testimony to the art of brand building and maintenance.'

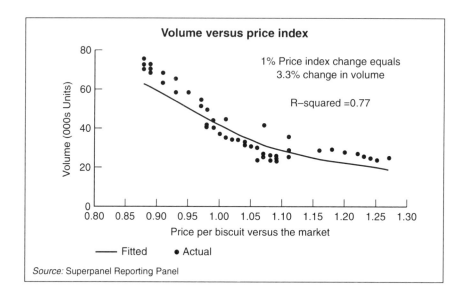

Figure 5.7

PRICE ELASTICITIES OF DEMAND

As with breakeven analysis, price elasticity and inelasticity are familiar concepts. With the vertical *y* axis indicating volume and the horizontal *x* axis showing price we can model hypothetical elasticity coefficients until the cows come home. Is our product or brand more or less elastic than the competition? Can we jack-up the price without affecting volume? Will a price cut make any difference to demand and therefore volume?

Widely different values can be obtained by expressing the elasticity of demand coefficient as:

$$E = \frac{\text{Change in } y \text{ (Volume)}}{\text{Change in } x \text{ (Price)}}$$

An answer less than one implies *inelasticity,* one is evenly balanced or *unitary,* more than one implies *elasticity.*

This is expressed graphically in Figure 5.6.

But what does all this prove for the hard-pressed marketing manager? The following price elasticity graph, produced by AGB from its *Superpanel* data on the UK biscuit market, suggests that for a 1 per cent price change there is a 3.3 per cent change in volume, an elasticity coefficient of 3.3 (Figure 5.7).

If this is true it is a frightening statistic for the likes of John Warren at United Biscuits and underlines the points made by Chris Wickham and John Wakely of Lehman Brothers.

But does the data actually mean anything in practical terms? Can it be used for predictive pricing? How is the elasticity of a single biscuit product affected by competitive pricing or other marketing activity? How is it affected by the sociodemographic character of the sample group? Do other environmental factors like the weather, the type of outlet through which the product is sold or the state of the economy distort the picture? Is the elasticity coefficient identical at all price levels?

For example, Pampers had to drop its price 17 per cent to regain only 3 per cent of market share. Presumably, as Pampers prices come closer to competitive products the ratio of per centage price cut to market share gain will dramatically improve. How predictable and monitorable are such changes?

There are econometricians, working in the business of price modelling, who think sense can be made from empirical data, to help inform the marketing process. By contrast, there are academics who believe that the number of data variables and inconsistencies make price elasticity modelling a complete waste of time. To the academics the commercial econometricians are no more than charlatans selling snake oil to gullible marketing people. In the words of Professor Andrew Ehrenberg, a leading academic in the marketing field,

> 'In lots of Eastern places leaders believe in tea leaves. They are even cheaper than computers! There is also an enormous amount of astrology around. People need support which is easy to reject when they want to and quite nice to accept when they feel like it!'

To the commercial econometricians such academics are unconstructive 'dogs in the manger'.

The academic view

Professor Andrew Ehrenberg, who was Professor of Marketing and Communications at the London Business School for many years, is one of the best known and most outspoken academics in the field. He is now Research Professor of Marketing at The South Bank University in London, a Visiting Professor at The Stern School of Business in New York, and undertakes a large number of research studies into pricing, advertising and other marketing techniques, on behalf of major, blue-chip organisations. He is highly sceptical of the advice given to companies by many commercial econometricians.

He casts doubt on the validity of many price and volume curves used in price modelling because they are often based on single sets of data (SSOD) rather than on multiple sets of data (MSOD). Unless a predictive curve has been validated by many repeat samples, which confirm relationships, then the predictive model becomes highly unreliable. Often commercial price modelling exercises are based on inadequate data samples for cost or practical reasons.

In addition, he questions the accuracy of many regression analyses based on the data collected. In order to produce a predictive model for price modelling it is necessary to define a *line of best fit* for the observed data. Yet he believes that it is often hard to match lines of best fit from a series of different samples to obtain a usable price: volume curve. In his words,

> '*I am an anti-statistician. It is obvious there is only one line that can fit two sets of data, which has to go through the means – Euclid proved it 2,000 years ago. The question is what happens with a third or fourth set of data?*'

Unless phenomena are routinely predictable, and they can be validated experimentally, it is impossible to produce useful predictive models. Ehrenberg uses the example of Boyle's Law, the 330-year-old law of physics which says that the pressure P of a body of gas varies inversely with its volume V under a great variety of conditions, ie that $PV = C$, a constant for that body of gas and for a given temperature T. This relationship can be demonstrated experimentally under a whole range of conditions.

He believes that just such a relationship can be shown to exist for *double jeopardy,* a predictable rule for all secondary brands. This rule states that the smaller of two brands will not only be bought by fewer consumers in a given time period (its penetration b) but that this smaller number of consumers will also buy it less often (their purchase frequency W). So when a small brand appears to be doing badly in its market it is in fact falling in line with an established fact of life for secondary brands; less people use them and those who do use them less often. A theoretical relationship can be defined as $W(1-b) = Wo$, a constant for the product category and a given length of time t. What is being predicted is not specific values for the variables but a predictable relationship between those variables. In the case of Double Jeopardy he argues that there is very clear and consistent evidence of the principle. In fact, the observed values for double jeopardy are often remarkably close to the predicted values using the formula. For example, one study of double jeopardy in the breakfast cereals market gave the results shown in Figure 5.8.

He goes on from this to argue that there is no such thing as brand equity – that special value of a brand over and above its basic sales and profitability – that extra premium which companies should be prepared to pay to acquire a brand. His thesis is that there is no such thing as a strong brand or a weak brand, just a big brand or a small brand. If one brand had inherent strengths and hidden properties that another brand does not have then the first brand should just keep getting bigger, but they don't. In Ehrenberg's words,

Breakfast cereals in the UK: quarter I, London, 1968*

Leading brands**	Proportion buying b	Average no. of purchases per buyer w	
	Observed	Observed	Predicted
Corn Flakes	0.42	3.7	4.0
Weetabix	0.27	3.3	3.2
Shredded Wheat	0.16	2.9	2.7
Rice Krispies	0.17	2.5	2.8
Sugar Puffs	0.11	2.5	2.6
Average	0.23	3.0	3.1

* Predicted from w=3.32/(1 − b)
** In market share order

Source: Predictability & Prediction, Prof Ehrenberg & J.A. Bound, *Journal of the Royal Statistical Society*, 1993, page 169

Figure 5.8

'From a narrow consumer perspective, brand equity merely reflects market share. Big brands generally score higher on consumer loyalty measures than small brands. This does not mean that big brands will necessarily grow bigger. It simply mirrors the fact that they are already big.'

He illustrates the double jeopardy issue with evidence from the cereals market, where 60 per cent of households buy Kellogg's Corn Flakes on average ten times a year while Shredded Wheat buying households (30 per cent of the population) purchase Shredded Wheat only six times a year on average. Tests of consumer loyalty to the two cereals reflect the relative size of the two brand shares. Similar patterns can be found in the petrol market between brands like Shell and Fina. In the car market, the differences in France and the UK, between Renault and Ford sales figures and consumer loyalty measures, provide another neat example. The two are mirror images of one another. In France Renault is dominant, in the UK Ford is. Because of the double jeopardy rule Ehrenberg advises marketing managers against pursuing illusory aspects of brand equity when the only thing which distinguishes between brands is size.

However, while Double Jeopardy may be measurable, as far as Ehrenberg is concerned price and volume relationships are often not reliably predictable. In the words of Boyle,

'. . . till further trial hath clearly informed me, I shall not venture to determine whether or not the intimated theory will hold universally and precisely either in condensation, or rarefaction.'

Unlike Boyle many of the commercial econometricians are prepared to form views about pricing relationships without sufficiently reliable evidence.

In fact, as far as Ehrenberg is concerned, all consumer products seem to have identical price elasticity curves. In an extensive field experiment with fast-moving branded consumer goods, Ehrenberg found price elasticities to be much the same for different products or brands, for prices going up or down, at different speeds, and irrespective of the brand's previous pricing history. These results differed radically from the view that individual products and brands have their own distinct elasticities.

The study tracked the performance of four brands in each of five product categories, offered by a mobile shop to a panel of 300 housewives, every two weeks for five months, to establish the sales effect of prices changing between +15 per cent and −15 per cent. The experiment generated a sequence of purchases made for real money, with interspersed consumption in the home, and at prices for any brand which could be varied at will, both over time and between controlled subgroups. The study also eliminated major interference factors like income effects, risk, incomplete information, search behaviour, and transaction costs.

The study showed the following variations in sales share for the one brand in each category whose price changed while the other three brands in the category remained fixed:

AVERAGE SALES – SHARES AT M + 15%, THE MID-PRICE M AND M – 15%

(Sales – Shares: Observed (O) and Fitted (F))

	Prices					
Sales calls 1 – 2, 5 – 6, 9 – 10	M + 15%		M		M – 15%	
	O%	F%	O%	F%	O%	F%
The 20 cases						
The variable-price brand	16	15	27	28	42	41
The fixed-price brands	84	85	73	72	58	59

Source: 'Generalising a Pricing Effect', Prof. Ehrenberg and L.R. England, *Journal of Industrial Economics*, Vol xxxix, Sept. 1990

Figure 5.9

The overall results of the study showed that:

• price elasticities did not vary by brand or product.

According to Ehrenberg this fact has been substantiated by other similar studies.

- a brand's share did not depend on how a given price level had been reached.

It made no difference whether prices had previously been higher or lower. This is consistent with the wide-spread experience that short-term consumer promotions and price cuts have no longer-term effects on sales levels.

- elasticity was lower if competitive brands were less substitutable.

This confirms normal expectations in marketing and economic theory but leaves open the question of the interaction between pricing and the degree or nature of product differentiation.

In the words of the research paper on the experimental results,

> '. . . it is no longer meaningful to talk in terms of a brand or a product having its own specific price elasticity. On the other hand, we have shown that many different brands and products are capable of having virtually the same elasticity under a given set of conditions . . . any particular elasticity is highly specific to a particular competitive situation and is likely to vary, for every brand or product, with the competitive context.'

So marketers should concentrate on total market elasticities rather than elasticities for their own brand alone.

Another aspect of pricing which Ehrenberg has recently researched is the area of price promotions and whether they confer any long-term benefits on a brand. In the introduction to a large-scale study on the sales effects of price promotion Ehrenberg reviewed the pressures which prompted price promotions; the competition, retailers, internal management seeking higher sales and increased long-term market share. However, while acknowledging that established brands in stable markets could increase short-term sales and market share through price promotions he concluded that there is no tangible, long-term benefit. They are simply expensive ways of boosting short-term sales volumes.

His conclusions covered four main measures:

- before-to-after sales
- before-to-after repeat buying
- the general level of repeat buying
- existing customers or new ones?

In the case of the first three measures there were no measurable changes in the before and after pattern of sales. In the last case there was evidence that the majority of new consumers were lapsed or irregular users of the brand, who largely reverted back to their previous buying patterns after the promotions. According to Ehrenberg the majority of consumers have a portfolio of two or three brands which they will habitually buy over time, and will switch tactically between. Low pricing at the time of a promotion simply flicks that switch for the short-term, giving the ambivalent consumer a reward for little return to the brand. In his view the number of genuinely new consumers gained from price promotions is tiny.

In many instances price is not the determining factor in brand loyalty. In fact, in Ehrenberg's view, 'Price is an indicator of quality! Most people, most of the time do not go for the lowest price.' But they will switch away temporarily if the short-term incentive is significant enough and they are familiar with the brand.

In summary, he concludes that, '. . . Price promotions for grocery products generally do not seem to influence brand-building, but undoubtedly have an immediate effect, at a cost.' He recommends that companies should gradually wean themselves and their retail customers off price promotions and invest the money in above-the-line advertising and other parts of the marketing mix, including product development, quality and long-term profitability. Ehrenberg cites the simple example of Tetley Tea which changed from square to round teabags – to fit the cup or mug – and took a 1 per cent lead in the teabag market over PG Tips, the previous market leader.

Admittedly, Ehrenberg also has major reservations about the value of advertising, arguing that it is far more to do with brand maintenance than brand building. This is an interesting concept for financial people to get to grips with. There is an assumption among many finance directors that multi-million pound advertising campaigns must inevitably result in higher sales. Ehrenberg suggests that after the money has been spent sales may remain static because the realistic target should have been to maintain rather than to optimise sales. In Ehrenberg's view advertising cannot be used to optimise brand sales, 'God is not an optimiser; only analysts and statisticians try to be!'

At the end of the day Ehrenberg attempts to offer insights, not specific advice, 'That's what management gets paid for – making decisions when they don't know the answers.'

The commercial econometricians' view

Commercial econometricians commit heresy by doing exactly what Ehrenberg refuses to do – optimise budgets, prices, marketing activities and sales. They are confident of their ability to help clients, and refute many of the academic views. For example, Paul Baker, a professional statistician and a Director of OHAL, a leading econometric modelling consultancy in the marketing field, suggests that some of Ehrenberg's conclusions come from biased and unrealistic theoretical studies.

According to Paul Baker the panel study on which Ehrenberg based his view that all brands in the same sector have identical elasticities was unrealistic because prices were made explicit and repeat purchasing cycles were identical for all products in the sample. 'In reality many consumers are only partially aware of brand prices, and the length of time between purchases can have a major influence on price perceptions and sensitivity. The more frequent the purchasing cycle the more sensitive the consumer is to price changes. Other environmental factors also confer different elasticities to individual brands within specific product sectors.'

OHAL, for example, has worked with Andrex for many years, tracking the performance of its toilet paper brand in one of the largest, and most frequently repeated, consumer purchase areas. It is one of the most price competitive consumer markets. Recently OHAL's proprietary modelling software, Brandpac, has been used to track the effect of different aspects of the marketing mix – advertising, price promotions, distribution and competitive activity – and to help forecast and increase sales volumes for different Andrex products. Brandpac is used to devise optimal marketing strategies, particularly in the context of pricing and advertising. Modelling has been done in both the UK and in the US, where a wealth of EPOS data is available for validating the model and where price promotions are a regular feature of the market.

According to Paul Baker the model is set up with empirical data on the price elasticity of the Andrex brand and the known trigger level for consumer response to advertising. It also incorporates base data about the seasonal weight of purchase and changing levels of product distribution and stock holding. Brandpac then operates as a 'what if' model, allowing different assumptions to be fed in to establish which combination of factors will result in the optimal cost, timing and weight of advertising, the optimal pricing structure and the likely resulting sales volume to plan production and distribution.

Certainly the whole emphasis of the OHAL approach is practical and based on forecasting in real markets. A paper by Paul Baker, published in the *Journal of the Market Research Society* in 1987, 'Econometrics for pricing research', reveals the practical rather than theoretical emphasis of his work. For example, in devising computer pricing models, he outlines ten golden rules:

- there is no such thing as positive price elasticity
- do not use annual data
- be very careful if there are trends in the market
- be very careful if your brand or market is seasonal
- be very careful in markets where brands have a range of sizes
- price and non price variables should be constructed with equal care
- not all data are suitable for price elasticity measurements
- one hour's thought plus 100 hours' computing = no result

- do not use lagged dependent variables
- the residuals from an equation must be acceptable.

One of the keys to success is constant validation of price modelling results against actual patterns in the market, which can be done by frequent cross-reference to known sales patterns. OHAL claims that the differences between forecast and actual results are often very small.

The down to earth informality and emphasis on producing workable models reveals the clear difference between the consultants and the academics. The latter take a detached view of experimental research and do not wish to get involved in practical decision-making. The former roll their sleeves up and try to create working decision-support models. The question is can they ever succeed or is the result a computerised fudge designed to intimidate marketing people?

Perhaps there is something in the fact that Andrex recently won an IPA advertising effectiveness award and has been highly successful at tracking and beating the market. No doubt the judgement of the marketing people and the advertising are largely responsible. But part of its success may be attributable to the assistance it receives from OHAL. Of course the academic view is that the elasticity factors and the relationships built into Brandpac are about as useful as computerised tea leaves or rune stones. Only the marketing director of clients like Andrex can reliably judge whether the models are helpful or not. Certainly the cost of such assistance is significant and yet the business is rapidly growing. So unless such clients are suffering from mass hysteria or an interest in astrology there could be something in it after all.

SOME COMMON PRICING BASES

When setting prices there is a wide range of approaches. For example:

1 *Loss leader* – deflated price to attract consumer into store.
2 *Offset* – low basic price with additional revenue from extras.
3 *Diversionary* – low prices on some products in range to give impression of value.
4 *Discount* – usually linked to specific time period to attract sales.
5 *Guarantee* – price inclusive of quality or performance guarantee.
6 *Conditional* – price conditional on connected purchases.
7 *Predatory* – aimed at killing the competition by selling below cost.
8 *Skimming* – exploiting market imperfections to make super-profits.
9 *Referential* – never knowingly undersold.
10 *Price-lining* – keeping price steady by altering product specification or quality.

11 *Contingency* – price tied to specific performance criteria.

12 *Cost plus* – all inputs plus agreed margin.

13 *Value* – whatever the market will bear.

14 *Premium* – extra charge for superior or nonstandard product.

SPECIAL PRICING CIRCUMSTANCES

The business of price modelling tends to work best for large volume consumer products operating in stable, relatively homogeneous markets with reliable distribution. However, many markets are neither tangible, homogeneous nor stable. The item being modelled may be a service rather than a product, it may be subject to the complications of segmentation or foreign exchange rates, and so on. Without exhausting every possible complication in the pricing area a few serve as an example of how difficult it can be to build accurate price models in real markets. For example:

Service pricing

Unless service providers are working at full capacity, which would be unusual other than for actuaries, insolvency practitioners or QCs, the marginal cost of providing a service is effectively zero. So what should the price be?

Differential pricing

Many products and services operate in markets where target audiences can be effectively compartmentalised. It is then possible to operate complex differential pricing structures for different groups which frequently change as circumstances change. A good example is airline or public transport systems in the service area, savings products in the financial area or perishable food products. How can this complexity and change be reliably modelled?

International pricing

Although Marlboro slashed its prices for the US market its premium prices were maintained in many world markets, notably the developing world and the Eastern bloc, where the brand has huge status. In some markets, different international pricing structures can create all sorts of 'grey' goods problems, with arbitrageurs organising parallel imports at lower prices. This affects products like Rayban in the sunglasses market, IBM in the PC market and many other high-value products. How to set, flex and integrate international pricing structures can be a hugely complex issue.

Many of these problems are modelled but the data to make accurate decisions, and the ability to manipulate the different variables is a major problem. The power of computer technology is helping with this but the accurate calculation of factors for the models must be some way behind, even if we believe in their validity.

ALTERNATIVE STRATEGIES?

Since the issue of price cutting hit the headlines many leading branded goods companies have dedicated themselves to reducing their cost base, reducing the complexity level, adopting EDLP and competing on product quality supported by more advertising, rather than costly store promotions. This has, and will continue to, put the squeeze on many secondary and tertiary brands.

For those manufacturers who cannot compete against the market leaders, who want to cut the level of trade support, and make a profit, are there new ways of working the system? Are there different distribution routes or product sizes? Are there opportunities in catering as opposed to retailing? In discounting as opposed to mainstream retailing? Should such companies participate in own-label or watch it develop without them? Is it possible to supply own-label, low-cost, low-marketed brands as well as high-marketed, high-cost brands? These questions are relevant to all FMCG marketing directors, not just when addressing marketing strategy, but also commercial strategy. They are particularly relevant to the middle order batsmen in the branded goods game.

Own-label?

Own-label price competition is so extreme that if all branded goods companies do is compete on claims they're likely to go out of business. If they can compete on claims and also create an added value through image and consistency, building a heritage, then they have some degree of protection. The brands which were able to survive the own-label onslaught in the UK were precisely those that had more to them than just being functional commodity products.

In both the UK and the US functional products have been swamped by own-label. They were turkeys waiting for Christmas. But some like Cotts, a Canadian cola and soda maker in competition with Coca-Cola and Pepsi Cola, made a virtue out of a necessity by becoming the leading own-label cola supplier in the US as well as supplying its own branded product. It has boomed since making the own-label decision. It would never have beaten the market leaders brand for brand but as the own-label, low-cost product with huge volume it has thrived.

Discount?

In the past the discount proposition often squeezed companies out of the market because there was nowhere for discount products to go. The independent trade was not dynamic enough to sustain a brand that had been removed from Boots, Sainsbury, Tesco, Asda, Gateway or any of the major retailers. If a brand wasn't in the top stores it didn't stand much chance of survival. The same is true today, and many more brands may go to the wall. But opportunities may now be emerging.

There are two sectors of trade emerging for many secondary brands: the discount wholesale and the discount retail sectors, which have particular requirements. They are not interested in offering advertising support for their brands, they are interested in offering a reasonable product at low cost to their consumers, and making a low but reasonable margin for themselves. Mega retailers are mainly interested in advertised brands, in line with their overall imagery of quality purveyors, and they are interested in significant promotional and marketing support, together with constant new product development ideas. They want to be first in with new products, as opposed to discounters who wait until the market is established, then buy the second or third brand at a discount.

So as the discount sector grows, two manufacturer strategies may become viable as opposed to one, particularly for smaller brands – in the past it was just a matter of trying to survive and make it into the top six chains which dominate the retail market. Now the discounters offer an alternative for secondary or tertiary brands which would otherwise die. Low cost and low price coupled with high volume could provide a viable profit strategy.

Fighting brands?

Brands are under pressure and many markets are down to own-label plus two or three brands. A manufacturer who concentrates on putting low cost but reasonably high quality brands through discounters with no advertising spend, no marketing spend and very low infrastructure could do well. Most quality manufacturers of products think there is only one way – to advertise, to promote, to use a panoply of marketing techniques and structure-up accordingly. But a contracted manufacturer with limited exposure in terms of capital set-up, good quality control and good cost control, and with only negotiating skills rather than marketing skills, could supply the discount trade at a price that is right. A brand that is being squeezed could become the fighting brand. This will certainly happen more and more over the next five years.

For example, according to Roger Scarlett-Smith of SmithKline Beecham Consumer Healthcare Division, in the toothpaste market, Ultra-Brite from

Colgate and SR from Gibbs seem to have become 'dealing' brands. With some heritage and public recognition as reasonable toothpastes, consumers will buy them at the right price, but they have the cost benefit of low levels of advertising support.

Conventional wisdom

Conventional wisdom has it that the strategies outlined are recipes for disaster, for the slow and painful death of the branded manufacturer. This may be true in many cases, and merely be a reaction to current circumstances. But there could be a profitable niche for some manufacturers who get the mix of such options right and maximise volume at very low cost.

CONCLUSIONS

There are many areas of uncertainty in both costing and pricing and many different ways they can be deployed to give companies competitive advantage. But in exploiting the techniques available for strategic decision-making there are a number of issues which many companies still need to address:

- the continued belief that cost and price data can be simply derived by finance
- the education of marketing people in subjective areas of costing and pricing
- the appointment of marketing accountants as liaison managers
- the selective use of modelling software.

Despite the academic objections and areas of uncertainty the need for pricing and marketing modelling is rapidly increasing. They may be crude but decision support systems will be in strong demand to help define optimal activity as markets become more complex and competitive. There is no doubt that the market for such systems is growing and will grow further. All those responsible for marketing should be familiar with the systems which are available and the techniques which can be used, albeit with caution. Theory may help us to bear our ignorance of the facts, but as markets become more competitive there will be a growing demand to apply theory and grope for the facts through the fog of conjecture.

Bibliography

'VW's Rocky Road', Alex Taylor III, *Fortune* Magazine, Issue 17 August 1993

'Brands – It's thrive or die', Patricia Sellers, *Fortune* Magazine, Issue 17 August 1993

'Tesco gets a cheap frill', Helen Slingsby, *Marketing Week*, 13 August 1993

Financial Aspects of marketing, Keith Ward, Heinemann Professional Publishing, ISBN 0 434 92221 8

Management Accounting: Strategic Planning and Marketing, Patrick McNamee, Butterworth/Heinemann, CIMA, ISBN 0 750 60339 9

Accounting for Competitive Marketing, J Ratnatunga, CIMA, ISBN 0 948 03642 7

Economics, Paul A. Samuelson, McGraw Hill, ISBN 0 07 054590 1

'Predictability and Price', A. S. C. Ehrenberg and J. A. Bound, Paper to The Royal Statistical Society, 18th November 1992

'Generalising a Pricing Effect', A.S.C. Ehrenberg and L. R. England, Article in *The Journal of Industrial Economics*, Volume XXXIX September 1990

'The After Effects of Price Related Consumer Promotions', A.S.C. Ehrenberg, K. Hammond, G. J. Goodhardt, Research Report on price promotions, July 1993

Marketing Audit Checklists, Aubrey Wilson, McGraw Hill, ISBN 0 07 707760 1

6

BUSINESS DEVELOPMENT IN THE 1990s

'One doesn't discover new lands without consenting to lose sight of the shore'
Andre Gide

INTRODUCTION

Change has been a constant theme of this book. The pace of change has been increasing in all areas of marketing, and the indications are that it will continue to increase as the decade goes by. Change in consumer wants and expectations, in the technology underlying new product development, in the products and services which emerge from the technological process, in the structure of markets, and in the channels for delivering products to the end consumer. New markets are being created overnight and existing markets are being turned upside down. Major redirection and massive reinvestment programmes are being called for in many familiar areas.

For example, banking and insurance – apparently sedate and highly conservative corners of the financial services sector – are being torn apart by technological forces. Technology is taking the emphasis away from physical delivery, through branch networks and extensive personal fieldforces, to online access. The products themselves are changing as technology is being applied to make investment and banking products more flexible and transparent. First Direct from the Midland, Armchair Banking from The Co-operative Bank, and Direct Line Insurance from the Royal Bank of Scotland are just the first wave of new services which will turn into a tidal wave in the nineties. On the negative side, branches are closing in the high street, and familiar faces are disappearing as they are made redundant. On the positive side are accessibility, stemming from in-home provision, increased choice and the opportunity for new markets to be created domestically and abroad, without the need for traditional, physical delivery mechanisms. In the past, UK insurance companies achieved low penetration levels in the EU because of local government restrictions and physical delivery problems.

The Co-operative Bank has failed to make major inroads into the south of England because it lacked a credible branch network. Pension and equity investment vehicles have traditionally been inaccessible and incomprehensible, which has limited demand. In the nineties these considerations will subside as consumers focus on flexible financial products and services, reliably and intelligibly delivered into their homes. Competition and the pace of change will accelerate.

One of the main constraining factors to date has been the conservatism of consumers, who have not believed in, nor understood how to use, the new technology. But, as the number of terrestrial and cable channels increases, and as retail operations pioneer in-home shopping, financial services companies will find new markets opening up to them.

This turmoil will apply across many sectors, demanding more and more from marketing and finance teams. It will no longer be enough for financial people to be good at controlling and reducing costs within established corporate and marketing structures. Companies will not be delivering the same products in the same way but will be using technology to change the fundamentals. They will not just be able to rationalise the cost structure but will have to fundamentally change it. Increasingly they will be reshaping their businesses. This brings with it a need for greater judgement and higher risk.

Innovation is risky and mistakes are costly. But there are very few markets where companies can continue as they have in the past. Growth is a prerequisite of fulfilling investor expectations, and market saturation demands a constant search for new ideas. If companies are not rapidly moving forward and changing they will be going backwards. There will have to be a change in attitude in many companies at corporate, marketing and financial levels. Instead of the zero sum game of tighter and tighter cost and production control, driven by clever new technology, there will have to be more visionary approaches. Financial evaluation will more often be made on the merits of large-scale, speculative developments and investments, with uncertain paybacks, rather than on edging up margins by paring down existing costs.

For those companies which have grown used to hugging the coastline of established practice it will be hard to strike out for the horizon and risk losing sight of the shore. But if companies do not leave shallow water they will never find new markets. Greater risk-taking has become a corporate necessity rather than a luxury. Paradoxically, a recent conference for marketing people managed to persuade 450 marketing directors to leave the shore in the greatest of luxury!

INNOVATE OR DIE

At the 1993 Marketing Forum, held on board the SS Canberra, several speakers dwelt on the subject of innovation. Mike Destiny, the Chief Executive of Foote Cone and Belding, Michael Peters, Managing Director of Identica, and Creenagh Lodge, Chairman of Craton Lodge and Knight, all stressed the need to build innovation into the marketing process, rather than to have it as some kind of add-on function or functional specialism.

In Creenagh Lodge's words innovation is 'the science of success'. Unfortunately, many companies have historically regarded the *new product development* function as the corporate geriatric ward, producing raffia-work baskets and placemats which are unravelled at the end of the process. Neither invention – the creation of mega changes, like the internal combustion engine, nor ingenuity – the clever use of existing ideas, like Wash & Go in the shampoo market, or Hair Styling Spray in the haircare market – have been treated as fundamental to marketing or corporate strategy. In the future they will have to be. Creenagh Lodge drew a comparison between the research and development efforts of many companies and Old Mother Hubbard. For many, research is a concept that hasn't been seriously considered since the second world war and development has concentrated on cost reduction exercises in the factory. As a result the cupboard is bare of new ideas which can feed through into the marketing chain.

By contrast, uncommercial boffins continue to invent things without a real conception of how they will be translated into products or services which consumers might want. Prestel is a perfect example of this. Its inventors thought how interesting it would be to combine a TV screen, a telephone link and a keypad to create an interactive information service, without thinking of consumer information needs. People don't buy the *Encyclopaedia Britannica* for its own sake simply because it's available on screen. CLK was therefore asked to 'infect' Prestel with marketing to make profitable use of its clever new technology. CLK helped Prestel 'reinvent' its service, focusing on real consumer needs. Its first targeted information service was Farmlink, which proved highly popular and useful, and has spawned a whole range of similar services. Prestel graphically demonstrates that innovation without marketing is a waste of time and money and vice versa.

Leading the field through innovation

Nothing could illustrate the importance of innovation linked to consumer appeal better than the example of Williams Grand Prix Engineering, the world championship winning Formula One team. At the marketing forum, Richard West, Director of Marketing Services for Williams, described how innovation is part of the fabric of Williams. It is the single reason the company has achieved so much, and is the credo of the organisation. But while the company has dedicated itself to technological innovation. Williams has also developed and exploited powerful brand values for both itself and for its sponsors. With 500 million people in 121 countries watching 5,000 TV hours of its cars charging to victory it is easy to see why global audiences associate the Williams brand with high-technology, sophistication, glamour, aspirational values and success.

It all began in 1977 when Frank Williams set up the company with a mission to show the larger players in the motor racing circuit that uncompromising standards and the quest for leading edge technology could beat the competition. He teamed up with Patrick Head who became technical director with a mission to build the most advanced cars in the world. The company has pioneered the use of light carbon fibre materials, hydraulics, aerodynamics and electronics, to build the most technologically advanced cars in Formula One racing. Williams has some of the most advanced research and production facilities in the sport, including one of the fastest and most accurate half-scale, moving-floor wind-tunnels in the world. With the exception of engines, wheels, tyres and brakes, all car parts are manufactured exclusively by the Williams team in the company's 86,000 square foot production facility at Didcot, Oxfordshire. For example, the Williams semi-automatic, electronically controlled gearbox cuts gear changing times from around $\frac{2}{10}$ th of a second to significantly less than $\frac{1}{10}$ th of a second, allowing the car's 500 kilo, 3.5 litre, 800 brake horse power engine to go from 0 to 140 miles per hour and back to 0 in around 5.1 seconds.

This is a business where the product parameters can change every year, as the ruling body alters regulations. For example, in 1994 Williams will have to build cars without its proprietary Active Ride suspension system, which is deemed too advanced for the rest of the Formula One world to compete with. In addition, while cars may look identical from race to race they are in fact reconstructed and altered every two weeks to fit the geography, climate and competition in each grand prix. Formula One is the science of new product development taken to its ultimate conclusion. The product is new every time it comes out to compete. NPD is a continuous process and if it stops the wins dry up. But NPD has not stopped.

In 1992 Nigel Mansell won the Drivers' Championship in a Williams car and in 1993 Alain Prost did the same. The Williams team has now won 11 Drivers' and Constructors' Championships in the 15 years since the company was set up. In reaching the pinnacle of this highly competitive sport Williams has introduced new ways of using carbon fibre composite materials, in addition to major developments in engine, gearbox, transmission, braking systems and vehicle design, many of which are now being marketed outside the area of Formula One. Renault, the team's engine supplier, is collaborating with Williams on the production of a new 16 valve Clio, JCB is using Williams high speed gear box technology in a new range of light-weight earth-moving equipment, British Rail is looking at the Williams Active Ride suspension system for use in a self-levelling train, a major car manufacturer is looking at the Williams fuel saving gear box system, which holds out the promise of a 10 per cent fuel efficiency gain, and many companies are looking at the use of its carbon fibre components. Williams is a genuine British success story in an area where success and failure are measured in hundredths of a second, and in which passing the chequered flag first is the only real test. Nobody remembers who came second.

Not all companies can be in the same position as Williams, but there are many important lessons. One is the need for commitment from a team of people who are the best in their field, and who are passionate about the market and the product. Another is putting long-term achievement ahead of short-term financial results; investments are high and payback is long term. Others are the application of research, the search for short turn-around times and the elimination of bureaucracy. At Williams, prevarication is impossible, with the hours ticking away before the next race. Many companies need to learn the same lessons.

Realising a vision

Williams is a very specific example of a team of people driven by a vision. A more commonplace consumer example of the same principle is the development of the Sony Walkman®. Sony's founder Akio Morita had a vision of miniaturised hi-fi systems to provide consumers with their own portable entertainment centres. He pursued his objective without a short-term regard for the cost because he was so convinced that this would create a whole new market. He proved that his vision was right and after millions of Walkman® sales, with myriad variants, the Walkman® remains a major source of revenue for Sony. It also led the company to integrate vertically into the 'software' end of the music business, buying into RCA records. Sony has now matured into a company which provides complete personal entertainment to the public, not just clever pieces of hi-fi hardware.

Why is it that many UK marketing companies have not been successful at creating fundamental dynamic changes in their markets. The Japanese have done it by making technology commercially friendly and acceptable. The UK was big in computers at one stage. Sir Clive Sinclair pioneered many ideas – the digital watch, the pocket calculator, the flatscreen mini TV, and the portable computer. Yet these innovations were not sustained in the markeplace.

Perhaps there are not enough links with academia. It has been said that the academic community in the UK is not sufficiently commercial in its own right. Bright young scientists in Japan and the US frequently go to bankers and say, 'I've had this great new idea, give me the money and I'll form a company.' Most academics in the UK would run a mile rather than see anybody with an accountant's suit on, or form a company. It's just not in their nature. Technology innovators are completely at odds with, and are not communicating with, the marketing innovators.

Perhaps there is not enough vision in the financial community. Sources of capital have admittedly increased in recent years, with many high-technology venture-capital funds scouring the market. But many are cautious, and look for proven technology rather than completely new technologies. Perhaps every company should have a venture-capital wing in its own right, funded and working to create venture-capital opportunities in markets which could then be integrated into the main company.

Some sectors are far more proactive than others. For example, in the pharmaceutical area links with academia are strong, investment levels in pure and applied research are high, and product development levels are astronomical. Glaxo, Wellcome and SmithKline Beecham each spend hundreds of millions researching and developing new treatments and products every year. Perhaps it is no coincidence that they have been some of the best performing and most profitable companies in the UK over the last ten years.

In the words of Roger Scarlett-Smith, Vice President of Marketing SmithKline Beecham Consumer Healthcare Division.

> 'One of the reasons SmithKline Beecham is such a successful organisation is because it has strong links with the academic world, finding breakthrough technologies for application in the marketplace. We are focusing on how high technology can be brought through from the pharmaceutical arm into the consumer area. Many other companies in the toiletries and food businesses don't link true innovation and the market place.'

Creating real product differences

The problem identified by Roger Scarlett-Smith lies behind the issue of own-label and its threat to food and other grocery brands. Unless brands can keep one step ahead technologically they rapidly degenerate into commodity products. This point was well made by David Robey, Divisional Marketing Director for Tesco, at the IPA's 75th Anniversary Conference in October 1992. He pointed out that not only had big supermarkets like Tesco spent huge amounts creating their own brand equities but in many cases had led their suppliers in the development of new products. Over the previous five years Tesco had launched 5,000 new food products, employing 250 people, conducting 10,000 technical factory audits and 2,000 consumer tests, with a product testing budget of £10 million. Tesco had pioneered ranges like Healthy Eating, Traditional Product, Nature's Choice and Green Choice. Its frozen confectionery line now vies with Sara Lee for market leadership in frozen cakes.

He made the point that

> '. . . there are too many me-too products. Products which are poor quality, products which offer poor value, products which have incorrect positioning, products which do not fulfil a real consumer need, products which have inadequate support, and in fact far too many so-called brands are actually not brands at all, and fail the brand definition test on virtually every criterion. These are not brands in my view, but what I would term manufacturer label products.'

Only investment in innovation and development can remove the threat of degeneration into the manufacturer label trap.

Investor or consumer focus?

The main obstacle is the cost and long-term commitment required to make an impact. Unfortunately, if you were to ask the chief executive of a typical Western company about his corporate strategy he is more likely to talk about *return on investment* or *investment yield*, whereas a typical Japanese CEO might talk about making his products go faster, look better, work more efficiently or have new features – reflections of a real consumer-oriented strategy. There is a fundamental difference in emphasis; consumer rather than financial.

In any strategic decision there is pain and gain, a negative and a positive side. For example, a typical decision an accountant might make is to try and reduce working capital. The good thing about reducing working capital is making more profit; the bad thing is running customers out of stock, so consumers buy competitor products. A typical decision a marketing manager might make is to spend more on product innovation or advertising; to develop new ideas or to tell people about the brand. The good thing is that over a period of time it builds brand loyalty; the bad thing is that as product innovation or advertising go up, profits immediately go down. The point is that the good part of an accountant's decision is felt almost immediately, and certainly within the current fiscal year. The bad part is almost always felt further down the road. The effects of salami-ing costs out of the product, tweaking down the quality, running down stocks are not felt for years. In marketing it is exactly the other way round. The negative side of a marketing decision is felt almost immediately in the profit and loss account, whereas the positive side is always a longer pay-back.

This trade off has historically impacted on the new product development process in many Western companies. It has been considered an expensive luxury and a discretionary item in the budget rather than a fundamental part of corporate strategy.

The CBI innovation trends survey

Because of its fundamental importance to the success of the UK economy, the CBI runs an annual innovation trends survey, which looks at how much companies are spending in this area. Innovation expenditure includes research and development, market research, academic links the use of outside consultants and licensing trade mark specialists, training and capital expenditure. The November 1992 survey, based on 425 responses, indicated that after a number of years, during which many of the indicators were pointing downwards, there has been a marked shift upwards in many areas. It suggested that product and process development times are shortening, with the most common period being in the one to two year category. Product life-cycles are also shortening. While the most commonly cited period is in the five to ten year category, more companies are reporting product lifecycles in the three to five year period. Companies are spending more on innovation, and the prime incentives are consumer demand for quality followed by price and competition. Variations are significant in the proportion of turnover spent on innovation. While 70 per cent of the sample spent 5 per cent or less certain companies in the electronics sector spent up to 14 per cent of turnover and certain companies in the chemicals sector spent up to 20 per cent. Most interestingly, nearly two-thirds of manufacturers cited profits directly resulting from investment in innovation over the last three years. 82 per cent reported market share gains and 78 per cent reported the development of new markets as a result of investment in this area.

These findings underline the benefits which can be obtained from well-planned and well-directed investment in innovation.

PROJECT PLANNING

Who writes the brief?

How can the lessons of Williams, Sony and the pharmaceutical giants be learned and acted upon by mainstream UK marketing companies. One of the problems which many companies still face is the view that marketing is considered a cosmetic exercise for dressing-up products developed by designers and production engineers. That marketeers should specify the kind of products required by consumers, and should expect designers and production engineers to meet their marketing briefs, is still an uncommon phenomenon

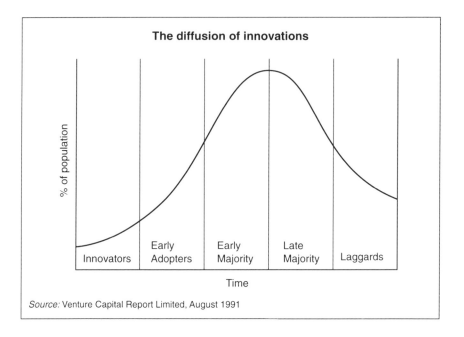

The diffusion of innovations

% of population

Innovators | Early Adopters | Early Majority | Late Majority | Laggards

Time

Source: Venture Capital Report Limited, August 1991

Figure 6.1

in many industries. In the words of Mark Sherrington, the Managing Director of The Added Value Company,

> '. . . *some companies I have worked with are completely overawed when the marketeers talk about changing the product. I have sat with design directors and they have asked "Why are you interested in the product specification? That's my job." They think of marketing as the bit you do after they have developed the product. Real marketeers get involved in specifying the product.*'

What are the key questions?

One of the key areas marketeers need to address is the balance between invention and innovation referred to by Creenagh Lodge. Invention implies complete novelty, innovation is simply the adaptation of what is already there; Wash & Go and the Pentel Rollerpen are good examples of the latter. What are the key questions?

1 How innovative can and should new products be?

In some cases like home banking, consumer take-up is slow because the concept is simply too new. For example, fromage frais did not take off in the

UK until it was dressed up in yoghurt pots. The key point is whether the new idea has a frame of reference for the consumer.

2 Can the company afford the time and money to establish the new concept?

New products need both time and money, even when consumers have a clear frame of reference. The exact balance between money and time depends on the novelty of the product, and the level of social endorsement by influential groups within the population. (See Figure 6.1).

How fast a product moves along the diffusion curve often cannot be assessed before the event. Who would have predicted the slow acceptance of the satellite dish despite heavy promotion? Who would have predicted the rapid acceptance of compact discs or bottled mineral waters despite their high costs? Some companies with more time than money have benefited hugely by exploiting the diffusion of minority endorsement into the main-stream market; The Body Shop is a perfect example of this.

3 Is there a demand for the new product?

Is there evidence of substantial consumer need for the new product? Sir Clive Sinclair's C5 and tobacco substitutes are good examples of products which sounded fine in theory. People ought to have been interested in environmentally friendly transport and healthier smoking. But in reality the average road user and smoker was not interested. Similarly, fashions like Sock Shop and Tie Rack were popular for a while but had no real substance. After a brief honeymoon both concepts ran into difficulties with fickle consumers.

4 Is the advantage sustainable?

Does the new product fit with the internal and external skills of the company.

5 Does the new product perform?

There are many examples of a great product idea which has been killed by underperformance against consumer expectations. Take the Black and Decker Paintmate, an idea to pump paint under CO_2 pressure direct to the paint roller, thus speeding up the DIY process for lazy home improvers. The product simply did not perform as expected.

6 Who is the project champion?

It is crucial that a strong individual with marketing flair and corporate clout leads the project.

Who owns the project?

Even in those companies where it is accepted that product development is the primary responsibility of the marketing function confusion can often arise about who 'owns' a project and therefore takes ultimate responsibility for its success or failure. For example, in many cases the new product development function forms part of the marketing department but is quite separate from day-to-day product management. At some point new projects have to move from one responsibility to the other but they sometimes get lost or delayed en route. The point at which products move across from development into product management can become confused, and vital time can be lost.

As products get closer to launch, new product development teams typically include specialists from many departments; marketing, finance, legal, research, production, distribution, sales and so on. The structure is often more of a matrix than a pyramid, and matrices can degenerate into tangled webs. In many cases a matrix is the only viable structure, particularly with multinational new product developments; matrices running across functions and geographic areas. But the trouble is that often no one square in the matrix takes ownership. Very often the owner of the project is not clearly identified. Even when the owner is clear, individuals making up the team have line responsibilities to their own functional heads, rather than to the project leader, and significant problems can arise with priorities.

Calling in the mumbo-jumbo specialists?

To help make sure things do happen and that all the required resources are available, new product development managers have a panoply of agencies at their disposal; qualitative and quantitative market researchers, product and identity designers, trade mark specialists, lawyers, marketing consultancies, advertising agencies and a new profession which came of age in the eighties – the NPD consultant.

In the 1980s, one of the big growth areas in the consultancy world was new product development. The retail market was voracious for new product lines. Large numbers of new products and line extensions hit the shelves, existing products were repositioned, budgets were high and many categories were in a growth phase. Large consultancies like KAE, CLK, The Creative Business, Interbrand, The Value Engineers and The Added Value Company brought extensive brands marketing, market research and promotional agency experience to clients with limited NPD expertise. Many smaller consultancies flourished. They represented a source of advice and a shoulder to cry on. Their services were much in demand among traditional FMCG companies and also in new sectors like personal financial products marketing.

They helped to systematise the process and to reduce the number of expensive failures. The nineties have seen some attrition and belt-tightening in the sector as marketeers have moderated their new business programmes, but the better consultancies have survived and thrived. After all, the need for new and repositioned products does not go away in recession. In many markets it becomes even more important than in the boom years.

However, John Murphy, the Chairman of Interbrand, is concerned that NPD agencies tend to over complicate and over elaborate the NPD process, something which has left a legacy of trepidation among marketing managers about the complexity of NPD. In his view, many processes are simply straight forward common sense and need not be either daunting or horribly expensive.

AGREEING AIMS, OBJECTIVES AND EVALUATION CRITERIA

Whether John Murphy is right or not, NPD consultancies claim to bring objectivity, comparative experience, extensive knowledge of relevant markets and the retail sector, and above all a systematic approach to the definition of aims, objectives and project success criteria. Those companies which adopt the geriatric ward approach to NPD, as described by Creenagh Lodge, are made to sit up and think by high quality NPD consultants. Perhaps more so than any other consultancy sector, NPD consultants have a strong vested interest in ensuring that tangible results come out of the process. Their work is totally invisible until new or repositioned products and services hit the market. Their portfolio of case studies may be lagged, for security and confidentiality reasons, but they ultimately have to demonstrate results. If they sense that their work will be sidelined or misdirected they often speak their minds and withdraw.

Some of the financial, corporate and market performance criteria they can be expected to review include:

- consistency with the corporate mission
- the climate of competition
- market potential
- range compatibility
- volume of sales
- buying and production economics
- marketing costs
- inventory costs
- working capital costs
- fixed asset costs

- profits and cashflows
- returns on investment
- payback periods
- possible exit costs.

They can be expected to thoroughly review threats and inhibiting factors, for example:

- extent of financial resources to support a launch
- availability of raw materials
- production capacity constraints
- price elasticities and demand limitations
- suitability of distribution and sales channel
- extent of production, distribution, marketing and management resources
- external threats; competitive, political or consumer
- timing constraints; when to launch if at all.

This rigour is a very useful discipline because many firms have a long tail of projects with little sense of the relative priorities attached to each, the order in which they are expected to hit the market and the relationship between the various different development projects.

BRAND CREATION OR EXTENSION

One of the perennial debates among marketing people is whether to develop entirely new brands or to develop existing brands. Fulfilling new market opportunities with new product concepts suggests new branding for genuine new products, but the desire to minimise risk suggests sheltering under the umbrella of an existing brand. A recent study in the US revealed that total promotion costs are 35 to 40 per cent less for brand extensions than for completely new brands. Initial trialling is higher and failure rates are only 30 per cent, compared with 50 per cent for completely new brands. A 1991 study by the UK based strategy consulting firm OC&C pointed to a 26 per cent saving on launch costs and a 20 per cent increase in success rates. With these statistics in mind it is hardly surprising that marketing people often opt for line extensions within existing brand franchises, rather than for launching entirely new brands.

In addition to the lower promotional costs and lower risks of failure, there are financial pressures to strengthen the value of existing brands. Brand valuation has given explicit values to brands which financial people are keen to support. The costs and complications of design and trade mark registration are also significantly lower with brand extensions, particularly if new products are to be launched worldwide. New products within existing brand portfolios are much quicker to reach the market than new products with entirely new brand platforms. In today's markets this is a major consideration.

But while new products can hide behind existing brands, and thereby reduce the risks of failure, many positioning problems can be created by indiscriminate brand extension. How much can the original target market for the brand be expected to support new products? How much cannibalisation and fragmentation of the original core brand is acceptable? What effect will many line extensions have on the strength of the original brand? Will the trade accept more and more stock keeping units (SKUs) under the same brand? Is the new product concept so far from the original brand that it would have been more logical to launch a completely new brand platform despite the higher risks involved?

While brand development is high risk and expensive it would be wrong to think that brand extension is low risk and cheap. All new product introductions are high risk, even brand extensions. Extending brands may fail, damage the extension or worse still damage the brand. For example, Levi jeans seriously damaged its brand franchise in the late seventies by a disastrous foray into the general leisurewear market.

Frankenstein and the meaning of life

Paul Walton, Managing Director of The Value Engineers, considered these issues in a recent paper *Frankenstein and the meaning of life*. In the paper he drew an analogy between the changing meaning of words and the changing meaning of brands to consumers. He uses the example of Samuel Augustus Maverick, a Texan lawyer who won a herd of cattle playing poker in the 1860s, and became a rancher by accident. Contrary to local practice he refused to brand his steers, then claimed that all unbranded calves were his. His name came to mean 'unbranded steer' or someone who refuses to follow the herd. Language inevitably adapts, changes and stretches over time to accommodate new facts of life, and the same principle applies to brands. But how far can brands be stretched? Words are many, brands are few. Language evolves without constraint. Brand evolution must be managed with care and control, otherwise a brand's highly condensed meaning to consumers can become confused.

Paul Walton outlines a number of 'start points' for brand stretching:

Format development

This consists of providing exactly the same brand experience in a different format. Recent examples are typified by Mars in ice cream. The key thought is not to allow production-based views of markets to interfere with fundamental similarities. Countlines are countlines whether they are ambient or frozen.

Feature development

Many brands are built on a strong functional feature like taste or a distinctive ingredient. SmithKline Beecham's use of Ribena as the definitive source of blackcurrant created a strong niche for a high value, ready-to-drink variant of Ribena, and from there by extension into a family of ready-to-drink juices.

Market transference

A strategy for moving the brand into new but related territory. The therapeutic brands of dentrifices have recently extended from caries and gum health into anti-plaque mouthwashes. Duracell, the brand leader in battery cells, has extended into torches.

Benefit transfer

This strategy applies the brand's consumer benefit to other markets where the benefit is relevant. Unigate's Shape has created a portfolio of dairy products built around the proposition of half the fat of standard products. Domestos in the UK has brought germ kill to the general purpose cleaner market.

Technology and expertise transfer

This strategy relies upon a more abstract reading of what skills go into the brand. Sony's Walkman® is about miniaturisation. Bic knows about disposability, hence pens and razors. Because Honda understands small motors it has extended from motor bikes into lawn mowers.

Prestige extension

Brands which trade more on imagery, especially in premium and super premium segments have found success in extending across a wide front of products. While this is especially true of designer brands like Lacoste and Pierre Cardin, Alfred Dunhill has done well in the upper mass market. Williams Grand Prix Engineering is now applying the same principle to its brand.

Consumer relationship transfer

This approach is less typical among grocery products but is very typical of grocery store brand owners and indeed many other retailer and service providers. Where broad brand values have been created and where there are reasonable barriers to entry, for example a consumer's relationship with a bank, it is not only easy to extend the product choice, it is a key success factor to recruiting new customers; Consider The Bodyshop, Visa Travellers Cheques and Benetton.

Paul Walton goes on to describe what he calls the *Swot* strategy as opposed to the *Sweat* strategy, the former employed by stronger brands, the latter by weaker brands. A *Swot* strategy involves development from strength to further invest in the brand against market opportunities. New products lead rather than follow the market. A *Sweat* strategy involves pragmatic extension from an average to poor position, to sweat the brand asset in the light of consumer opportunities or competitor threats. The latter approach is typified by force fitting existing company equities with production feasible product concepts, usually for short term reasons like profit shortfalls or to block competitors. New products usually follow rather than lead the market. Economy is the main reason for adopting this approach and there is a real threat of confusing the consumer.

Creating a brand extension blueprint

Paul Walton concludes by setting a blueprint for brand extension:

Set a brand strategy within the portfolio

Decide the investment strategy for the brand. Is it to milk the brand equity for short-run profit generation? Is it to maintain the brand by keeping the offer up to date without a fundamental shift in meaning? Is it to invest in the brand against the needs and opportunities of an evolving market?

Define the meaning of the brand

Define what is to be extended. What does the brand mean to the consumer, its proposition, its core values and its properties? A brand equity study can establish the relative mobility of the marque and by exploring potential futures establish legitimate areas for development.

Define a mission for the brand

A three to five year view should be constructed to show where the company wants the brand to be and consider the consequences for development of the medium-term brand mission. The mission must take account of national, international or global issues where applicable.

Achieve the mission

What are the critical success factors for achieving the mission? What are the negotiable and non-negotiable aspects of brand meaning which must be present in any future brand extension? Are the visual characteristics of the brand defined? How must core values be reinforced or modified over time? What renovation work is needed before further extensions are completed? Is there a simple consumer logic for extensions? In new markets does the brand provide an appropriate reference point for the consumer? Do the new market's values sit well with the brand?

Monitor progress

What are the key steps? Are the milestones defined? What are the implications for trade development and category management? How must brand tracking research be modified? At what point must brand stretching stop or be reversed? What checks are in place to prevent dilution of the brand equity?

Brand extension must not be allowed to threaten the underlying structure of brand syntax. Evolution must be planned, managed and monitored. If it is not then the results may not be as intended. In this context it is interesting to note that Frankenstein was the name of an inventive philosopher. But he has gone down in history as a self-destructive monster.

Over-extending the brand franchise

Unfortunately, many marketing people have massively over-fragmented existing brands. This guarantees a lower pay-back, because there is so much fragmentation into the main brand, creating high fixed costs. Many marketing people have overlooked the opportunity to launch new brands. Some would argue that Unilever provides case studies on both sides of the equation. In the case of Persil the fragmentation of a simple product range into myriad versions of the basic product creates the risk of consumer confusion. Admittedly the quality of the range extensions and the extent of promotional support minimise the risks, but the Persil brand appears to have been stretched quite far enough for consumers. By contrast, when Unilever launched a mild shampoo range it could have simply extended the Pears range but instead it decided to launch Timotei, which has become a huge brand platform in its own right, appealing to consumers far removed from traditional Pears loyalists.

In Mark Sherrington's opinion the next ten years will see a market correction, with the pendulum swinging back towards new brands. 'Half the projects we are doing at the moment are in the area of brand structures, helping clients sort out the fact that they have parent brands, sub brands and disparate extended brand ranges. That will get sorted and people will launch far more new brands.'

A niche too far

Another area where Mark Sherrington believes there will be a fundamental correction is in the area of niche marketing. Oversegmentation of markets has led to the excessive development of niche brands. But while production strategies, based on flexible production facilities, mean that more and more product variants can be delivered, there is a growing danger of over-fragmenting brands. In his words,

'. . . niche branding has gone crazy. What marketeers should be doing is considering that in any market there are only four or five key purchase dynamics. In the car market they are "does it look good is it safe, is it economical to run, is it spacious"? and so on. These are basic purchase dynamics and what marketing people should concentrate on is understanding what those dynamics are, and making incremental improvements in those areas. For example, insurance is a product most people buy but never use. In many ways the product is the promise of prompt, efficient claims settlement. But insurance companies hate the whole idea of making claims easier. One insurance company told me that making the claims process simpler and quicker would cost money. People will want to claim more often! But no company I know can develop its product or build its brand without spending money. It cost British Airways a fortune when it upped its service levels. Improving the core benefit of insurance – claims settlement – is going to cost money. In the insurance example the company should concentrate on good claim settlements, rather than worrying about niche insurance products for small target groups. By understanding key purchase dynamics, and by making incremental improvements in them, it will be possible to appeal across a range of niche markets. I think there will be a "back-to-basics" movement in the nineties as consumer segmentation swings back towards fundamentals.'

Premium product extension

One of the more common marketing practices of the 1980s was the creation of premium products within brand portfolios. Either the main product itself or a variant of the product was driven up the market, and certainly up the price bracket, by adding premium attributes. In the words of Mark Sherrington,

'. . . marketeers went mad at the end of the 1980s and convinced themselves that by sticking a bit of gold and the word "premium" on a few things they could automatically jack-up the margin by 15 per cent. Companies have got to add real value or consumers will find them out. Many of them are now getting found out!

The one thing marketeers forget at their peril is that 95 per cent of good branding is good product. The twiddly bits at the end, important as they are, and much as they can give the product an edge, are only five or ten per cent. No amount of great marketing can save a duff product. That is why genuine brand development normally involves real product development which costs money.

Often people devote all their efforts in NPD to coming up with a facsimile of what their competitors are doing already, and the whole NPD process is devoted to making an acceptable rip-off of the competitor and not coming up with anything different. Even if you come up with a wonderful pastiche of what is already there, people don't have any reason to buy it, because all it is is an imitation, albeit a good imitation. Why should they go to the brand they don't love, even if they recognise it is acceptable packaging and quality?'

USES AND ABUSES OF MARKET RESEARCH

One of the central pillars of NPD is understanding what the consumer might or might not want. One of the fundamental questions must be what price can a new product sustain without killing demand? One problem with market research is concluding on broad public reactions to new products based on a few specific tests; research samples are often relatively small, and drawing conclusions can sometimes be difficult. Another problem is gaining a realistic impression of how products will be received in real life situations, rather than in artificial research situations. If a consumer in a research group or hall test says they will use the product can the public be relied upon to do so when the product finally hits the shelves? How does the product interact with other social and cultural factors at the launch date? How will the consumer react to the product, the price, the packaging, the advertising and the on-shelf display? Which of several different routes is the optimal one? Few market research techniques can precisely predict the extent or the depth of demand with enough sensitivity to assess whether volume demand will be present when a new product is launched at the agreed price. As many new product launches depend for success or failure on minor price fluctuations this can be a major problem.

Problems which crop up time and time again are the costs of multilayered research, timing constraints, and confidentiality. One of the main issues, apart from the basic interest in the product, is what price can be charged. This is critical because if the price is set too low the product may become unviable and be scrapped, or be launched and make insufficient profit. If the price is set too low at launch it is hard to fundamentally shift pricing structures at a later date. By contrast, if the price is set too high a potentially winning product may be stillborn, withdrawn from the shelves as the sell-by date is reached and the product is delisted.

Some of the possible research techniques used in the NPD process are:

1 Qualitative concept research among small but representative consumer groups. These sessions typically last a few hours and involve half a dozen target consumers. At the initial stages qualitative groups may be assessing very broad concepts and product parameters, but as the NPD process comes closer to launch they may include prototypes, samples, price trade-off analysis and specific promotional materials. They are intended to give pointers for subsequent validation but all too often qualitative research findings are treated as though they have quantitative validity. They are also said to be excellent at gauging interest and trial but to be an inadequate way of assessing repeat usage.

2 Quantitative research by way of omnibus surveys or large samples may be of use, particularly at an early stage to spot market gaps. The difficulty with large-scale research of this kind is that it takes time, money, and runs the risk of being either too vague or of spilling the beans to the competition.

3 Placement tests, where product is put into a representative sample of consumer homes, can be very useful to test consumer reactions and to feed back comments into the development process. These have the advantage of putting products into a real consuming environment.

4 Hall tests, where larger groups of consumers are exposed to the product concept, pricing and promotion take smaller sampling techniques one stage further, but suffer from a measure of artificiality.

5 Test markets can be very helpful but are often impracticable for a variety of reasons. For example, many supermarkets may not co-operate, the competition may employ spoiling tactics, or test areas may not coincide with TV areas. Some manufacturers test products in mini-vans or individual shop tests, using a small selection of shops to test-launch the products. However, these alternatives to a full test lack the support of relevant advertising and their validity as predictors of a national roll-out has to be questioned.

6 Trade research with buyers from key retailers is becoming increasingly important. If one or two of the key retailers refuse to list the new product after launch all the hard work may have been wasted. The problem on the other hand is that many of the supermarkets are now so active in the area of own-label NPD that confidentiality becomes a major consideration. It has even been suggested that some retailers watch their suppliers NPD activities

with interest, see which new products succeed, and then launch similar own-label products after a short gap. Branded manufacturers effectively become the test marketing function for the retailers.

7 Modelling using market maps, consumer segmentations and the results of micro-tests may be of use but the results have to be taken with a large pinch of salt until the product is in the market proving the models were correct.

One of the dangers with all research is that every technique has major conceptual flaws. A great deal of experience, judgement and gut feel have to be employed interpreting and taking action on the results. For example, research taken at an introductory phase in development may be out of date by the time a product is ready to go, and the product may have taken liberties with one or two of the initial research findings. Judgement has been used as to whether this will undermine the process or not. Research should be an aid to decision-making not a replacement for decision-making.

At one end of the spectrum are those who slavishly follow the results of the various research techniques. At the other are those who conclude that the cost, complexity and flawed objectivity of many techniques mean that gut feel is the only worthwhile approach. Somewhere in between is a happy medium.

John Murphy has strong opinions about the contribution of market research,

'A lot of the blame for unsuccessful NPD can be laid at the feet of market research. People go out and ask consumers daft questions, or very badly-designed market research. Consumers feed back characteristics of the brands they think you ought to be developing, which are often the characteristics of the brands they know and love, so they feed back a template for developing a "me-too" brand.

'A lot of the qualitative work that goes on is almost fraudulent. I've sat in on four or five presentations in the last five years where things have been researched and I don't believe the research company has actually done the work properly. I'm not saying they didn't run qualitative groups, but certainly the person who wrote the reports didn't sit through them and probably didn't read the material that came out. Companies make profound decisions on the basis of glib research summaries of this sort. I can think of two cases where I've been so astounded by what the research company said that I asked for the tapes. In neither case had the person giving the over-view attended any of the groups. They were then unable to find the tapes – they had mysteriously gone missing! It was like Watergate!'

He goes on to describe one recent NPD exercise he was asked to become involved with,

'The entire world positioning on a new brand was done on the basis of two qualitative research groups, one in London, one in Paris, and a fifty page report. A major packaging issue came up – the British company wanted one type of packaging and the foreign company wanted another. So the British company spent over £50,000 on 2,000 face-to-face interviews to ask people the difference between various packages. The qualitative research was grossly inadequate. The client made multi-million pound decisions on the basis of two qualitative groups and the researcher's interpretation. They spent £50,000 on making a decision on the basis of a totally inadequate tool. It was like opening a tin of baked beans with a dentist's drill.'

In John Murphy's view successful NPD is about being hard-nosed and commonsensical, about asking, 'Why should the consumer buy this? What's different about it from the products already on the shelf?' He does not think companies need grossly elaborated market research and huge quantitative studies. In fact, in his view a lot of market research companies have become extremely cynical. 'We all know that if we are making decisions we ought to research them first. So market research companies are in the position of being God and they know it. Some think that because they already know the answers, why bother to do all the work?'

There is no doubt that many marketing and NPD people often spend very inappropriately on market research. A significant proportion of market research is commissioned inappropriately and often misleadingly. The irritating thing for policymakers is that poorly briefed and executed market research can be used to close down valid discussion on the basis that whatever hypothesis is being discussed 'has been researched and discounted'. Policymakers need to fully understand and agree with the type, quantum and conclusions of market research conducted if they want to avoid leading their companies into costly NPD disasters.

To avoid both excessive market research costs and expensive failed launches a key issue is to review new products frequently. There is an unfortunate tendency to let NPD teams go their own way until it is too late. In the words of Graham Turton, a partner in Price Waterhouse Management Consultants practice,

'Companies who are successful at NPD have systems for making sure that the money going into NPD is geared to how well new products are starting to perform. Companies should start off with an idea and a small research budget. As the idea progresses it should be given more money and as it gets nearer to commercial value real money should be fed into it. Projects which don't pass various hurdles should be chopped. That is the successful way to do NPD, but I suspect a lot of NPD is done by people who are charged with the responsibility. They go away and develop pro-

ducts up to the final stage before market testing or serious internal review takes place. Budgeting and controlling NPD should be subject to rigorous review at all stages; as an idea, as a concept and as a working prototype.'

SIMPLIFYING THE LOGISTICS OF LAUNCHING NEW PRODUCTS

The sort of NPD exercise which is close to the heart of a down to earth chap like John Murphy is the kind adopted by many retailers. As he says, 'M&S are successful because they don't produce products themselves, they lean on their suppliers to do it. For example, they might come up with an idea for selling large bags of peanuts, so they get a supplier to put some sieves in the factory, bag them up and if they sell, fine, if not, they do something else.'

One successful and well established supplier of chilled, short-life products to leading retailers has a direct and simple NPD process. Little market research is done because the retailer's shelves are the main source of market research. Its NPD process stages are simple and direct, as follows:

- priority setting
- concept development and screening at kitchen with provisional costings
- concept presentation to retail customer
- factory trial and scale up exercise
- preliminary agreement with customer and timing plan
- further factory trials
- confirm final launch plan with customer
- final factory trial
- pre-production run
- launch
- debrief and learn.

Apart from the logistics of sourcing and producing a quality product, and the difficulty of ensuring that initial ball-park cost estimates can be replicated in factory production runs there are few NPD complications. The process has the advantage of speed and the one drawback that if a product fails the recall and cancellation costs can be high. However, it is generally a highly successful system for both parties.

Unfortunately, the relative certainty of this type of NPD is not available to many branded manufacturers who have to throw themselves at the mercies and the vagaries of the full blown NPD process.

DOES THE SALESFORCE HAVE A FUTURE?

The case of close retailer relationships in the NPD process highlights the issue of what role the salesforce has to play in the future. In many instances such a large proportion of a company's business is done through a small number of key contact points that it brings into question the need for and role of the sales team. In many cases even a key account handler may seem unnecessary, the relationship being managed by marketing, NPD, production and senior management.

In addition to the concentration of buying points in many companies the shift towards flatter management structures and integrated teams means that there has also been a merging of disciplines within companies. In many cases it is not entirely clear what the conventional sales person brings to the party. As a result of this challenge the sales function has been thinking long and hard about its own product positioning. The sales function is being forced to recreate itself for a new business environment. One manifestation of this regeneration process is partnership selling, which redefines the saliency and significance of the sales role.

Partnership selling

The modern approach to sales management can be termed *partnership selling*. It emphasises:

- understanding the client's business
- a customer rather than a factory-led approach
- salesman promoting service not just products
- customers regularly supplied with useful information
- whole company is customer focused
- speedy response to customer queries
- building long-term relationships
- salesmen don't sell on price
- salesmen are problem solvers not just order takers
- salesmen are paid on customer satisfaction not just on sales achieved
- senior directors and managers are directly involved in selling
- the salesman is the key contact
- the salesman is a business person.

This new approach is increasingly leading to the splitting of the sales function; one team to get new business, one to service existing customers. The emergence of the supersalesmen and women – a more entrepreneurial, business generating individuals within the sales function is one which may help many companies escape from the stranglehold on their business of conventional sales channels, which are narrowing the options for profitable growth.

CUTTING OUT THE MIDDLE MAN

For one of the real challenges in the nineties will be not only establishing better relationships with existing customers but also finding completely new distribution channels. Some of the developments which the new breed of business generating salespeople may investigate will include:

- interactive direct line shopping systems
- screen based shopping
- computerised directory shopping
- network marketing.

The recent link-up between Bell Atlantic and Telecommunications Incorporated, to create the world's largest telecommunications and cable TV system is a foretaste of things to come. If the combined group can also succeed in taking over Paramount Studios the combined conglomerate will provide telephony, computing and entertainment in one package to millions of homes. If such a combine can be created it will not be long before other integrated networks are created to compete. The impact on day-to-day life could be as dramatic as the invention of the internal combustion engine, the telephone, the television or the computer, changing consumer habits and buying patterns out of all recognition. In terms of NPD the interactive visual capabilities open up huge opportunities for researching and testing new products. The touch-screen ordering and home delivery mechanisms which will be developed create huge opportunities for new product placement and long-term sales delivery. New methods for selling, perhaps even bypassing the all powerful retailer, will grow apace. The business capabilities of the new breed of sales people will be at a premium.

CONCLUSIONS

The business environment is moving faster and becoming riskier by the day. New technologies and systems are creating the means for producing new products and for delivering them direct to the home. Innovation in all its guises is at a premium. In this environment the need for well-informed and imaginative financial strategies is critical. The critical factors are resource allocation and capital rationing. Rather than the blind forms of cost paring and investment control that many companies have experienced in the past, there will need to be a more informed and integrated approach in the nineties if the new opportunities are to be properly exploited.

Bibliography

Practical Business Development, Peter Kraushar, Holt, Reinhart and Winston, ISBN 0 03 910614 4

Planning and Control of New Product Marketing, D. Garbutt, Bourne Press, ISBN 0 94 803626 5

Marketing Audit Checklists, Aubrey Wilson, McGraw Hill, ISBN 0 07 707760 1

CBI/Natwest Innovation Trends Survey, Issue 4 November 1992

'The Marketing of New Products', Paul Walton , Venture Capital Report, August 1991

Frankenstein and the meaning of life, Paul Walton, The Value Engineers

Partnership Selling, Achieving added value from your sales force in the 1990s, Business Marketing Services Limited

7

DOES BRAND VALUATION HAVE A FUTURE?

'It is perfectly easy to be original by violating the laws of decency and the canons of good taste'
Oliver Wendel Holmes

THE INTERBRAND PHENOMENON

When John Murphy, the rumbustious Chairman of Interbrand, the world's leading brand valuation consultancy, established Interbrand in the early seventies, little did he realise the effect he would have on the stuffy world of accountancy.

Interbrand began life as Murphy's vehicle for creating catchy names for biscuits, chocolate bars, toiletries and many other everyday products. Hobnobs and Boasters biscuits, the Rover Maestro, Chanel's male fragrance, Antaeus, and more recently, the Ford Mondeo, are just a few of the many brands created by Interbrand. Whether his jovial modesty is entirely justified or not, Murphy claims to have cracked product names on his way to work; to have charged the client a large fee by the coffee break, and to have spent the rest of the day finishing *The Times* crossword.

Had Murphy left it at that he would probably just be running a profitable marketing consultancy. But in the eighties he recruited two bright chartered accountants, Michael Birkin and Paul Stobart, who helped create and promote the concept of brand valuations in financial accounts. They set off a huge debate within the accountancy profession which has still not been satisfactorily resolved. There are many who consider brand valuation to be a complete irrelevancy to the business of managing large enterprises. Merchant bankers dismiss the whole idea as a desperate attempt to dress up the balance sheet of companies under threat of takeover. In the words of one,

> *'You can make up any values you like and put them on the balance sheet but no one in the City is going to take the resulting balance sheet seriously. We simply add back the values we have no faith in and draw our own conclusions.'*

The advocates of brand valuation argue that it is such narrow-minded City opinions and the inadequacies of existing accounting conventions that created the need for brand valuation in the first place.

WHY NOT ACCOUNT FOR BRANDS?

The purpose of financial accounts

At the heart of the debate is the question of what financial accounts are meant to convey. Should they simply record historical transactions for interpretation by technical users, or should they be meaningful documents for nontechnical users? Should the balance sheet strictly record historical events and be simply a parking place for expenditures halfway between the cash-flow statement and the profit and loss account, or should it be a genuine statement of value? Do arbitrary valuations and revaluations have any place in a set of meaningful financial accounts?

One wing of the accountancy profession believes that financial accounts should record only historical transactions, as these have a solid basis in fact. Interpretations of real company values should be the responsibility of users, after analysis of all relevant external facts, provided both in the Notes to the Accounts and from elsewhere.

The criticism levelled at this approach is that many users receive a set of accounts which bears little relevance to the operations of the commercial enterprise and that professional investors have a major advantage in terms of understanding the real financial issues affecting the business.

The other wing of the accountancy profession believes that financial accounts should recognise current asset values at the period-end and that the associated profit and loss account should include charges for the depletion of those current asset values rather than long-outdated historical values.

The criticism levelled here, is that arriving at accurate valuations is almost impossible and that they change from period to period. Arbitrary valuations and revaluations also remove the ability to compare similar companies on a like-for-like basis. Nondepreciation of valuations and revaluations is imprudent but depreciation of them could give nonsensical results, if there is a long-term upward trend in value. Arbitrary depreciation charges carried to the profit and loss account, which reduce *Earnings Per Share*, have the perverse effect of reducing a company's value. However, taking changes in asset values straight to the balance sheet, without touching the profit and loss account, opens the door to all sorts of creative accounting.

Current cost accounts

One attempt to resolve this dilemma was the ill-fated introduction of Current Cost Accounting in the late seventies. This was an attempt to provide users with a set of historical cost accounts side-by-side with a set of fully revalued current cost accounts – the best of both worlds. Unfortunately, this worthy objective was shot to pieces by the backwoodsmen. The work involved in preparing and auditing current cost accounts was considered onerous and the conceptual justification for many of the current cost adjustments was held to be questionable. Many commercial accountants did not understand the method of calculating current cost adjustments and had no idea what the revalued, adjusted accounts were telling them. The initiative was ignominiously scrapped.

After the current cost accounting debacle, the conflicting approaches have coexisted in an uncomfortable fashion, the net result of which is that we now have neither one thing nor the other. The basis of financial accounts remains historical cost but with one or two specific inclusions for revaluations, most notably for property.

A conceptual framework

What is needed is an overarching theoretical framework defining the purpose and content of financial accounts within which individual accounting treatments can have some context and relevance. The International Accounting Standards Committee has put forward, in 'The Framework for the Preparation and Presentation of Financial Statements,' the concept that accounts should enable users to make economic decisions concerning the size, timing and certainty of future cashflows. Corporate and individual cashflows may be the heart of the matter but a specific UK accounting framework reflecting this approach has yet to be agreed.

Against this background, it is possible to see why accountants have been unwilling to entertain the introduction of new categories of intangible assets in balance sheets, particularly where the valuations are subjective.

Michael Renshall, ex-chairman of the Accounting Standards Committee encapsulated the concerns about brand valuation when he said '. . . it is an approach which comes close to the capitalisation of future profits, a concept which makes conventional accountants deeply uneasy, not least because of its obvious uncertainty.'

THE BIRTH OF BRAND VALUATION

There had been disquiet, with the failure of accountants to recognise intangible assets in company accounts for many years, before the subject finally became a hot one in the late eighties. There had been some rumblings, but the first organisations to actually do something about the issue were the publishing giants News Corporation and United Newspapers, which in 1984 and 1987 respectively capitalised acquired titles.

The impact of the 'corporate raiders'

However, the wider impetus for brand valuation came from the corporate raiders and asset strippers. They targeted brand-rich companies, which, because of the prevailing accounting conventions, failed to reflect the true value of brand assets in their balance sheets.

Although it was apparent that advertising and marketing expenditure influenced customer buying behaviour long after specific campaign periods, it was not considered sensible by the accountancy profession to carry forward any part of the cost to be matched against future revenues. The 'prudence concept' defeated the 'accruals concept' every time, in the absence of tangible proof that there was a direct link between expenditure in one period and sales in the next. The year-end valuation of intangible assets was held by accountants to be too uncertain to give them carrying values, and without a reporting requirement, little time was spent calculating theoretical brand valuations.

The perfect market theory

It was assumed that analysts and professional investors were shrewd enough to appreciate the underlying value of a company's brand portfolio and to reflect this in the share price. Unfortunately, this assumption ignored the impact on stock prices of short-term income dips, heavy investment programmes and uncertain perceptions of management performance.

It also overestimated the ability of the market to spot hidden values. Without effective investor relations programmes pointing out the facts, it hardly seems surprising that analysts failed to recognise the true value of brands, or of the companies that owned them.

Takeovers expose the problem

The problem had developed over many years. As early as 1978 Allied Breweries was considered by many in the City to have paid an excessive price for the J Lyons brand portfolio, although the commercial value of its brands was significant. Then in 1986 Hanson Trust paid £2.3 billion for the Imperial Group. In 1988 Nestlé paid £2.5 billion for Rowntree'. Alarm bells rang in the boardrooms of many underperforming branded goods companies. Large, blue-chip companies with respectable but unstartling financial histories and sagging share prices suddenly found themselves in the firing line.

A realisation that not all analysts could spot hidden value where it was not explicitly shown in the accounts led to a reappraisal of how intangible assets in general, and brands in particular, should be disclosed. The fact that Hanson eventually disposed of much of the Imperial portfolio, leaving the huge tobacco interests for a net price of under £200 million, demonstrated the dangers of relying on conservative financial reporting practices.

The watershed came with the Goodman Fielder Wattie (GFW) bid for Rank Hovis McDougall (RHM) in 1988. In its defence document, RHM played heavily on the power of its various brands and the fact that GFW's bid was an attempt to get them on the cheap.

> *'RHM owns a number of strong brands, many of which are market leaders, which are valuable in their own right, but which the stockmarket tends consistently to undervalue. These valuable assets are not included in the balance sheet, but they have helped RHM build profits in the past and provide a sound base for future growth.'*

The first brand valuation

After fighting off GFW, and in case there was any doubt about the arguments put forward in the heat of the bid battle, RHM's 1988 accounts incorporated the first independently prepared balance sheet valuation of a brand portfolio. A figure of £678 million was included under intangible assets, being the valuation of both internally generated and externally acquired brands.

Many observers were confused by the company's statement that the valuation 'only recognises the value of the brands as they are currently used by the Group and does not take into account their future prospects, or indeed, their worth in the open market.'

If this wasn't the market value of the brands why bother to include the figures at all? In the notes to the accounts, RHM further qualified its novel treatment, which was apparently based on property valuation methods, with the words,

> *'The Group has valued its brands at their current use value to the Group in conjunction with Interbrand Group plc, branding consultants.*

> *'The basis of valuation ignores any alternative use of a brand, any possible extension to the range of products currently marketed under a brand, any element of hope value and any possible increase in value of a brand due to either a special investment or financial transaction (eg licensing) which would leave the Group with a different interest from the one being valued.'*

The headscratching and arguments begin

The RHM action provoked much headscratching and argument within the accountancy profession. But most importantly, and regardless of the conceptual or technical methodology used in the valuation, it set off a discussion which significantly raised awareness of the brand valuation issue. Interbrand had suddenly propelled itself into poll position in a debate which drew in not only finance departments but marketing departments and the board.

Most marketing people found the debate among financial people, about the rights and wrongs of brand valuation, extremely puzzling. Surely, it was obvious that legally protectable and saleable brands, often developed over decades, with vast marketing resources behind them, had an inherent value? Interbrand had arrived, and the results of its new approach were to be found not only in balance sheets but also in a growing recognition of brands as assets within companies.

The proof of the pudding

Whether RHM's actions were ultimately fruitful is open to question as the company eventually lost its independence in a takeover tussle between Tomkins plc, the miniconglomerate, and Hanson Trust. Tomkins made it clear that it would not include brand valuations in its accounts, and Interbrand's brand valuation service was dispensed with, at least for external reporting purposes.

However, the original reason RHM adopted brand accounting was to avoid being snapped up on the cheap. As many analysts consider the £950 million paid by Tomkins to have been a very full price for RHM the popularisers of brand valuation may still get the last laugh.

A DEFENSIVE TECHNIQUE TURNED TO ACQUISITIVE ADVANTAGE

The takeover of RHM saw the disappearance of the only major company which had included both internally generated and externally acquired brands on its balance sheet. The inclusion of both internally and externally derived brands in the RHM balance sheet seemed like a logical and consistent policy to the layman, unversed in the ways of the accountancy profession. But, to those in the know, RHM's attempt to include internally generated brands in its balance sheet was heresy.

Internally generated brands

The problem with internally generated brand valuations is that any form of capitalised sum is effectively a reinstatement of expenses previously written-off to the profit and loss account. Without an externally verifiable transaction to support such an internal brand valuation there is a clear danger of manipulation.

With externally acquired brands at least a known sum has been paid to a third party, and that it exceeds the value of identifiable, tangible assets. In the old days, the difference between tangible asset values and the amount paid was referred to simply as 'goodwill' and was held to relate to an indeterminate mix of intangibles – customer loyalty, staff knowledge, distribution channels, trademarks, patents and brand values.

Breaking up 'goodwill'

In *Creative Accounting* Ian Griffiths characterises 'goodwill' as simply the result of '. . . *the accountancy profession's slavish devotion to the principle that for every debit there shall be an equal and opposite credit . . . something which exists only in the mind . . . like the wind, you cannot see it or hold it but you know it is there.'*

But as the brands debate took off, and as methodologies were developed to quantify brand values, goodwill was split up into its component parts, one of the most significant being brand valuations.

The particular attraction of identifying brand valuations separately from the rest of goodwill is that in the UK brand valuations can currently be stated at cost in the balance sheet, need not be amortised and are subject only to annual review and confirmation of the carrying value by the directors. By contrast, normal accounting rules for goodwill involve either writing-off the full amount direct to reserves or amortising it over the expected useful life of the acquisition, to a maximum of 40 years.

As the first option significantly erodes reserves, and therefore Shareholders' Funds, and as the second decreases Earnings Per Share it is easy to see why many acquisitive companies were converted to the concept of brand valuations, at least in relation to acquired brands.

Scale of the goodwill issue

A brief look at the scale of goodwill figures paid in the late eighties illustrates why the brand valuation approach might be particularly attractive to acquisitors.

Examples of goodwill payments in the 1980s

Acquiror	Vendor	Goodwill as % of price paid
Nestlé	Rowntree	83
Grand Met	Pillsbury	88
Cadbury Schweppes	Trebor	75
United Biscuits	Verkade	66

In the case of WPP, the holding company for advertising agencies Ogilvy & Mather and J Walter Thompson, the practice of writing goodwill off direct to reserves rather than amortising it through the profit and loss account resulted in negative equity. The implications of this for banking covenants and media recognition agreements exposed the ridiculous consequences of UK goodwill accounting rules and highlighted the incentive to adopt brand valuations on acquired brands.

The need to comply with Stock Exchange 'Yellow Book' rules concerning shareholder approvals during takeovers, created just one more incentive to opt for brand accounting. In 1989 the International Stock Exchange allowed the inclusion of intangible assets in the Class I tests for shareholder approval of capital transactions. By capitalising acquired brands, and therefore Shareholders' Funds, companies could raise the threshold for shareholder approval of specific transactions.

The profession struggling to catch up

Recent pronouncements in this area include 'Accounting for intangible fixed assets', Exposure Draft 52 of the old Accounting Standards Committee, published in 1990, which specified that brand valuations could be separately identified from goodwill, but only if:

- the historical costs associated with the asset are known or ascertainable
- the characteristics of the asset can be distinguished from goodwill and other assets
- its costs can be measured independently of goodwill and other assets.

In late 1993, the newly formed Accounting Standards Board issued a paper on alternative accounting treatments for goodwill and intangibles. In essence, the ASB proposes three 'building block' methods together with a number of hybrids. The three alternatives are; immediate elimination (currently favoured by 96 per cent of UK groups). Capitalisation with amortisation over a maximum of 20 years (currently favoured by 4 per cent of UK Companies), capitalisation with an annual review of carrying value by 'ceiling test'. Under this last method values would be maintained until they could be shown to be stated at too high a value, at which point the excess would be subject to write down.

The paper also suggests that many identifiable intangibles, currently dealt with as separable assets, should be treated as goodwill. Goodwill would include all intangibles other than those having a clearly defined legal identity and a known life. Brands would be returned to goodwill. The argument will run for some time before the ASB attempts to turn its 'white paper' into firm 'legislation'.

One thing UK standard setters have always agreed upon is that internally generated brand valuations should not be capitalised.

Of course none of this would be possible in the US which insists that all goodwill amounts, however described, should be written-off consistently over a period not to exceed 40 years. The opportunity to write-off direct to reserves or to create a nondepreciable asset seem to be particular vagaries of the UK accounting system. In the US acquisitors are all in the same boat when it comes to hitting Earnings Per Share with the cost of acquisitions.

Vested interest in high brand valuations

In fact, with the current rules in the UK, acquisitive companies have a vested interest in high post-acquisition brand valuations.

However, when the ASB revises its rules on goodwill and its component intangibles we will still be left with the odd fact that a company like United Biscuits has acquired brands like Verkade on the balance sheet but its core McVitie brand is not on the balance sheet. Similarly we will have a variety of food and drink companies with huge brand valuations in their asset figures while a brand like St Michael is nowhere to be seen in the M&S accounts.

Examples of acquired brand valuations

Company	Capitalised brand valuations	Goodwill reserve	Net shareholders funds
	£million	£million	£million
Grand Met	2,492	(2,205)	3,759
Guinness	1,395	(1,327)	3,571
Ladbroke	377	(2)	2,512
United Biscuits	156	(306)	866
WPP	350	(856)	(253)

(*Source*: Report and Accounts dated 31 December 1992 except for Grand Met, 30 September 1992, and United Biscuits, 2 January 1993)

It seems ironic that a technique which was developed specifically to help defend companies from aggressive takeover and to highlight the value of a company's brand portfolio has become just one more handy accounting technique for acquirors seeking to get round the rules on goodwill, to enhance balance sheet values and Earnings Per Share.

WHAT IS A BRAND ANYWAY?

We all think we know what brands are, but before looking at brand valuation methodologies it is worth considering brands in a bit more detail. Of course, the actual term is American and is supposed to have originated in the Wild West when the cowpokes branded their steers, although they did this more to protect ownership than to guarantee quality. Predictably there are more world brands with American parentage than from anywhere else, and the USA has arguably contributed more to the development of modern marketing thinking.

American academics have certainly done their bit, one of the best known being Philip Kotler who defined a brand as '. . . *a name, term, sign, symbol or design, or a combination of them which is intended to identify the goods or services of one seller to differentiate them from those of competitors.'* (Marketing Management)

J Hugh Davidson takes the definition one step further to encapsulate the psychological benefits intrinsic in brands '. . . *brands enable consumers to identify products or services which promise specific benefits. They arouse expectations in the minds of customers about quality, price, purpose and performance. A brand stands out from commodities because commodities lack identity.'* (Offensive Marketing)

In other words brands have personalities in their own right whereas commodities do not.

Within the broad generic definition there are also a number of brand types:

- consumer goods brands
- industrial brands
- service brands
- corporate brands.

In addition to the product or service itself, physical attributes which typify a brand are trademarks, packaging and consumer presentation, forming a definable personality expressed in its marketing communications.

When considering a brand valuation certain key questions have to be asked:

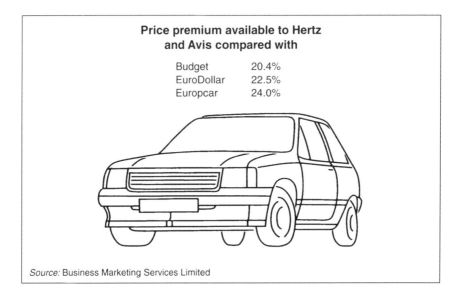

Figure 7.1 (a)

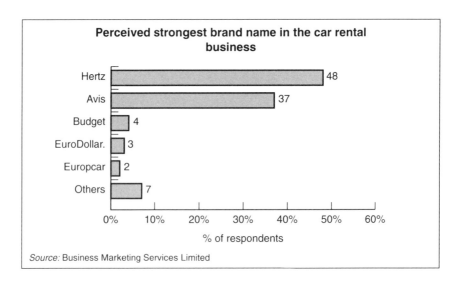

Figure 7.1 (b)

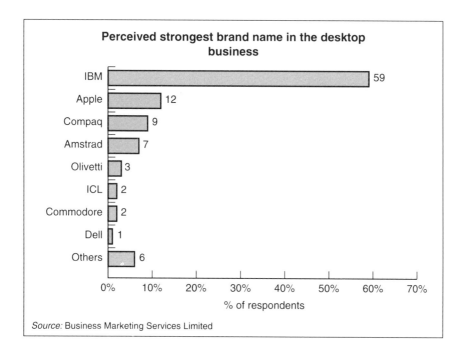

Figure 7.1 (c)

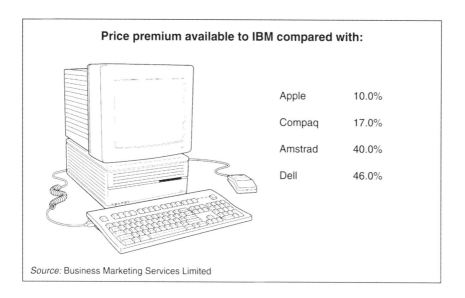

Figure 7.1 (d)

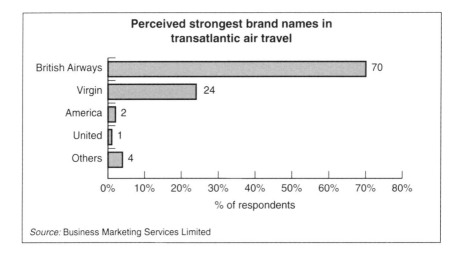

Figure 7.1 (e)

Figure 7.1 (f)

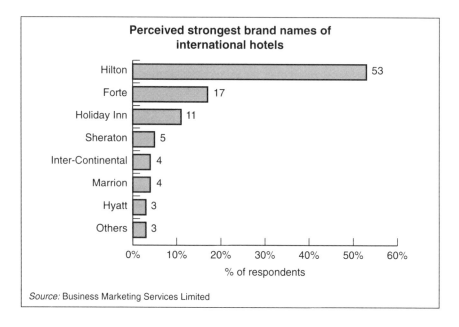

Figure 7.1 (g)

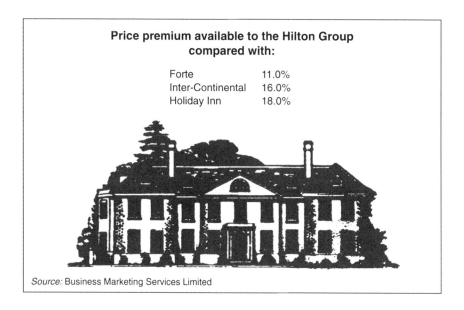

Figure 7.1 (h)

- is the brand clearly identifiable?
- is title to the brand unambiguous?
- could the brand be sold separately from the business?
- is there a premium value over the equivalent commodity product?

If the answer to any of these questions is 'no' there is little value in pursuing the valuation process because the results are likely to be inconclusive.

EMPIRICAL EVIDENCE OF BRAND VALUES

Few marketers are in doubt that brands have a value but there have not been many studies to quantify what consumer premiums particular brands command. One interesting study which has been undertaken was conducted by the industrial market research consultancy Business Marketing Services in 1992. One hundred and forty-one senior purchasing managers in the top 500 UK companies were interviewed to establish brand values associated with business-to-business brands. Respondents were asked to rate brands out of 100 and then state what price they would be prepared to pay for each brand. The sectors considered were car rental, desk-top computers, transatlantic airlines and international hotels. The rating and price premiums are shown in Figures 7.1 (a) to (h).

Consumer oriented studies of this type may help to define price premiums for mainstream consumer brands.

BRAND VALUATION METHODOLOGIES

Having determined that there is a clearly identifiable brand to be valued what is the best approach to a valuation exercise?

There are many sceptics who have little faith in the robustness of the theories and methods employed by the branding consultants. To the sceptics, brand valuations are just hocus pocus using unsophisticated mathematical formulae and a raft of subjective financial data. The results are viewed as little better than informed guesswork.

To these sceptics, the branding consultants are close cousins of the cowboys who gave us the term in the first place. It has to be said that many of the critics are from the accounting establishment which tried to kill the whole idea when it was first mooted, so their comments have to be taken with a pinch of salt. Are they just 'flat earthers' muttering to themselves as Interbrand discovers the new world of marketing theory? Or are they right?

Unfortunately, many of the 'flat earthers' also work for large accountancy firms which tried to get in on the brand valuations act until the Institute of

Chartered Accountants let it be known that should a firm both produce and audit a brand valuation it would constitute a conflict of interest. As a result many stopped providing the service and concluded that brand valuation methods had never been theoretically sound in the first place.

Despite the partisan nature of much criticism the reliability of valuations remained a major concern until in 1992 Arthur Andersen reported on the subject in *The valuation of intangible assets* (Arthur Anderson/Economist Intelligence Unit, 1992). The authors concluded that '. . . *there are indeed methodologies for valuing intangible assets that are well understood and applied by many different types of practitioner.*'

Andersen's research indicated that many intangible assets are identifiable, separable and capable of systematic valuation and have been valued effectively in a number of different contexts, for example in:

- taxation – agreeing values with the Inland Revenue
- licensing – for the determination of royalty rates
- borrowing – where funds are borrowed against intangible assets
- acquisitions – of both companies and separable brands
- financial reporting – intangible asset reviews are now a regular occurrence.

Andersen's conclusions are in marked contrast with a report produced in 1989 by the London Business School, which suggested that brand valuations tended to be flawed by subjectivity, inconsistency, and an inability to separate the brand from the rest of the business. The Andersen report concluded that a great deal of progress had been made by brand valuation practitioners since the earlier report.

Andersen identified a wide variety of techniques for brand valuation including cost based, market value, royalty, brand contribution and other economic value approaches.

In practice the cost based approach is often inappropriate because cost data on the development or purchase of brands is usually historic and may not be relevant to the current value of the brand. The two market based approaches are generally impractical because there is often little open market or comparable market information.

However, the bulk of valuations involve economic valuation models using some form of earnings multiple or discounted cashflow analysis. Such models are based on the identification of cashflows attributable to the brand. The starting point is accounting profit which is subjected to various adjustments and the removal of timing differences, to render the earnings stream as a cashflow stream.

Of the many consultancies now conducting such valuations, Interbrand remains the market leader and by far the most experienced player in the market. As it invented the whole brand valuation business it is worth looking at its methods in some detail. Set out below is its basic approach, although each exercise is clearly tailored to the specific circumstances.

The Interbrand model

According to Interbrand the value of a brand, like that of any other economic asset, is the worth *now* of the benefits of future ownership. In order to calculate brand value one must identify clearly:

- the actual benefits of future ownership, in other words the current and future earnings or cash flows of the brand
- the multiple or discount rate which needs to be applied to the brand earnings to take account of growth and risk.

Brand strength

Interbrand's approach is based on the premise that brand strength determines a discount rate, or multiple, which is then applied to brand earnings to arrive at a capital value. In certain situations Interbrand calculates the capital value by discounting expected future brand earnings, using a discounted cashflow (DCF model). In other situations it applies a multiplier to a stable stream of historic brand earnings (annuity model).

A strong brand should provide a high level of confidence that brand earnings will be maintained, and result in either a low discount rate or a high multiple. Conversely, a weak brand gives a lower level of confidence in future earnings, so the discount rate must be high, or the multiple low.

The determination of the discount rate, in the case of DCF valuations, or the multiple to be applied to brand profits, in the case of annuity valuations, is derived from an in-depth assessment of brand strength, as it is brand strength which determines the reliability of a brand's future cashflow. The assessment of brand strength requires a detailed review of the brand's positioning, the market in which it operates, competition, past performance, future plans and risks to the brand. In the Interbrand model the brand strength is a composite of seven weighted factors, each of which is scored according to clearly established and consistent guidelines. These key factors are as follows:

Leadership

A brand which leads its market is generally a more stable and valuable property than a brand lower down the order. To score highly in the area of brand leadership a brand must be a dominant force in its sector with a strong market share. It must be able strongly to influence its market, set price points, command distribution and resist competitive invasions.

Stability

Long established brands which command consumer loyalty and become part of the 'fabric' of their markets are particularly valuable and are normally afforded high scores.

Market

Brands in markets such as food, drinks and publishing are *prima facie* stronger than brands in, for example, high-tech or clothing areas as these markets are more vulnerable to technological or fashion changes. A brand in a stable but growing market with strong barriers to entry will thus score particularly highly.

Internationality

Brands which have proven international acceptance and appeal are inherently stronger than national or regional brands. Significant investment will have been incurred in the geographical development of such brands and they are less susceptible to competitive attack. They are, therefore, more robust and stable assets. Moreover, by no means all brands are capable of crossing cultural and national barriers so those that are must be considered particularly valuable.

Trend

The overall long-term trend of the brand is an important measure of its ability to remain contemporary and relevant to consumers, and hence of its value.

Support

Those brands which have received consistent investment and focused support usually have a much stronger franchise than those which have not. While the amount spent in supporting a brand is important the quality of this support is equally significant.

Protection

A registered trade mark is a statutory monopoly in a name, device, or in a combination of the two. Other protection may exist in common law, at least in certain countries. The strength and breadth of the brand's protection is critical in assessing its overall strength. Indeed, if the legal basis of the brand is suspect it may not be possible to apply a value to the brand at all.

Example of comparative brand scores

Brand A	Leading international toiletries brand
Brand B	Leading international food brand
Brand C	Secondary national UK drinks brand
Brand D	Small regional UK brand in fragmented market

Strength factor	Maximum score	Brand A	B	C	D
Leadership	25	18	19	10	6
Stability	15	12	10	5	11
Market	10	7	6	8	6
Internationality	25	16	6	2	0
Trend	10	6	5	7	5
Support	10	8	7	8	4
Protection	5	5	3	4	3
Total	100	72	56	44	35

The brand audit

When assessing brand strength a detailed audit is conducted by Interbrand in conjunction with the marketing management. Once a thorough understanding of the brand, its market, competitive factors, trends and promotional activities have been acquired the brand is scored.

The Interbrand scoring method could be criticised on the grounds that there are other attributes of brand strength, that the total weighting between attributes is arbitrary or that the percentage score for each brand is subjective, but the method has the benefit of extensive experience behind it, with more than 250 individual brand valuations having been conducted worldwide by the consultancy.

In a sense Interbrand's method creates its own momentum because of implicit comparison and verification by reference to previous brand valuation exercises. This is something that few other consultancies and no clients could claim. Armed with the brand strength score Interbrand then derives a discount rate for its DCF model or a multiple for its annuity model, one being the reciprocal of the other. For obvious reasons the discount rate is never lower than the rate which would be achieved on a risk free investment. Account is also taken of prevailing interest rates and of the multiples being paid in the marketplace for brands or for companies in the same sector.

On the basis that new and developing brands are weak for some time as they mature, and that old and dominant brands reach a point where there is a diminishing rate at which the brand can continue to strengthen, Interbrand uses a classic 's' curve when attributing a discount rate or multiple to a given brand (see Figure 7.2).

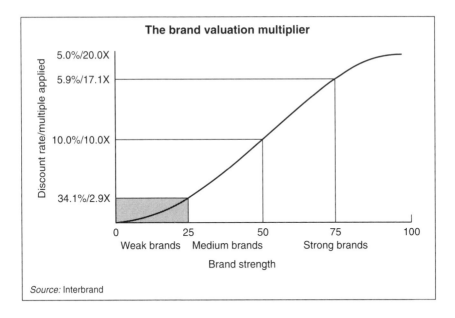

Figure 7.2

The relevant DCF or multiplier is ready for application to agreed brand earnings.

Brand earnings

In the Interbrand model brand profitability over time is a key factor, but to arrive at a balance sheet value Interbrand does not simply apply a discount rate to post tax profits. Firstly, not all of the profitability of a brand can necessarily be applied to that brand. A brand may be essentially a commodity product or may gain much of its profitability from nonbrand related factors. The elements of profitability which do not result from the brand identity are therefore excluded from the calculation. Secondly, the valuation itself may, in the case of the annuity model, be materially affected by using a single, possibly unrepresentative, year's profit. For this reason a smoothing element is introduced; generally based on a three-year weighted average of historical profits. Finally, the future profit projections for the brand can frequently be optimistic and the DCF model must incorporate a thorough review of expected performance.

According to Interbrand the following issues therefore need to be considered in calculating brand earnings:

Determining brand profits

Since it is the worth of the brand to the business which is being valued it is important that the profits on which the valuation is based are clearly defined. For balance sheet purposes the profit used in the calculation should be the fully absorbed profit of the brand after allocation of central overhead costs and before interest charges. Interest costs are ignored on the basis that funding chosen for the brand is irrelevant to the brand's performance.

Elimination of private label production profits

The profits to which a discount factor or an earnings multiple are applied must relate only to the brand being valued and not to other, unbranded goods which may be produced in parallel with the brand, but which are not sold under the brand name. These profits may be separately identified by the company through its accounting systems; alternatively, judgement may be needed in assessing the extent of such profits based on production volumes, sales values or other methods. Interbrand contends that the elimination of own-label profits is entirely feasible.

Remuneration of capital

To apply a discount rate or multiple to the unadjusted profitability of a brand potentially overvalues the brand because it would then reflect the value of other assets employed in the business, for example the distribution systems, the fixed assets, or the management. Interbrand therefore eliminates the return on capital which would have been achieved on the production of a nonbranded good. This then leaves a residual return which reflects the return on capital for the brand alone. If a suitable return is not deducted for the other assets employed there could be double counting on the balance sheet.

Taxation

The discount rate or multiple is always applied to post tax profits. It is therefore vital that all the reported earnings are collected on the same basis. A tax rate is normally applied which is the medium-term effective tax rate for the company.

Weighted historical earnings

In order to avoid erratic capital values from the annuity model a weighting factor is applied to historic earnings. This ensures the use of a prudent and conservative level of ongoing profitability with the multiple. Typically a

Calculating Brand Earnings

		Year -2	Year -1	Year 0	Year 1	Year 2	Year 3	Year 4	Year 5	Year 6	Year 7	Year 8	Year 9	Year 10
Trading profits	$000s	750	795	850	925	985	1,050	1,060	1,100	1,150	1,150	1,150	1,150	1,150
Profits from own-label manufacture	$000s	-275	-275	-250	-300	-300	-300	-300	-300	-300	-300	-300	-300	-300
Brand trading profit	**$000s**	**475**	**520**	**600**	**625**	**685**	**750**	**760**	**800**	**850**	**850**	**850**	**850**	**850**
Capital employed	$000s	3,500	3,600	3,700	4,000	5,500	5,600	5,600	5,700	5,700	6,000	6,000	6,250	6,250
Charge for Capital @ 5.0%	$000s	-175	-180	-185	-200	-275	-280	-280	-285	-285	-300	-300	-313	-313
Brand profit before tax	**$000s**	**300**	**340**	**415**	**425**	**410**	**470**	**480**	**515**	**565**	**550**	**550**	**538**	**538**
Tax payable @ 33.0%	$000s	-99	-112	-137	-140	-125	-155	-158	-170	-186	-182	-182	-177	-177
Brand earnings	**$000s**	**201**	**228**	**278**	**285**	**275**	**315**	**322**	**345**	**379**	**369**	**369**	**360**	**360**
Inflation	$000s	8.0%	5.0%	4.0%	3.0%	3.0%	3.0%	3.0%	3.0%	3.0%	3.0%	3.0%	3.0%	3.0%
Brand earnings constant money	**$000s**	**228**	**239**	**278**	**276**	**259**	**288**	**286**	**298**	**317**	**300**	**291**	**276**	**268**

MULTIPLE OF EARNINGS

Brand earnings	$000s	228	239	278
Weightings		1	2	3
Weighted Average	$000s	257		
Provision for decline		0		
Brand earnings	$000s	257		

DISCOUNTED CASH FLOW

		Year 1	Year 2	Year 3	Year 4	Year 5	Year 6	Year 7	Year 8	Year 9	Year 10
Brand earnings*	$000s	276	259	288	286	298	317	300	291	276	268

*This example assumes Earnings and Cash Flow are interchangeable – i.e. Capital Expenditure equals Depreciation

Figure 7.3

Calculating Brand Value, Earnings, Multiple and DCF Methods

	$000s	Year -2	Year -1	Year 0	Year 1	Year 2	Year 3	Year 4	Year 5	Year 6	Year 7	Year 8	Year 9	Year 10
Brand earnings	$000s	201	228	278	285	275	315	322	345	379	369	369	360	360
Inflation	$000s	8.0%	5.0%	4.0%	3.0%	3.0%	3.0%	3.0%	3.0%	3.0%	3.0%	3.0%	3.0%	3.0%
Brand earnings constant money	$000s	228	239	278	277	259	288	286	298	317	300	291	276	268

MULTIPLE OF EARNINGS

	$000s	Year -2	Year -1	Year 0
Brand earnings	$000s	228	239	278
Weightings		1	2	3
Weighted Average	$000s			257
Provision for decline				0
Brand earnings	$000s			257

Brand strength score/Multiple value

Strength	Multiple	$000s
72	16.37	4,204
56	11.87	3,048
44	8.13	2,088
35	5.46	1,402

DISCOUNTED CASH FLOW

	$000s	Year 0	Year 1	Year 2	Year 3	Year 4	Year 5	Year 6	Year 7	Year 8	Year 9	Year 10
Brand earnings	$000s		277	259	288	286	298	317	300	291	276	268
Base discount rate (strength score of 72)			6.11%	6.11%	6.11%	6.11%	6.11%	6.11%	6.11%	6.11%	6.11%	6.11%
Discount factor		1,000	1,061	1,126	1,195	1,268	1,345	1,427	1,515	1,607	1,705	1,810
Discounted cashflow	$000s		261	230	241	226	221	222	198	181	162	148

	$000s	
NPV of cashflow to year 10	$000s	2,091
NPV of cashflow beyond year 10	$000s	2,283
Total NPV of cashflow	$000s	4,374

Brand strength score/discount rate value

Strength	Multiple	$000s
72	6.11%	4,373
56	8.42%	3,186
44	12.30%	2,198
35	18.32%	1,492

Figure 7.3 continued

weighting of 3 for the current year, 2 for the previous year and 1 for the year before that is used. The aggregate earnings are then divided by the sum of the weighting factors; 6 in this case. If forecast future earnings are significantly in excess of the weighted average profit value, and are expected to remain at this level in the foreseeable future, Interbrand reviews the weighting allocation. Historical profits may have been depressed by factors which are now under control, and it may therefore be more reliable to give a higher weighting to more recent earnings.

Restatement of profits to present day values

When the annuity model is being used rather than the DCF model it is necessary to bring past profits onto a comparable basis with current profits by adjustments for inflation.

Provision for decline

In a brand valuation based on an earnings multiple rather than a DCF calculation future brand profitability must be reviewed to see whether future earnings levels will be maintained. If they will not it would be imprudent to arrive at a brand valuation based on past profit levels which will not be sustainable in the future. If weighted average historical earnings are below forecast future brand earnings no provision for decline is necessary. But where weighted average historical earnings are above the forecast future brand profits a provision for decline may be necessary.

Brand valuation

Figure 7.3 illustrates the calculation of brand earnings and the calculation of brand values based on the brand scores and discount factors referred to above.

It can be seen that stronger brands achieve higher values even where the brand earnings are the same because of the impact of the brand score on the discount factor used in the calculation.

Synergy premiums

Something which needs to be noted is that Interbrand valuations do not attempt to estimate the incremental portfolio value of a brand if it is incorporated in a range of related brands, nor does it account for acquisition premiums paid for other strategic reasons.

A good example of this type of premium arose in the acquisition of Corsodyl by SmithKline Beecham. In that case a higher price was paid than might have been suggested by a normal brand valuation because it was a unique product, with a tremendous heritage, the gold standard product for mouth infections, recommended by both doctors and dentists. Corsodyl integrated perfectly with the rest of the company's oral hygiene range, creating the perfect platform for detailing of other dental products.

Is it all mumbo jumbo?

With all these qualifications does the ultimate result actually mean anything? Would companies actually consider using the method if it were not for the need to redescribe goodwill as a more desirable, nondepreciable asset?

One person who thinks that brand valuations are of little value is David Damant, an international consultant with Credit Suisse Asset Management in London, who believes that there is a logical fallacy in the whole process. According to Damant, current international accounting theory seeks to allow investors to calculate future cashflows of the business. If balance sheet asset values are themselves based on capitalised cashflows the whole process becomes circular.

Huge margin of error

Others acknowledge the inherent value of brands and the benefits of valuing them but argue that the length of the valuation process and the number of assumptions and judgements needed to get to the final result make the figures of little use.

In the words of John Warren, Group Finance Director at United Biscuits,

'. . . at the end of the day you have to ask "does the method arrive at figures which seem sensible?" If you are looking for a pragmatic tool it is a pragmatic approach, and the auditors like it because they've got something to check!'

John Murphy's response to the accusation that brand valuations are arbitrary is blunt,

'. . . they are not. Look at brand values over the recession compared with property values. People are happy to put property valuations in their balance sheets and think they are hard valuations. But they have been shot to ribbons, whilst brand values and intangible values have held up. The question is whether the valuation method is reproducible and comparable. Virtually everyone in the brand valuation business uses the Interbrand methodology. I would put it to you that the valuations it produces are more comparable than the valuations you would get if two different valuers went out to value the same piece of land in Docklands.'

THE POWER OF SELF INTEREST

John Murphy goes on to point out that brand valuation is likely to continue in balance sheets because there is now a general recognition that brands have values separate from the products and companies that underlie them, because valuation methodologies are maturing. They are now more widely accepted and, above all, because it is in companies interests to include them.

Murphy feels that the argument has been won in the accounting context even if its opponents have not formally admitted defeat. Meanwhile he has moved on to new pastures.

For the real growth in the use of brand valuation principles is in other contexts. It is this fact which means that the brand valuation debate is not simply an irrelevant argument among accountants or a quaint reminder of the desperate takeover defence of the eighties.

Interbrand now conducts more brand valuation work for nonbalance sheet purposes than for the balance sheet.

The main applications are for:

Transfer pricing

Several large food groups now hold their trade marks and brand names centrally and license the use of them back to their national subsidiaries. For example, Nestlé holds all of its worldwide brands in Switzerland.

Arm's length royalty payments are made for the use of brands. Lower tax rates in the country of brand ownership mean that such a policy has major fiscal advantages. Brand valuation techniques are used as a way of substantiating royalty rates charged, and many tax authorities, particularly in the USA, are prepared to acknowledge brand valuations as a basis. The more valuable the brand, the higher the rate that can be justified to the tax authorities.

A nice wheeze

In fact, corporations must rejoice when tax authorities take an accommodating stance because the reality is that the tax system bears brand costs twice; once on the revenue expense of promoting the brand in the local market and then on the royalty payments. If marketing activity increases the brand value presumably royalty rates based on brand values also increase. A nice wheeze for those who can get away with it.

The 'Delaware Dodge'

In the USA a number of companies have used the 'Delaware Dodge'. They avoid corporate taxes in their home states by transferring brands into properly constituted investment companies in Delaware, which charges no State corporate taxes. Operating companies wishing to use the brands pay royalties to the Delaware holding company, thereby reducing operating revenue and avoiding local corporate taxes. It is easy to see the benefits of this type of technique for international corporate tax planning and as it becomes more prevalent there is a growing need for independent valuations.

Tax avoidance

More and more companies are transferring the ownership of brand names offshore to tax havens and charging royalties back to their operating subsidiaries. This naturally minimises local tax payments but will increasingly attract the attention of tax authorities. In fact, some tax inspectors are beginning to ask why companies with brands held in the UK are not charging for their use. In John Warren's words,

> *'We are very aware of tax authorities getting keener on ensuring companies get paid for the use of brand names, although most of the brand names we use overseas are not UK brand names.'*

Licensing and franchising

Many companies allow associate companies to use group brand names, often without charge. Interbrand research indicates that one third of companies charge nothing for the use of brand names, one third charge only a nominal amount while only one third charge royalties of between 5 and 10 per cent of sales. Many companies also allow external licensing and franchising of their brands. In either case there is a strong commercial value in establishing the real value of the brand in question, and more and more companies are using brand valuation principles to this end.

Significant management benefits accrue because operating companies do not take for granted the use of valuable assets. Just as they would pay for the use of central research facilities or for shared production facilities operating companies also pay for brands they are using. The charge made for use of a brand is seen to relate directly to the value of the asset actually being licensed

Takeover defence

RHM is a case in point of the extra value which brand valuations can extract for shareholders in the event of a takeover being mounted. It is interesting to note the difference in price for shareholders of brand rich companies since the branding issue became big news. When Rowntree was taken over by Nestlé many shareholders bailed out at well below the final price, thinking they had achieved the full economic value. Compare this with the later assault on RJR Nabisco by KKR where few shareholders can have regretted the perceived appeal of the underlying brands.

Acquisition planning

Brand valuations have played a significant role in mergers and acquisitions activity. Potential acquirors of branded goods companies, and their investors and bankers, have used brand valuations to provide comfort that the price being paid for a company can be substantiated by reference to the value of specific intangible assets as well as the tangible assets being acquired. The brand valuation model creates a consistent basis for assessing brand and portfolio additions, even if other circumstances ultimately determine the outcome.

Investor relations

Many large organisations refer to the brand equities which have been built up and brands are frequently referred to in investor relations presentations. As valuation methods gradually become more embedded, there is an obvious opportunity to use hard numbers in expressing what is currently a soft argument.

Internal marketing management

Whether valuations are conducted internally or externally the ability to use brand valuations and revaluations as a management technique is becoming increasingly prevalent. A number of large, blue-chip companies now calculate brand earning streams and valuation models as tools for all concerned in brand management. In the future brand valuation and management manuals are likely to feature in many more large blue-chip organisations.

   Not only does this give the marketing director an opportunity to assess the success of brand strategies, it also gives the group chief executive the opportunity to assess the success of particular management teams. One international company has introduced brand valuation manuals for all their brand managers worldwide to monitor brand values themselves, and include a report on the growth or decline in brand value as part of their regular reporting procedure.

Resource allocation

The consequence of valuing individual brands is that investment and reinvestment can be planned on a more sensible and systematic basis. At present, marketing resource allocation is often done on an intuitive basis.

Understanding brand values can be useful in managing portfolios of brands. For example, when allocating advertising budgets between brands, launching new brands, phasing out brands, setting discount policies or extending brands overseas. One of Scandinavia's largest drinks companies, with a portfolio of national and international brands, used the results of a brand valuation to develop just such a branding strategy.

Brand development

The disciplines associated with the brand audit, review and valuation process form key elements in a strategic approach to brand extension and development. For example, the marketing director of a UK financial services company whose corporate name is also a significant consumer brand, used the results of a brand valuation exercise to identify the potential increase or decrease in brand value that would result from stretching the brand into various new product areas.

Forensic brand valuations

Brand valuation techniques have been used by lawyers, for example, in the UK High Court 'passing off' case in which the value of the Gucci brand was being threatened by an illicit use of the Gucci name. It was also used as evidence for Nescafé in the Monopolies and Mergers Commission enquiry into soluble coffee. In these situations brand valuation has been useful as a way of explaining to nonmarketing audiences the role of brands, and the importance their value has for the companies which spend so much acquiring and maintaining them.

THE FUTURE OF BRAND VALUATION

The argument about brand valuation has moved a long way since RHM's groundbreaking action in 1988. It seems clear that the argument has been driven by corporate self-interest. Techniques have been developed and refined to substantiate the need for credible accounting disclosure. But in achieving this end a new industry has been created.

To a large extent the accounting debate has masked the other uses brand valuation techniques can be employed for. Inevitably there must be strong commercial reasons for further development of brand valuation methods and for their use in other contexts. There seem to be many emerging reasons.

At times John Murphy must have felt like General Custer, without friends or reinforcements. The establishment cavalry has finally arrived, and the debate is now less about *whether* and more about *how* to value brands.

Whether John Murphy ultimately turns out to be just another cowboy or a marketing Columbus only time will tell. But at present the odds seem to be stacked in his and Interbrand's favour.

Bibliography

Brand Valuation, Edited by John Murphy, Business Books Limited, 1991, ISBN 0 7126 5020 2

Accounting for Growth, Terry Smith, Century Business, 1992, ISBN 0 7126 5764 9

Creative Accounting, Ian Griffiths, Sidgwick & Jackson, 1986, ISBN 0 9477 5281 1

'The Valuation of Intangible Assets', A Report By Arthur Andersen The Economist Intelligence Unit, 1992, ISBN 0 8505 8611 9

'Accounting for Intangible Fixed Assets', ASC Exposure Draft 52 (1990)

Marketing Management, Philip Kotler, Prentice Hall, ISBN 0 13 556267 8

Offensive Marketing, J Hugh Davidson, Penguin, ISBN 0140 09 1173

Framework for the Preparation and Presentation of Financial Statements, International Accounting Standards Committee, July 1989, 167 Fleet Street, London EC4A 2ES

8

BUDGET ALLOCATION AND CONTROL

'Money, like dung, does no good till 'tis spread'
Thomas Fuller

INTRODUCTION

Marketing budgets have rapidly escalated in the last 20 years as the pressures of competition, retailer expectations and available media and marketing techniques have expanded. The simple certainties of the sixties and seventies have been shattered. A cosy mix of TV advertising, some trade discounting and an affable salesforce have been replaced by complexity, aggression and a host of difficult choices.

What impact do different business and brand strategies have on the budget setting process? What brand value does a given level of investment create, and how does the investment flow back as sales in future years? Is the scale of spend worthwhile? What should the marketing budget be as a proportion of retail unit price or total turnover? What should the above and below the line split be? Have trade promotions, discount offers and extra product promotions become insidious ways of price cutting, or are they genuinely promotional? Who controls and monitors the whole process?

In this chapter we consider a number of the general issues concerning the budget setting process, look at the imperfections in the way marketing and finance functions derive and control budgets, and review some common budget methodologies. Finally, we review an attempt to put hard numbers on the levels of advertising and marketing spend needed to launch, maintain and extend brands in the current market.

PROFITABILITY OR MARKET SHARE

Mass market or niche

One of the fundamental issues facing companies is whether to go for mass markets, seeking high market share, high volumes, the economies of scale, ever-reducing costs and tight price competition, or whether to opt for a niche position, with lower market share, low volumes, product differentiation, limited economies of scale and a premium price.

For some organisations market share is an obsession and a proof of corporate virility. For example, it is alleged within the car trade that during the recent recession some of the leading car makers supplied new cars to the rental trade, and to dealers in the Channel Islands, at discounts of up to 35 per cent in order to maintain their market share at any cost. Others apparently registered cars which had not been sold to massage the figures. In the end such tricks caught up with the market in the form of cheap recycled cars with low mileages, which dented new car sales figures. But in the obsessional world of market share growth the future can often be forgotten.

In terms of marketing budgets the high volume market share strategy implies lower relative promotional support than the latter, certainly in terms of marketing spend per unit sold. It also implies less above-the-line support. The low volume, high value strategy implies higher marketing spend per unit and as a per centage of profits. It also implies more above-the-line spend.

More product or more brand support?

The vogue for free product and extra value packs in the food sector is evidence of manufacturers playing off the back foot, taking a short-term profit hit to defend market share for the long-term. The corollary has been a decrease in brand-building promotional expenditure to help cover the cost of defending market share. However, the dilemma facing many companies is whether the investment will ever be repaid. These tactics have been a short-term means of holding onto market share in the face of stiff competition and retailer pressure, but whether there will be a long-term increase in consumer loyalty, and whether such tactics will generate trade loyalty, is uncertain.

Branded or own-label?

Many branded goods manufacturers are also faced with the decision as to whether they should utilise spare capacity and absorb costs, by producing own-label products side-by-side with their brands. Some, like United Biscuits and Heinz, do so quite happily. Others, like Kellogg's, refuse to do so; their on-pack boast, 'We don't make cereals for anybody else' has even become part of the brand proposition.

Does own-label necessarily represent a surrender in the battle for strongly branded products, or is it a mere commercial expedient. From the marketing budget perspective, opting for high volume, low branded output implies lower margins and less marketing support. As a result some have been caught in a commodity trap and have seen the strength of their core brands decline in exchange for certainty of volume.

Strategy dictated by market dynamics

Such decisions are fundamental to company strategy and to the nature and disposition of marketing budgets. Should companies slug it out for every market share point, and for every unit of extra production volume, or is it more intelligent to be selective, targeting specific geographic and demographic segments? Should companies defend the integrity of branded products without own-label dilution?

To a large extent the question of whether marketing strategies should be driven by market share, profitability or by some other measure is dictated by the economics of the specific business sector? For example, in many process and manufacturing industries the maintenance of market share is crucial to profitability, and the two objectives become indivisible. Market share is often critical to profitability where bulk buying of raw materials is important, and where the fixed costs of production can only be fully recovered on substantial production runs.

In many food manufacturing processes large-scale forward purchasing, and the fixed costs of factory and equipment investment, dictate that full production must be maintained. The marginal costs of individual batch runs are only one small part of the total costs which need to be recovered. Losing market share, and therefore factory throughput, can be disastrous to overall company performance.

Roger Scarlett-Smith, Vice President of Marketing Consumer Healthcare Division of SmithKline Beecham, comments that in the dynamics of his market there are,

> 'three key targets; sales, market share and profit. If we are hitting all three in terms of growth then we are doing fine, but if any one of those drops we look closely at what is going wrong and react accordingly.'

In many cases integrated production processes dictate the need to maintain market share of by-products as well as the primary product. For example, in the oil industry the composition of a barrel of crude is such that if demand is high for products from the lighter end of the barrel, like petrol or lubricants, the refinery will inevitably continue to produce heavier products, like diesel or fuel oil, as part of the 'cracking' process. In this context it is essential for the oil company to maintain or increase market share in the heavier products, to balance output from the refinery.

Premium products need stronger branding

For those companies where economies of scale are not crucial to market competitiveness, or for those companies which have marked out a specific, high profit niche, the importance of service levels, intangible product benefits and consumer brand preference are dramatically higher, to avoid encroachment by lower cost producers. Consequently a higher proportion of sales and profits is likely to be allocated to the marketing budget as the best means of establishing and maintaining a consumer franchise. Within the total marketing budget the importance of brand image advertising is more significant than discounting, sales promotion and trade support.

Brand image or product sales priority?

A perennial problem for all marketing people is the relationship between long-term brand image and short-term sales patterns. On one hand brand management must create long-term brand values while on the other it is obliged to hit short-term sales targets. Activity that does one sometimes does not do the other. The ideal is to have all marketing activity integrated so that long-term brand equity is created while short-term sales are maximised.

Ideally, all promotional money should be spent in a way which is in line with long-term brand strategy. In an early phase of a product's life promotional activity should generate trial and awareness. In a mature stage it should generate continuity of purchase and loyalty. But in both phases tactical activity should stress brand values.

Very often there are opportunities to link promotional activities in some way with the advertising theme and brand benefits, to create added-benefit from the short-term activity. Similarly there are often opportunities to use an advertising idea to create short-term promotional themes. But all too often the linkages are missed or ignored. Brand managers, and many promotional agencies, do not think hard enough about how to spend money on tactical activity which produces both a short-term result and contributes to strategic brand image building. It can also be difficult to persuade advertising agencies to use long-term advertising messages to short-term effect. Many are still seduced by the belief that the purity of the brand should not be sullied by crude salesmanship in the marketplace.

This is not a view shared by many clients. For example, Anthony O'Reilly, Chairman of H. J. Heinz, commented in *AdWeek* on 26 October 1992,

> '*Marketing is certainly more than advertising to disinterested or inattentive television viewers. In recessionary times hand-to-hand combat in store promotions is what builds and sustains brands.*'

Finding the right balance

The question is where the balance should lie between the long-term brand image promotion and short-term promotional trench warfare. Unfortunately for the purists there are few empirical studies which tangibly demonstrate the link between long-term investment in brand image and the increased sales volumes and premium prices which most marketing people intuitively believe result from such investment.

Studies have been undertaken by many large consumer goods companies in an attempt to track the relationship. For example, one of the leading cola brands has extensively researched the relationship between historical advertising investment and sales impacts many years after the original campaigns. The recall of discontinued advertising campaigns long after the event, is compelling with qualitative research demonstrating consumer awareness and brand preference. But there is as yet no foolproof methodology for quantifying the sales effect.

The Institute of Practitioners in Advertising has attempted to create a framework for this kind of evaluation with its Advertising Effectiveness Awards, in particular the longer and broader effects category. But while useful, these awards provide only a dossier of persuasive evidence, rather than a generally applicable model.

Seductive appeal of short-term budget modelling

By contrast there are many models which purport to demonstrate the relationship between short-term promotional techniques and actual sales, and are offered as tools for planning budget allocations. For example, a few years ago Anderson and Lembke, a London based business-to-business advertising agency, developed a computer modelling system which took a number of campaign parameters, including target audience numbers, expected response rates, expected sales conversion rates, known revenues from marginal product sales and expected repeat sales levels, to produce an 'ideal' campaign budget.

This kind of model is interesting, but leaves many fundamental questions unanswered. For example, how much does brand image advertising increase the short-term response and sales conversion rates implicit in the short-term campaign model. Clearly, a well-known and well-regarded brand will command better response and purchase rates, as well as higher selling prices, than an unknown brand. But how can these factors ever be seriously tracked and fed back into the budget allocation process?

Big end or little end?

The discussion about image versus short-term sales activity occasionally takes on the appearance of the debate in Gulliver's Travels about which end the egg should be opened. Many in advertising believe that the egg can only be cracked from the image end while many in direct marketing and sales promotion believe passionately in the tactical end. The theological debate seldom allows for compromise between the two opposing camps.

Pressure on under-advertising brands

However, as FMCG companies cut their investment in brand image advertising, in the depths of the recession between 1990 and 1993, many brands came under intense pressure.

A similar phenomenon took place during the 1979 ITV strike, which exposed many premium brands to almost three months without TV advertising, and resulted in significant sales and market share declines. A study, by Andrew Roberts of DMB&B, into the strike's effect on traditionally TV advertised brands, indicated an average drop in sales of 4.5 per cent with a 2.4 per cent loss of market share. Heavily advertised brands saw a drop of 9 per cent of sales and a 6 per cent loss of market share. It was demonstrated that for every £1 not spent on TV the advertisers lost £2.80 of sales.

Pure long-term brand-building has been cut by many firms under the pressure of recession and rebuilding brand franchise will not be easy, particularly in many food sectors. Once above-the-line budgets have been given away to consumers as price cuts or extra product, or as increased margins to the trade, clawing back revenue to invest in brand-building will not be easy. It seems probable that as the recession ends many companies may have to take a margin and profit hit in order to reinvest in long-term brand-building.

For example, John Warren, Group Finance Director of United Biscuits, acknowledges that, while the recent vogue for free product promotions has proved *'a cost-effective way of maintaining consumer up-take, such offers don't actually increase consumption or defend long-term brand position.'*

ABOVE, BELOW OR THROUGH THE LINE?

The 1992 WPP Annual Report and Accounts reviews trends in the marketing services business worldwide.

'Despite the recession, which was particularly severe in Anglo Saxon markets such as the United States, Canada, United Kingdom, Australia and New Zealand, two well established trends continued to dominate the marketing services marketplace.

First, media advertising grew faster in non United States markets, particularly in Latin America, Continental Europe and South East Asia.

Second, non media advertising activities (public relations, market research, design, sales promotion, audio visual, incentives and specialist communications such as direct and healthcare) continued to grow faster than media advertising throughout the world.' (see Figure 8.1, p.216).

Worldwide marketing services expenditure 1992 ($bn)

	USA	UK	France	Germany	Japan	Rest of World	Total
Media advertising	136.2	13.8	10.7	13.9	36.0	73.4	283.9
Public relations	12.6	2.0	0.8	0.9	3.3	1.8	21.4
Market research	2.8	1.1	0.7	0.8	0.7	2.1	8.1
Non-media advertising							
Graphics & design	16.2	4.7	1.6	1.9	7.3	2.6	34.3
Incentive & motivation	2.7	0.7	0.3	0.5	0.9	1.5	6.6
Sales promotion	154.3	16.7	10.7	11.6	40.2	65.3	298.7
Audio visual communications	3.5	0.7	0.6	0.7	0.8	1.3	7.7
Specialist communications:							
Real estate	1.1	0.2	0.1	0.3	0.7	0.5	2.9
Financial communications	1.4	0.5	0.1	0.3	0.8	0.2	3.4
Ethnic	1.6	0.2	0.1	0.1	0.1	0.3	2.4
Public affairs	5.8	1.4	0.5	0.6	1.4	0.6	10.3
Direct mail	26.4	4.9	2.5	3.3	8.0	11.0	56.2
Recruitment	4.0	0.5	0.2	0.7	0.9	1.5	7.8
Healthcare	4.5	0.8	0.5	0.7	1.3	1.1	8.9
TOTAL	**373.0**	**48.3**	**29.4**	**36.2**	**102.5**	**163.2**	**752.6**

Source: Industry associations, goverment associations; WPP estimates

Figure 8.1

This suggests that while advertising continues to grow, particularly in less well developed consumer markets, in more sophisticated markets below-the-line activities are increasing in popularity (see Figures 8.2 and 8.2, p.217).

Advertising – the foundation stone

At the 33rd World Advertising Congress, held in Barcelona in September 1992, Michael Perry, Chairman of Unilever PLC, gave the following unequivocal endorsement of above-the-line advertising, as the foundation stone of strong brands,

'The major assets of a consumer business, overwhelmingly, are its brands. They are of incalculable value. They are our heritage. They sustain the current business. They represent our future. Once you have understood that, you know your central task. You must invent, nurture and invest in brands. You must develop and maintain your brand equities. And when you have grasped that, you understand that advertising is at the heart of your business. New brands are brought into the world through advertising. Innovation is promoted and promulgated by advertising. Established brands are sustained by advertising. Great product concepts need great advertising to become great brands.'

UK marketing services expenditure 1982–1993

	Media Advertising		Sales promotion		Public relations		Direct marketing	
	£bn	%	£bn	%	£m	%	£m	%
1993	7.97	4	9.84	5	1,228	2	929	6
1992	7.70	2	9.37	3	1,204	−1	876	3
1991	7.55	−5	9.10	2	1,210	0	851	5
1990	7.95	−1	8.88	8	1,210	9	810	10
1989	8.00	10	8.25	13	1,110	17	735	14
1988	7.26	17	7.30	12	950	16	645	12
1987	6.18	12	6.53	7	816	15	575	11
1986	5.50	24	6.10	11	708	18	517	10
1985	4.44	9	5.50	10	600	20	470	9
1984	4.06	13	5.00	25	500	16	430	6
1983	3.58	14	4.00	14	430	23	405	9
1982	3.13	11	3.50	17	350	27	370	19
10 year historic growth rate	9.4%		10.4%		13.1%		9.0%	
5 year historic growth rate	4.5%		7.5%		8.1%		8.8%	

Source: Advertising Association; Post Office, Keynote; DMPA; ISP; Hollis; IPR; PRCA, WPP estimates

Figure 8.2

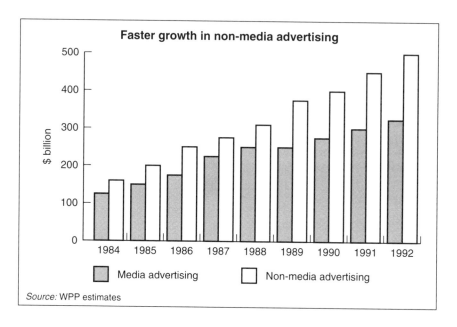

Faster growth in non-media advertising

$ billion

1984 1985 1986 1987 1988 1989 1990 1991 1992

◼ Media advertising ☐ Non-media advertising

Source: WPP estimates

Figure 8.3

A number of studies have been undertaken to quantify the impact of advertising on brands. For example, Taylor Nelson-AGB tracked the performance of 104 FMCG brands between 1977 and 1982 and found a marked difference between the 15 most and 15 least successful brands (see Figure 8.4).

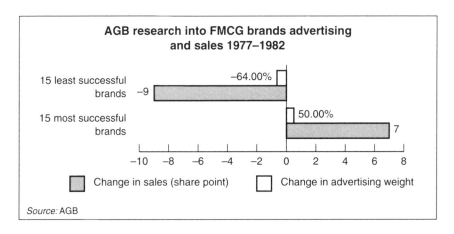

Figure 8.4

Many other variables affected the outcome of the study, including pricing, new products and changing consumer tastes but the impact of advertising seems convincing.

A new study by Taylor Nelson-AGB published in 1991, which looked at the impact of the recession on brands in 1989 and 1990 gave a similar message. Of the 25 per cent of brands which increased their advertising spend by £1 million or more the average sales increase was 13 per cent, with an average increase in market share of 1.5 points.

A third study, the Billett Consultancy/AGB Report 1993, looked at the effect of advertising and the recession on 127 FMCG brands in the first six months of 1992, compared with the first six months of 1991. Looking at the top and bottom third of brands in the study it seems that even in a declining market advertising is a prime determinant of market share growth (see Figure 8.5 a and b, p.219).

There are few who disagree with the view that advertising is crucial, particularly in the context of mass market FMCG products. In the long run no brand becomes a major brand without significant advertising support.

Promotion – the fabric

However, there are circumstances where other promotional techniques are more appropriate to establish a position in the market, to target specific audi-

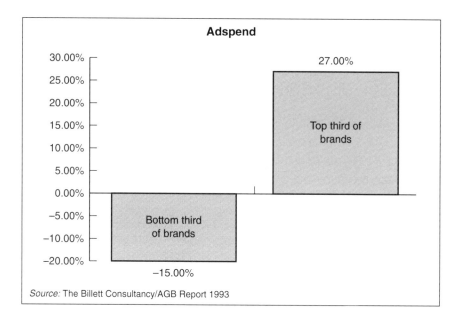

Figure 8.5 (a)

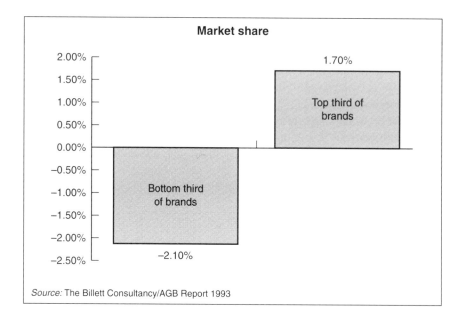

Figure 8.5 (b)

ences or to maintain brand loyalty. While advertising may be the foundation stone of the brand, there needs to be a well-designed, promotional structure built upon it. In the words of Tim Crull, Chairman and Chief Executive Officer of Nestlé USA, in a presentation to the American Association of Advertising Agencies annual meeting, reported in *Advertising Age* on 3 May 1993,

> '. . . advertising remains a key and critical part of the successful marketing mix. But if advertising is to continue to serve as the anchor in the overall marketing plan, agencies must come up with more than clever messages. Agencies must help clients develop compelling advertising concepts that will serve as launching pads for the broad range of other marketing tools available. That list includes packaging, in-store promotions, direct mail, direct response, product 0800 numbers, database marketing, coupon redemption programmes, cable programming – to name a few.'

In the current climate of corporate accountability, every part of the communications mix must work to maximum effect, and to do so each element must be consistent. Synergy between the various promotional techniques ensures that brands achieve maximum effectiveness from limited promotional budgets. Every element must reinforce the central brand proposition.

'Advertising is the answer, now what's the question?'

One might argue that the integration argument is no more than common sense. But for many years common sense failed to penetrate the tribal world of marketing communications. For many, the line, *'Advertising's the answer, now what's the question?'* typified, and continues to typify, the views of the advertising industry. It has only gradually and reluctantly been accepted that the upmarket world of advertising needs to work seamlessly with downmarket disciplines like direct mail, sales promotion and public relations. A rearguard action is still being fought by those who either have not accepted or do not relish the idea. In fact, the advocates of integration can never be quite sure whether they are pariahs or pioneers.

From one pioneer . . .

One of the earliest exponents of this holistic approach to marketing communications was David Bernstein, who set up The Creative Business in the early seventies with integrated communications as its credo. At the outset The Creative Business was condemned as a 'jack of all trades and master of none', by those who were used to the division of marketing communications into separate disciplines. David Bernstein recommended complete integration of brand communications, and for many years was a lone voice preaching the idea of 'through-the-line' communications. His views on corporate and brand communications have subsequently created an industry of integrated communications consultancies and agencies. Even mainstream advertising agencies are now paying lip service to the integration concept, although the number which are fundamentally changing their operations is limited.

Lintas is one which, because of its connections with Lever Brothers and Unilever, has developed the concept. Leo Burnett claims to be 'channel neutral'. Bartle Bogle Hegarty has a constellation of high quality below-the-line operations to match its above-the-line reputation. Many agencies have 'politically correct' integration presentations and a range of below-the-line services of varying quality and scale. But the segregation of activities into separate profit centres perpetuates integration problems, differences of opinion and quality of delivery. Many conventional agencies have not yet accepted that a demand exists, or that there is a necessity to do anything more than give a cosmetic appearance of integration.

. . . To another

By contrast, the most recent and most ardent convert to the holistic approach is the irrepressible Kevin Morley, ex-Managing Director of Rover, who set up KMM in 1992 as an integrated, through-the-line agency to handle all Rover's promotional activity. He has subsequently picked up work from ITT, Sally Line, Scottish & Newcastle Breweries, Pedigree Petfoods, St Ivel and British Airports Authority. His pungent criticism of more conventional advertising agencies has antagonised the advertising industry, and his application to join the IPA was ignominiously rejected, despite billings in excess of £100 million.

In his words, what he has done is an inevitable consequence of the way clients are looking at their marketing budgets,

> 'With integration you save money at both ends. If you have 59 agencies you have 59 Managing Directors and 59 Mercedes Benzes. At Rover we employed people just to make sure that the six or seven agencies we used were all on the same strategy. This involved huge fixed costs and confusion of purpose. We guaranteed to give Rover a better service for less money, and we have.'

Morley cites one simple example of the way traditional agency relationships create nonsensical results,

> 'When I was Managing Director at Rover the story went round that "Kevin doesn't like blue cars," which was rubbish because I was driving one. The truth was that the TV ad, the poster and various other materials

featured a red Metro, but some idiot had decided to put a blue Metro on the brochure! People don't think. They were "proving their creativity". That won't happen here.'

Fortunately for Kevin Morley he is in the unique position for an agency chief of having been Managing Director of his main client and remaining as a nonexecutive director of it. He benefits from a combination of roles, and commands an authority which is not always present when budgets are being set and agreed.

WHO CONTROLS THE BUDGET SETTING PROCESS

Gladiatorial combat

In many companies there is an adversarial event which takes place once a year, known as the annual budget round, when specific marketing proposals and their financial costs are fought over by marketing and finance people. In practice, the event seldom lasts for just one round and it seldom ends without one or other participant being badly bruised.

In fact, this annual spectacle often owes more to the traditions of gladiatorial combat than to modern management theory. The combatants tackle their opponents, using every trick and subterfuge at their disposal, until the adjudicating dignitaries give one or other contestant the thumbs up.

Budgetary sclerosis

Budgets are frequently set for the whole of the next financial year, which generally does not even start for several months. In many cases there is little room for flexibility in either direction once the relevant financial year is under way. As the year in question actually unfolds few marketing people will admit that part of the budget allocation has proved unneccesary and few finance people are able or willing to release additional funds, even if a genuine case for increase can be made.

In some companies, any deviation from budget is strictly 'verboten' and an institutionalised 'jobsworthy' mentality sets in. Eyes glaze over at the concept of intelligent flexing of budgets and ridiculous situations can develop in more strictly managed firms. Towards the end of the financial year some marketing departments have the air of refugee camps waiting for a UN relief convoy to arrive.

Many agency people will, at one time or another, have helped out at the financial year end, either by billing in advance to absorb unused budgets, or by billing late to push activity into subsequent budget period. Financial gerrymandering of this kind is a time-honoured tradition and a reflection of the partnership which frequently develops between client and agency. However, the need for this kind of game says little for the managerial system of the companies involved and points to a fundamental problem with the way the process operates in many companies.

Victor Ludorum

The problem is that the process is seen to be controlled by one or other functional department, with victors and vanquished, and a prize which, once won, will not be surrendered lightly. In 'marketing' oriented companies the marketing people often win the contest. In 'finance' oriented companies the finance people are usually the victors.

Certain FMCG companies spring to mind as archetypes of the marketing oriented approach, and several industrial conglomerates typify the other extreme. For example, it is said that Lord Weinstock of GEC casts an eye over even relatively insignificant expenditure which, if true, must dampen enthusiasm for taking expensive marketing risks.

In many companies the marketing people are seen as over-optimistic supplicants for funds while the finance director plays the role of cynical realist, pouring cost water on daft ideas and making the final decisions about budget allocations.

Left- or right-brained approach

Particularly in the recession, finance has tended to dominate the process. While this has no doubt helped with cost control it has not necessarily helped with the identification and agreement of bold new strategies to market companies out of trouble.

Professor Peter Doyle of Warwick University Business School is well-known for his views that 'left-brain' dominated companies are unlikely to achieve the marketing innovations and breakthroughs that more 'right-brain' dominated organisations can achieve. John Warren, Group Finance Director of United Biscuits, reflects this view,

> *'A Board dominated by accountants is probably not going to be very imaginative and is unlikely to break into new markets and create those new, added-value sectors which are the life blood of FMCG companies.'*

The ideal solution is a genuine partnership between the two protagonists which allows for mutual agreement of objectives and goals. A partnership approach which allows for subsequent common ownership of budgets, and flexing in both directions as circumstances dictate.

In the words of John Warren,

> *'I think there should be healthy balance. You don't want companies which are run by marketing guys with really bright ideas, without someone acting as devil's advocate saying, "hold on, do you recognise the risks we're taking, what proof have we got, how many projects can we afford to have going on at any one time?" You need to have those two perspectives. Who is the winner and who dominates at the end of the day depends on the company, but if one side dominates completely the result is very unhealthy.'*

Balancing act

A number of companies are increasingly recognising the need for more effective co-ordination. At United Biscuits, relevant financial data are available to the marketing function and financial decision. Support systems are shared between marketing and finance personnel, who work closely together. At Whitbread, marketing project teams include management accountants as an integral part of project teams rather than as simply financial, technical or information support personnel.

In addition, the Chartered Institute of Management Accountants has promoted and developed the concept of the marketing accountant, and is developing the concept through professional training. It is now more widely accepted that transfers and secondments should occur between the marketing and marketing finance disciplines.

BOTTOM UP OR TOP DOWN?

The $64,000 question

One of the $64,000 questions in every annual budget round is what method should be used for determining the initial size and scope of the marketing budget.

Should the financial shape of the business for the forthcoming year be sketched in outline upfront so that bids can fit within a 'realistic' financial framework? In other words should marketing budgets be set from the top down?

Roger Scarlett-Smith, Vice President of Marketing for the SmithKline Beecham Consumer Healthcare Division believes that in many organisations,

> *'Budgets are often set on "what we spent last year and what we can afford" rather than on the specific objectives that are to be achieved.*

Allocations of money don't generally change to reflect changing needs. They tend to evolve rather than to move forward in jumps, which means they are usually lagging real requirements.'

Top down?

The top down approach inevitably tends to reinforce historical strategies and historical experience. Marketing plans tend to be shoehorned into preordained expenditure limits with much less of a tendency to take risks or suggest radical departures from past experience.

The top down approach also promotes a feeling among finance people that the marketing budget is an overhead dictated by what the Profit and Loss Account can support rather than what the business needs to operate profitably. Plus, the top down approach leads to a mechanistic derivation of budgets which often owes little to commercial logic. For example, Graham Turton, a partner in the Marketing Division of Price Waterhouse Management Consultants recalls,

'. . . a large food company based in the UK where the advertising budget could be whipped away centrally to massage results if required, and where the spend on advertising each year had been through different product and brand managers within half a dozen operating divisions, all saying "I had this amount last year, I want 10 per cent more for inflation", with no account taken at all of the market share that the brand had, the growth of the market it was in, or competitive threats. We went through all these issues and identified the competitive position of each brand and what level of advertising each needed to sustain its position in the marketplace, and whether it was capable of growing by spending more money or not.

'We found a number of cases where far too little was being spent. If the company didn't spend radically more those brands were going to lose position, because of competitive pressures. New products were coming out, which everyone knew about but nobody had accounted for in the advertising spend.

'We found other cases where the brands were in such a dominant position, in small markets with significant barriers to entry, that the brands needed a much lower level of advertising to sustain their position. The company could actually get much more profit out of these brands and feed it back to where it really needed to spend the money.'

What Price Waterhouse Management Consultants did was to take an objective overview across the organisation, which comprised a number of different divisions and many different brands. Perhaps surprisingly, a complete review of this sort had not previously been undertaken internally.

Or bottom up?

So, should marketing management pay no attention to historical or practical 'realities' and prepare budgets on a bottom up basis? By looking at required marketing tasks, marketing management can map out the ideal budget to achieve brand objectives. This approach inevitably results in a broader, more task oriented budget and usually implies a higher bid for funds. The danger with this approach is that a 'blue sky' agenda for budget setting takes longer and creates false expectations, which are often subsequently dashed when final budgets are set.

Achieving a synthesis

In practice, there is no simple answer. Most organisations develop a synthesis of the two approaches. The important issue is whether the balance between the two approaches is appropriately weighted. There are certainly many companies where one gets the impression that the finance function informs the marketing function how much it has to spend and simply asks for a summary of its spending proposals. In other companies the marketing function dictates what is going to be spent and instructs the finance function to construct an appropriate Profit and Loss Account to fit.

Neither approach is particularly satisfactory. But how many organisations have achieved a synthesis of the two methods in a way which produces effective results for their organisations as a whole? In the opinion of Graham Turton of Price Waterhouse Management Consultants,

> *'Not many. I think a lot are spending a lot of money on marketing in the broader sense, with agencies, research companies and consultancies, but that spend tends to be at a lot of different levels with nobody taking a high level, fundamental view of specific brand objectives and overall business needs.'*

IDENTIFYING BRAND EARNING STREAMS

One surprising problem facing many companies is, in fact, understanding the basic profit and loss of different brands at different output levels. John Murphy, the Chairman of Interbrand, claims to have seen many brands which have been starved of promotional support because there has been an absence of rigour in the annual evaluation of brand cost and revenue streams. In this situation, strong brands, within indifferent brand portfolios, can be starved of investment. Because of inertia, historical mistakes in marketing budget allocation are often not reversed in subsequent annual budget rounds.

Key profit ratios

Two key management ratios in determining marketing budgets must be the ratios of marketing spend to gross product margin and to net product margin. Marketing budgets must ultimately fit within the profit contribution of the product. However, it can often be extremely difficult to determine margins on either individual runs or for total brand activity. It can be equally difficult to allocate costs between branded and own-label production

What is the variable cost?

A huge problem for many large-scale manufacturing businesses is determining what the variable cost of the product actually is. Clearly, the determination of what can be spent incrementally on marketing is largely determined by the marginal contribution of additional sales. Unfortunately, many traditional management accounting systems have failed to accurately distinguish between fixed and variable costs, throwing production and brand profit and losses into confusion.

Activity based costing to the rescue

To tackle the fundamental problems about budget derivation caused by the uncertainty of brand contribution and profitability statements, the last few years have seen an upsurge in interest in 'activity based' costing systems. Far greater attention has been paid to the definition of fixed and variable costs and the allocation of all costs, including many overheads, to specific production activities.

Some of the thorny problems with activity based costing are:

- time requirements
- sophistication of computer systems
- training of personnel
- subjectivity of cost allocation decisions.

Where activity based costing systems work well they work very well. Where they work badly they are a recipe for confusion and internal strife. However, this is the way that companies will be forced to go as pricing and promotional decisions become more critical in tight markets.

Where does the marketing budget start and finish?

One of the perennial problems in many organisations is where budgets start and finish. Is a '4 for 3 offer' the responsibility of production, sales or marketing? Is a trade 'promotion' a cost of sale or a marketing cost? Is a discount up to the sales or the marketing manager? Which budget gets cut to pay for it? In a well-run company this should pose no difficulties, but all too often definition of responsibility is unclear, leaving scope for misunderstanding.

Who is profit responsible

One of the fundamental problems concerns who should take profit responsibility for the brand? In the US it is common for the brand manager to be almost an 'intrapreneur', the managing director of his brand. This is not as common in the UK and Europe, where responsibilities have tended to be functional, and where the level of experience of marketing management has been less well-rounded. It is a trend which will almost certainly gather pace as the need for an integrated view of brand profits becomes more pressing.

BUDGETING OPTIONS

When the marketing and finance team sits around the table, with a 'top down' budget figure, a 'bottom up' budget figure and a variety of 'what if' budget figures, taken from historical and prospective activity based management accounts, the juggling act begins. There are other pointers – a number of theoretical methods have traditionally been used for determining marketing budgets, but each leaves a great deal open to subjective debate. Some of the more widely recognised benchmarks are:

1 Percentage of historic sales

What should the per centage be for a given industry, and is it appropriate to tie budgets to turnover figures which may fluctuate wildly? If sales decline should the budget be reduced to keep the marketing per centage stable or should it be increased to recapture lost sales?

2 Percentage of expected future sales

How is it possible to anticipate accurately what future sales might be, and how can budgets be flexed on a timely basis if actual sales differ dramatically from expectations?

3 Unit percentage method

How appropriate is it to allocate a fixed per centage of product price for marketing and promotion? Does the per centage remain affordable and relevant as product costings vary with raw materials and process costs change? Step functions in cost profiles, occurring as production volumes rise and fall, can significantly alter what is affordable or appropriate for marketing activity.

4 Competitive parity

Is it sensible to set marketing appropriations in the context of competitor spends which may be hard to ascertain and fundamentally flawed in terms of strategy?

5 Share of voice

Is there a correlation between 'share of voice' in consumer communication channels and product sales, and, if so, how is it actually possible to define future budget strategies which maximise market share while minimising promotional costs?

6 Marginal method

How much will sales increase for each incremental increase in marketing expenditure and does the law of diminishing returns apply?

7 Target sum method

What will it cost to achieve the required promotional task and can it feasibly be recovered from likely sales?

Pragmatic approach to budget setting

Which of these benchmarks is most useful for a given company depends on the strength of the brand, the market sector and the state of the competition. It also depends on the specific objectives for the brand. For example, is the objective to launch a new product or line extension, to reposition a brand within a different geographic or demographic segment, to reinforce a strong brand in a growing market, to maintain a brand in a stable market, to milk a dying brand, or to support a 'fighting', discount brand?

In practice, many companies begin with a fairly arbitrary per centage of sales and escalate the figure with inflation each year. It is often no more scientific than that, and few marketing people look comprehensively at the different methods each year.

Traditional ad/sales ratios

While the ratio of marketing spend to profit margin is the ultimate measure, and while a number of benchmarks may be considered, at a practical level the most commonly watched measure is the advertising to sales ratio. This is often set by reference to external factors – what the competition is doing – rather than by a scientific assessment of what is needed.

In many cases deriving the ad/sales ratio can be a fairly random and subjective affair. Tony Ayers, Chief Executive of Media Audits, the advertising consultancy, makes the following observation,

> '*Many companies need to consider their advertising to sales ratios more carefully. They've got to learn the marginal cost of generating additional sales. For example, I sometimes wonder whether clients know what the effect of withdrawing half a million pounds from their advertising budgets would actually be. For example, spending £100,000 in London as opposed to £100,000 in Yorkshire gives a much greater result in Yorkshire because you can buy twice as many consumer contacts in Yorkshire as London. Yet many companies blindly opt for London because it's sexier. Clients are often not looking at a proper marginal costing system when they assess their advertising and marketing allocations.*'

The future

As markets become more crowded, as niche marketing becomes more of a reality, and as the costs of marketing continue to rise, there will be a growing pressure for branded goods manufacturers to concentrate in specific geographical or demographic segments. This will result in more frequent and fundamental reappraisals of the scale and disposition of marketing budgets.

More organisations will need to test the relevance of different budget allocation methods as a matter of policy. From a strategic management perspective this will provide a spur to fresh thinking about individual brands and their markets.

ADVERTISING: PROMOTIONAL BALANCE

An integral part of agreeing the total marketing budget is determining the balance of expenditure between different marketing and communication channels. A crude measure of the split is given by the ratio of advertising to total marketing and advertising expenditure. While there are few reliable statistics on the norms for specific products or industries it has been said that there has been a gradual move below-the-line. This fact is borne out by WPP estimates of marketing expenditure trends, which show a definite increase in nonadvertising promotional spend in developed markets like the US and UK. It is often said that in the last 20 years many FMCG products have moved from a majority of their budgets being spent on advertising to a majority being spent on promotional activity.

Balancing advertising and promotional activity

It is impossible to generalise because every situation and product is different. In some cases artificial constraints, like advertising bans on cigarettes and infant milks, distort the picture. It also depends on the product sector, the historical reliance on advertising, or other types of promotion, and on the importance of branding in the category. For example, many commodity food products have less entrenched brands than the petfood sector. Where branding is less important there tends to be a lower advertising/promotion ratio.

The advertising/promotional split is also partly definitional. Are price cutting, extra value offers and certain types of trade support part of the pricing and distribution structure of the product or part of the marketing budget?

Inverting conventional budget relationships

However, perhaps due to media cost increases, and perhaps to the increasing sophistication of new below-the-line techniques, there does appear to have been a move away from advertising as other techniques have developed.

Special circumstances can also turn the conventional balance on its head. For example, Häagen Dazs and New Covent Garden Soups, strong and fast-growing brands in the premium ice cream and fresh soups markets respectively, both launched and developed exclusive brand positionings through public relations before allocating significant proportions of their marketing budgets to advertising.

More companies are reappraising the primacy of advertising, at least under specific conditions like product launch, or where precise audience targeting is required. In certain circumstances direct marketing, sales promotion, sponsorship or public relations may lead the promotional thrust, with advertising, in a supporting role, only entering the fray once the groundwork has been laid.

It has been suggested in the past that many of these techniques are more tactical than conventional advertising, but boundaries and roles are beginning to blur as budgets grow, sophistication increases and as intergration becomes more of a reality.

DISCRETIONARY BUDGET OR FIXED COST?

One of the problems facing many FMCG companies is that while they theoretically have significant discretionary control over their marketing budgets the reality is that many budget lines are fixed, either through consumer expectation or trade pressure.

For many FMCG companies, money spent supporting the price-proposition to consumers, and trade margins for major customers, are classified as part of the marketing budget, but withdrawing or changing either is an extremely difficult exercise. In addition, many retailers either implicitly or explicitly dictate the level and nature of marketing communications spend as a prerequisite for gaining shelf space. Advertising is often a prerequisite for a branded goods manufacturer wanting to get on shelf in Sainsbury, Tesco or any of the major multiples. Manufacturers have to spend a significant amount on promotions, or they are perceived not to be active enough by the trade.

Because it is visible and expensive many companies opt for TV advertising as a demonstration of loyalty to the trade, but often fudge the cost of their campaigns by taking offpeak or regional spots rather than mainstream network time.

Very similar principles apply in the financial products field, where broker channels have an expectation that generous broker margins and extensive promotional support will be built into the product cost. In an environment where competition is increasing, consumers are becoming more discerning. Where direct marketing channels are making significant inroads into conventional financial products markets this creates major pressures.

FLEXING BUDGETS

Consumer product and service companies tend to set budgets once a year for internal management purposes, and for external marketing agencies to plan their campaigns. At regular intervals, usually monthly or quarterly, most organisations seek to review both internal and external financial performance and consider whether changes are needed. Some companies attempt to track activity continuously but often only consider fundamental changes formally on a quarterly or on an ad-hoc basis.

Unfortunately, reviews often tend to be a one-way process, whereby if things are going well marketing budgets are held steady but if performance is below expectations the budget is cut. For example, in the course of promoting an insurance product with a high marginal contribution to profit, and which was trading ahead of budget, the marketing manager suggested increasing the marketing budget to achieve incremental sales. The response came back down the line that there was no need because the existing budget targets were being met and the predetermined marketing budget appeared to be working well. An opportunity for unexploited sales and profit potential was missed.

In a sense this is understandable. It is easier to plan activities in the knowledge that fundamentals will not change. In addition, there are a number of other factors which militate against a truly flexible approach to budgets:

1 Reliability of internal information

For all that has been said about the onward march of technology and the information revolution it remains the case that many organisations are simply unable to pull all the required information into a sensible format to make flexing decisions on a timely basis. Not only is it necessary to gather production, stock and sales figures, it is also necessary to produce timely, accurate internal financial reports, including product sales and profitability reports and cashflows.

2 Gathering external data

Information must be gathered from various external agencies, as to amounts spent and committed, together with an idea of time required to book or cancel activities if sensible flexing of budgets is to take place.

3 Getting decision-makers in one place

In many cases the annual review is one of the few times when all the relevant decision-makers get together in one place without interruption. With foreign-owned subsidiaries or foreign organisations promoting in the domestic market it may literally be the only time key decision-makers visit the market and sign-off plans. This can create an inertia which is hard to avoid.

For example, many US corporations and foreign government-funded marketing programmes involve major administrative routines, which need to be completed if any fundamental shift in the disposition of budgets is to take place. Oddities can arise where shifting exchange rates totally alter the shape of budgets. The value of sales and the cost of marketing activities may be totally different from plan within months of sign-off. Yet flexing plans can cause major difficulties.

4 Cultural and political dimensions

As described above there is often an uneasy relationship between the disciplines in many organisations which militates against a free and frank reappraisal of budgets. Even within marketing departments there are political barriers to the flexing of budgets between projects or brands.

Flexibility as a weapon in the strategic battle

The difficulty of changing the ground rules in many organisations cannot be stressed enough and there is unlikely to be rapid change except where there is a major shift in company strategy or culture from the top. The pressures of the market and the advance of new management approaches may achieve this, but many will be waiting for some time for the strategic advantage which can be conferred by a truly flexible response to budget setting and allocation.

However, there can be little doubt that in the next decade the marketing organisation which is able to respond flexibly to changing circumstances, and to increase as well as decrease activity, based on high quality, timely data, will be in a winning position.

OPTIMAL TIMING OF MARKETING EXPENDITURE

Seasonality

In each product sector there is a seasonal consumer buying pattern which companies ignore at their peril.

For example, Sodastream, the fizzy drinks dispenser, sells well in early summer and pre-Christmas, Clairol hairdryers sell well in the pre-Christmas gift rush. By contrast, while there may be a higher weight of sales for Sodastream mixer concentrates and Clairol haircare consumables in the pre-Christmas period the demand pattern is much more evenly spread throughout the year.

Many consumer markets have similar dynamics which individual companies cannot break, and the timing pattern of marketing expenditure tends to be driven by seasonal cycles. If you are not promoting summer holidays in January, lawnmowers before Easter, suntan lotion in the summer and dressed turkeys in December you are not seriously in those markets.

Each market also has its own trade-buying cycle, staggered before the consumer cycle. The gap between the two cycles depends on the logistics of the product and the trade supply chain. The fashion market demands up to a year's gap between trade and consumer activity, while the PC software gap is considerably shorter. The timing and weight of trade and consumer marketing activity depends on specific market logistics, so to a large extent the parameters for altering timing of activity are heavily constrained.

Practicality

For each activity which might be included in the marketing plan there are practical constraints on the delivery of the finished product. However fast agencies work, it is virtually impossible to short-circuit the timetables for a brochure, a TV commercial or a placed feature in selected editorial. The specification, development, production and approval process is one of the constraints. The physical timescales of outside suppliers and the relevant media are others. For example, glossy magazines usually close their editorial pages several months ahead of the publication date. Christmas issues of high quality titles, which hit the news-stands at the end of November, are therefore being put to bed by mid-summer.

Unfortunately, there are many occasions when practical timing issues are forgotten or ignored and it becomes a case of macho deadlines and tears on the pillow when deadlines are missed. Not only does it improve the relationship between client and agency when plenty of time is given to complete the agreed programme but there is almost certainly a major cost implication, as rushing for deadlines always results in higher charges and costly adjustment of the everyday glitches that arise in producing communications materials.

Sequencing

Some decisions about the relative timing of marketing activities are obvious. It is clear that consumer activity for a Christmas product will not shift much volume if it takes place in January. It is also unlikely that launching trade activity after consumer activity has begun will produce a sensible distribution pattern!

There are also conventional views about the timing and weight of different techniques. For example, intensified promotional (PR) activity at the time of an advertising burst is held to create additional 'noise' for the product and to extract greater response and memorability for the advertising. It is often said that image advertising needs to lay the ground for subsequent price or promotional activity.

However, many of the decisions are taken on a purely judgemental basis, either by the agency or by the client, or a mixture of both. Views are often subjective and are skewed by personal prejudice, experience or by commercial self-interest.

THE COST OF LAUNCHING AND MAINTAINING A BRAND IN THE 1990s

The question which comes up time and time again is 'How much does it actually cost to launch and maintain a brand? Forget the theory, give me a practical guide, based on evidence from the market, of what is being spent, in what proportions and what it is achieving.'

This is easier said than done, because there is no single source of information on what competitive branded goods companies are actually spending across all their marketing activities, and few are likely to subscribe to a monitoring service that will provide such critical information to the competition. However, the following are some of the sources of information;

Register-MEAL for adspend, the marketing press for declared levels of marketing support, observation of specific markets, and hearsay.

To see whether I could get closer to some guidelines on required marketing spend levels I asked Mark Sherrington, Managing Director of The Added Value Company, a fast-growing, branding and marketing consultancy. Mark Sherrington spent over ten years with Unilever, latterly with primary responsibility for the Persil brand – the UK's largest consumer products brand. Then, in 1990, he and Peter Dart, a Unilever colleague, saw the need for a consultancy which bridged the gap between the world of the brand manager and conventional marketing services agencies.

Answering questions about the scale and split of budgets is a regular part of this 50 strong consultancy's work, for a wide range of branded goods and service companies. In fact, in order to satisfy a number of its clients The Added Value Company recently conducted a review of necessary budget levels based on actual companies in 1991, 1992 and 1993. Their review considered the likely cost of launching a new brand, range extending or relaunching an existing brand and maintaining a large grocery brand. The study also looked at retail sales trends and advertising spend trends of the top 20 grocery brands.

Because of the difficulty of gathering absolutely accurate data The Added Value Company used a number of published sources, then applied various assumptions in arriving at estimates of the amounts likely to have been spent by brands in establishing and maintaining their market positions. The resulting tables are no more than informed guesswork. However, it may be helpful to see the thought process behind the assumptions made, and the spends which the exercise suggests are required to launch and support brands in the 1990s.

Costs of launch, relaunch or range extension

The summary of the research in the three areas suggests that on average there is no significant difference between the cost of brand launches, brand relaunches and range extensions. Big players in the market tend to spend over £10 million when brands are being launched, relaunched or range extended. The median for all the brands studied is just over £3 million (see Figures 8.6, p.237, 8.7, p.238, 8.8(a), (b) and (c), p.239–241).

Costs of supporting large grocery brands

The summary of the research separates the results for the top 20 grocery brands, measured in terms of estimated retail sales, from a larger sample of leading brands. The table, which is based on sales and marketing data for the year ending August 1992, suggests that the top 20 brands had significantly

Summary of M&A Support for . . .

Brand Launches

Brand	Company	Category	Est M&A
Pantene Pro V	P & G	Shampoo	£14.3m
Golden Wonder Nik Naks	Dalgety PLC	Snacks	£9.6m
Cadbury's Time Out	Cadbury	Confectionery	£7.0m
Average – Top 3			**£10.3m**
Median of total sample			£3.1m

Brand Relaunches

Brand	Company	Category	Est M&A
Fariy Excel	P & G	HH Cleaners	£13.4m
Bells Whisky	UD	Spirits	£10.8m
Findus Lean Cuisine	Findus	Ready Meals	£9.6m
Average – Top 3			**£11.3m**
Median of total sample			£3.1m

Range Extensions

Brand	Company	Category	Est M&A
Gillette Series	Gillette	Male Toiletries	£16.0m
Twix Ice Cream Snack	Mars	Ice Creams	£12.1m
Acti Brush Mouthwash	Colgate	Dental care	£7.2m
Average – Top 3			**£11.8m**
Median of total sample			£3.1m

Source: The Added Value Company

• There is no significant cost difference between launching, relaunching or range extending brands.
• Big players tend to spend over £10m on M&A when brands are being launched, relaunched or range extended.

Figure 8.6

higher advertising spends and total marketing spends than their competitors in absolute terms. However, the top 20 brands needed to spend less as a per centage of sales on marketing activity than their competitors (see Figures 8.9 and 8.10, pp.242–243).

One of the most interesting of the assumptions made by The Added Value Company is the difference in expected above- to below-the-line spend ratios by product category. The review suggests that less well-branded sectors like biscuits will have a lower above-the-line commitment (with a 50:50

Methodology Used to Estimate M&A Spends

● Spend estimates sourced through the Marketing press (ie: Marketing, Brand Strategy, etc).

● Spend estimates are given in two forms:
  – Advertising support, or
  – Marketing support

(Note: NO MEAL data brand launches, relaunches or range extensions less than one year old).

● When 'Advertising Support' was given, M &A spends were estimated by:
  – Discounting the ' claimed' advt ———▶ Estimate of actual advt spends
    support @ 10%
  – Assume actual advertising spend is
    70 % of total M&A Spend.
  – Inflation actual advt spend @ 30% ———▶ Estimate of below-the-line spends
    (This assumes a 70:30 split between
    above-the-line and below-the-line)

  – Adding

● 15% of actual ad spend for brands ———▶ Estimate of production costs for
                                           brands with budgets < £2m

● £300,000 of actual ad spend for brands ———▶ Estimate of production costs for
                                               brands with budgets > £2m

  – Adding £250k ———▶ Estimate of research costs

● When 'Marketing Support' was given, M&A spends were estimated by:

  – Discounting 'claimed' marketing ———▶ Estimate of actual M&A
    support @ 25% spends (This
    assumes that the company
    spokespersons overclaim M&A
    by 25% in the marketing press)

Source: The Added Value Company

Figure 8.7

expected ratio) than a highly branded and heavily advertised sector like coffee (with a 70:30 expected ratio) (see Figure 8.11, p.245–247).

According to The Added Value Company's estimates Persil and Ariel each spent over £20 million per annum on advertising in 1992, building and maintaining their brand equities and sales levels. Fairy Excel had the next highest advertising spend at just over £11 million.

The 71 brands included in the table had an average advertising spend of £4.4 million and a median spend of £3.4 million. The top 20 brands spent in the range

M&A Support for Brand Launches

Launch Year	Brand	Company	Category	Est M&A (£m)	Est. Advt spend	Claimed M&A/ Advt spend
1992	Pantene Pro V	P & G	Shampoo	£14.3	£9.6	£10.7
1992	Golden Wonder Nik Naks	Dalgety PLC	Snacks	£9.6	£6.3	£7.0
1992	Cadbury's Time Out	Cadbury	Confectionery	£7.0	£4.5	£5.0
1992	Clusters*	Cereal Partners	Cereal	£6.7		£8.9
1991	Golden Grahams*	Cereal Partners	Cereal	£6.0		£8.0
1992	Lucky Charms	Cereal Partners	Cereal	£4.9		£6.5
1993	Multi Cheerios*	Cereal Partners	Cereal	£4.9		£6.5
1992	Dove Cleansing Bar	Lever	Soaps	£4.4	£2.7	£3.0
1986	Hob Nobs (1986)	McVitie's	Biscuits	£3.1	£1.8	£2.0
1993	Riva	McVitie's & Terry's	Confectionery	£3.1	£1.8	£2.0
1992	Mr Tom Peanut Crunch Bar	Hosta UK	Snacks	£3.1	£1.8	£2.0
1992	Insignia Olympian	P & G	Male Grooming	£3.1	£1.8	£2.0
1992	Kemps Hard Pack Yoghurt Range*	AP Ross	Yoghurt	£3.1	£1.8	£2.0
1993	World Skips*	KP	Crisps	£2.7	£1.6	£1.8
1992	Capers Potato based Wheat Bran Snack	KP	Crisps	£2.4	£1.4	£1.8
1993	HJ Heinz	Heinz	Premium Soups	£2.0	£1.1	£1.5
1992	Rocky Biscuits Countline	Foxy Biscuits	Biscuits	£1.7	£0.9	£1.2
1992	Cadbury Dairy Milk Tasters	Cadbury	Confectionery	£1.7	£0.9	£1.0
1992	Ferrero Fresco Mint*	Ferrero	Confectionery	£1.5		£1.0
1991	Kinder Bueno	Ferrero	Confectionery	£1.5	£0.8	£2.0
1992	Wall's Too Good To Be True*	Birds Eye Wall's	Ice Cream	£1.4		£0.9
1992	Nestlé bianco white chocolate*	Nestlé	Confectionery	£1.1		£1.8
1993	GW Crunch 'n' Munch Toffee Popcorn*	Dalgety PLC	Snacks	£1.1		£1.5
1992	Healthy Options Complete Balanced Meal*	Birds Eye Wall's	Frozen Foods	£1.1		£1.5
1992	La Laitere Premium Yoghurt Range*	Chambourcy	Yoghurt	£1.1		£1.5
	Average Spend			**£3.7**		
	Median Spend			**£3.1**		

– claimed M&A spends discounted @ 25%

Source: The Added Value Company

Figure 8.8 (a)

M&A Support for Brand Relaunches

Launch Year	Brand	Company	Category	Est M&A (£m)	Est. Advt spend	Claimed M&A/ Advt spend
1992	Fairy Excel Washing up Liquid	P & G	Detergents	£13.4	£9.0	£10.0
1992	Bells Whisky	UD	Spirits	£10.8	£7.2	£8.0
1992	Findus Lean Cuisine	Findus	Ready Meals	£9.6	£6.3	£7.0
1992	Golden Wonder Pot Noodles, Rice based snacks	Dalgety PLC	Snacks	£7.0	£4.5	£5.0
1992	Beechams Powders and Hot Remedies Range	SB	OTC Pharma	£4.7	£2.9	£3.2
1992	Gino Ginelli Frozen Pizzas	Birds Eye Wall's	Pizzas	£4.4	£2.7	£3.0
1992	Bisto Fuller Flavour Gravy Granules	RHM	Sauces	£4.4	£2.7	£3.0
1990	Cadbury's Boost	Cadbury	Confectionery	£4.2	£2.5	£2.8
1992	Red Rock Cider	Taunton Cider Co	Cider	£3.8	£2.3	£2.5
1992	Walls Sausages*	Van Den Berghs	Foods	£3.8		£5.0
1993	Quavers*	Pepsi	Snacks	£3.7		£4.9
1992	KP Hula Hoops*	KP	Crisps	£3.4		£4.5
1992	Mars Bar	Mars	Confectionery	£3.1	£1.8	£2.0
1992	Pond's Performance	Elida Gibbs	Skin Care	£3.1	£1.8	£2.0
1992	Simple Skin Care	Smith & Nephew	Skin Care	£3.1	£1.8	£2.0
1992	Golden Wonder Crisps*	Dalgety PLC	Crisps	£2.6		£3.5
1992	Menumasters*	Birds Eye Wall's	Frozen Foods	£2.6		£3.4
1992	Drfiters Chocolate Bar	Nestlé	Confectionery	£2.5	£1.4	£1.6
1992	Tango*	Britvic	Beverages	£2.4		£3.2
1992	KP Skips	KP	Crisps	£2.4	£1.4	£1.5
1991	Phileas Fogg Adult Snacks	UB	Crisps	£2.4	£1.4	£1.5
1992	Harmony Protective Hair Care Products*	Elida Gibbs	Hair Care	£2.3		£3.0
1991	Golden Wonder Fun Pots*	Dalgety PLC	Snacks	£2.3		£3.0
1992	Skittles Sugar Confectionery	Mars	Confectionery	£2.2	£1.3	£1.4
1992	Rafaello Confectionery	Ferrero	Confectionery	£1.7	£0.9	£1.0
1992	Scott's Porage Oats	Quaker Oats	Porridge	£1.4	£0.7	£0.8
	Average Spend			**£4.1**		
	Median Spend			**£3.1**		

– claimed M&A spends discounted @ 25%

Source: The Added Value Company

Figure 8.8 (b)

M&A Support for Range Extensions

Launch Year	Brand	Company	Category	Est M&A (£m)	Est. Advt Spend	Claimed M&A/Advt spend
1993	Gillette Series	Gillette	Male Toiletries	£16.0	£10.8	£12.0
1993	Twix Ice Cream Snack	Mars	Ice Creams	£12.1	£8.1	£9.0
1992	Colgate Acti Brush Mouthwash	Colgate	Dental Care	£7.2	£4.7	£5.2
1992	Sun Progress	Lever	Dish Wash	£5.1	£3.2	£3.5
1992	Fiendish Feet Fromage Frais	St Ivel	Fromage Frais	£3.8	£2.3	£2.5
1992	Del Monte Presse Fruit Based Soft Drink	Del Monte	Beverages	£3.1	£1.8	£2.0
1992	Kingsmill Wholemeal Loaf	Allied Bakeries	Bread	£3.1	£1.8	£2.0
1991	Terry's Truffle Moments Chocolate & Truffle Bar	Terry's	Chocolate	£3.1	£1.8	£2.0
1992	McVitie's San Marco Main Meal Pizza	Ross Young	Pizza	£3.1	£1.8	£2.0
1992	Napolina Pizzeria	Napolina Ltd	Pizza	£3.1	£1.8	£2.0
1992	Sure Powerstick for Men	Elida Gibbs	APD	£1.8	£1.0	£1.1
1991	KP Lower Fat Crisps	KP	Crisps	£1.7	£0.9	£1.0
1993	Peperami Hot Spicy Snacks	Mattesons Walls	Meat Snacks	£1.7	£0.9	£1.0
1992	Knorr Stir & Serve Soups	CPC	Soups	£1.3	£0.7	£0.8
1992	Nescafé Espresso Instant Coffee	Nescafé	Coffee	£1.0	£0.5	£0.5
1992	Rowntree's Fruit Juice Drink	Nestlé	Beverages	£0.8	£0.4	£0.4
1992	Branningans Pan Style Crisps	KP	Crisps	£0.6	£0.2	£0.3
	Average Spend			**£4.0**		
	Median Spend			**£3.1**		

– claimed M&A spends discounted @ 25%

Source: The Added Value Company

Figure 8.8 (c)

Summary of Ad Spends and M&A Spends for Large Brands

	Top 20 Grocery Brands	Total Sample
Ad Spend		
- Average	£6.9m	£4.4m
- Median	£5.7m	£3.4m
M&A Spend		
- Average	£11.9m	£7.9m
- Median	£10.2m	£6.7m
Retail Sales		
- Average	£177m	£91m
- Median	£152m	£66m
Ad Spend/Retail Sales*		
- Average	4.1%	5.8%
- Median	3.0%	5.3%
M&A Spend/Retail Sales*		
- Average	7.0%	10.6%
- Median	5.2%	10.2%

* Calculated from individual brand ratios

Source: The Added Value Company

Figure 8.9

£1 million to £22 million on advertising with an average advertising spend of £6.9 million and a median spend of £5.7 million (see Figure 8.12, p.248).

Amongst the larger sample of 71 brands Radion, Fairy Excel, Surf and Kenco each apparently spent over 16 per cent of sales on advertising alone in 1992. The average advertisement spend as a proportion of sales was 5.8 per cent, with a median spend of 5.3 per cent. Considering the advertising to sales ratios of the top 20 brands there is a relatively wide spread, although the average ratio was apparently 4.1 per cent with a median figure of 3.0 per cent (see Figure 8.13, p.249).

According to the research Radion, Fairy Excel, Surf, Gillette Sensor and Kenco each spent over 25 per cent of sales on marketing in 1992. The average and median marketing to sales ratios of the 71 brands included in the survey came to 10.6 per cent and 10.2 per cent of sales respectively.

What this study suggests, when all its assumptions and simplifications have been excused, is that a major national marketing initiative for a top 20 branded grocery product could cost in the region of £7 to £15 million. Supporting such a marketing initiative in subsequent years could cost between £6 and £8 million.

Methodology Used to Estimate Annual Marketing Spends

- **Marketing spends** = **Above-the-line spend** plus
  Below-the-line spend plus
  Cost of production plus
  Cost of research

- **Above-the-line spend** : **MEAL figure adjusted for media discounts**
  - TV spend discounted by 10%
  - All other media discounted by 40%

- **Below-the-line spend** : **Dependent upon category's promotional activity**

  Above to the-line-below-the-line ratios

	50:50	60:40	70:30
Products	Biscuits	Canned Food	Paper
	Confectionery	Condiments	Coffee
	Personal Products	Detergents	Edible Fats
	Snacks	HH Cleaners	Pet Foods
	Frozen Foods	Tea	
	Ready Meals	Yoghurt	
	Soft Drinks	Cereal	

- **Cost of production** : **12% of Actual MEAL Spend for brands with advertising budget less than £3 million**
  - Cost of producing advert = 10% of above-the-line
  - Agency commission = 17.7% of cost of production
  - Includes PR, repeat fees, handling fees, etc.

    or

    £350,000 for brands with advertising budgets between £3–£10 million

    or

    £750,000 for brands with advertising budgets greater than £10 million (i.e. at least two TV films)

- **Cost of research** : **£250,000 per year**
  - Includes all research activities associated to the brand ie: tracking studies, U&A studies, ad hoc projects, etc

Source: The Added Value Company

Figure 8.10

Methodology Used to Estimate Total Brand Retail Sales

● **Total Brand Retail Sales** : **Brand's Grocery Sales**
plus
Brand's non-Grocery Sales

● **Brand's Grocery Sales** : **Estimated by Nielsen Market Research**
  − Brands used are included in the Top 100 grocery brands

  − Source: UK's Top 100 Brands; CheckOut Magazine; Dec 1992 issue

● **Brand's non-Grocery Sales** : **Dependent upon category**

  − Assume all categories grocery retail sales account for 90% of brand's total sales. (i.e: grocery:non-grocery ratio = 90:10)

  EXCEPT ...

  − Biscuits, Snacks, Soft Drinks, Personal Products and Confectionery where grocery sales account for 55% of the brand's total sales (i.e: grocery:non-grocery ratio = 55:45)

  − Non grocery sales assumptions are based on the 1992 UK Marketing Pocket Book

---

Source: The Added Value Company

Figure 8.10 (continued)

Advertising and retail sales growth trends of top 20 brands

While this analysis (see Figure 8.14) is of interest it raises as many questions as it answers.

There is, for example, no obvious correlation between total marketing spend and retail sales trends. It could be that while certain of the brands cut advertising expenditure they increased other promotional expenditure to compensate. Nor are there product volumes associated with the stated retail sales levels. Manufacturers may have decreased price, either overtly, through trade support. or with extra product offers to boost sales at the expense of the competition. It would be fascinating to know what the brand profit and loss statements looked like over the two-year period.

Estimated M&A Support for Established Brands

(*Source:* Nielsen/MEAL; Aug 1992 Mat)

	Brand	Category	Grocery Sales	Retail Sales	Total MEAL	% TV	Adj MEAL	Est M&A	Adj Meal as %	Est M&A as %
1	Persil	Detergents	£237.2	£264	£27,022	75%	£22,293	£38,156	8.5%	14.5%
2	Coke	Soft Drinks*	£237.0	£431	£6,182	86%	£5,298	£11,197	1.2%	2.6%
3	Ariel	Detergents	£224.4	£249	£22,566	99%	£20,253	£34,754	8.1%	13.9%
4	Andrex	Paper Products	£193.0	£214	£7,343	77%	£6,108	£9,325	2.8%	4.3%
5	Nescafé	Coffee	£177.8	£198	£7,807	95%	£6,909	£10,470	3.5%	5.3%
6	Whiskas	Pet Food	£150.3	£167	£9,629	95%	£8,521	£12,773	5.1%	7.6%
7	PG Tips	Tea	£135.6	£151	£9,478	88%	£8,189	£14,248	5.4%	9.5%
8	Flora Margarine	Edible Fats	£131.5	£146	£5,079	95%	£4,499	£7,027	3.1%	4.8%
9	Walkers Crisps	Snacks*	£125.0	£227	£5,195	98%	£4,645	£9,889	2.0%	4.4%
10	Robinsons Squash	Soft Drinks*	£123.0	£224	£2,417	91%	£2,108	£4,719	0.9%	2.1%
11	Tetley	Tea	£120.7	£134	£10,489	88%	£9,063	£15,704	6.8%	11.7%
12	Pampers	Paper Products*	£112.1	£204	£5,824	95%	£5,154	£7,963	2.5%	3.9%
13	Heinz Baked Beans	Canned Food	£104.0	£116	£1,264	81%	£1,065	£2,153	0.9%	1.9%
14	Pedigree Chum Dog Food	Pet Food	£101.5	£113	£8,658	99%	£7,767	£11,695	6.9%	10.4%
15	Heinz Soups	Soup	£100.8	£112	£2,590	93%	£2,276	£4,317	2.0%	3.9%
16	Kellogg's Cornflakes	Cereal	£92.1	£102	£7,227	100%	£6,504	£11,440	6.4%	11.2%
17	KitKat	Confectionery*	£84.8	£154	£4,468	87%	£3,847	£8,295	2.5%	5.4%
18	Anchor Butter	Edible Fats	£83.5	£93	£2,589	100%	£2,330	£3,858	2.5%	4.2%
19	Ribena	Soft Drinks*	£79.8	£145	£3,807	99%	£3,420	£7,440	2.4%	5.1%
20	Bold	Detergents	£78.6	£87	£7,924	100%	£7,132	£12,486	8.2%	14.3%
21	Daz	Detergents	£78.6	£87	£7,844	100%	£7,060	£12,366	8.1%	14.2%
22	Pepsi	Soft Drinks*	£76.0	£138	£5,022	92%	£4,399	£9,399	3.2%	6.8%
23	Muller Yoghurt	Yoghurt	£74.2	£82	£2,539	100%	£2,285	£4,332	2.8%	5.3%
24	Birds Eye Steak House Burgers	Frozen Foods	£72.6	£81	£1,964	100%	£1,768	£3,998	2.2%	5.0%
25	Birds Eye Menu Master	Ready Meals	£69.4	£77	£3,217	79%	£2,693	£5,958	3.5%	7.7%

Figure 8.11

	Brand	Category	Grocery Sales	Retail Sales	Total MEAL	% TV	Adj MEAL	Est M&A	Adj Meal as %	Est M&A as %
26	Kleenex Toilet Tissue	Paper Products	£67.9	£75	£3,657	78%	£3,050	£4,957	4.0%	6.6%
27	St Ivel Gold Spread	Edible Fats	£60.5	£67	£4,440	80%	£3,730	£5,928	5.5%	8.8%
28	Weetabix	Cereal	£60.2	£67	£8,570	85%	£7,328	£12,813	11.0%	19.2%
29	Fairy Excel	HH Cleaners	£59.5	£66	£12,735	99%	£11,423	£20,039	17.3%	30.3%
30	Felix	Pet Food	£59.3	£66	£3,341	85%	£2,857	£4,674	4.3%	7.1%
31	Clover	Edible Fats	£55.7	£62	£1,818	69%	£1,467	£2,522	2.4%	4.1%
32	Comfort	Detergents	£54.7	£61	£8,581	85%	£7,337	£12,828	12.1%	21.1%
33	Mars Bar	Confectionery*	£53.8	£98	£3,382	99%	£3,033	£6,666	3.1%	6.8%
34	Ski Yoghurt	Yoghurt	£53.7	£60	£1,911	65%	£1,519	£2,964	2.5%	5.0%
35	Lenor	Detergents	£52.6	£58	£4,847	80%	£4,071	£7,385	7.0%	12.6%
36	Lurpack Butter	Edible Fats	£52.1	£58	£1,261	0%	£756	£1,421	1.3%	2.5%
37	Golden Wonder Pots	Snacks*	£51.9	£94	£4,407	97%	£3,927	£8,453	4.2%	9.0%
38	Kellogg's Frosties	Cereal	£50.9	£57	£3,081	85%	£2,635	£4,957	4.7%	8.8%
39	Typhoo Tea	Tea	£47.3	£53	£4,338	75%	£3,579	£6,565	6.8%	12.5%
40	Nescafé Gold Blend	Coffee	£46.8	£52	£6,758	98%	£6,042	£9,231	11.6%	17.8%
41	Heinz Tomato Ketchup	Condiments	£41.8	£46	£1,329	67%	£1,065	£2,152	2.3%	4.6%
42	Bisto Gravy	Condiments	£41.6	£46	£4,252	70%	£3,447	£6,346	7.5%	13.7%
43	Lucozade	Soft Drinks*	£41.0	£75	£4,198	85%	£3,589	£7,778	4.8%	10.4%
44	Heinz Spaghetti	Canned Foods	£40.3	£45	£874	100%	£787	£1,656	1.8%	3.7%
45	Maxwell House	Coffee	£40.1	£45	£5,218	95%	£4,618	£7,197	10.4%	16.2%
46	Twix	Confectionery*	£39.2	£71	£4,457	85%	£3,810	£8,221	5.3%	11.5%
47	Fairy Detergent	Detergents	£38.8	£43	£5,170	100%	£4,653	£8,355	10.8%	19.4%
48	Colgate	Personal Products	£38.4	£70	£3,757	100%	£3,381	£7,362	4.8%	10.5%
49	Tampax	Personal Products	£37.6	£68	£1,996	95%	£1,767	£3,995	2.6%	5.8%
50	Kellogg's Crunchy Nut Cornflakes	Cereal	£36.3	£40	£5,851	89%	£5,073	£9,055	12.6%	22.4%
51	McCain Oven Chips	Frozen Foods	£36.1	£40	£2,609	90%	£2,270	£5,061	5.7%	12.6%
52	Cadbury Dairy Milk	Confectionery*	£36.0	£65	£2,402	100%	£2,162	£4,834	3.3%	7.4%
53	Kellogg's Rice Crispies	Cereal	£35.9	£40	£3,652	92%	£3,199	£5,932	8.0%	14.9%
54	Tango	Soft Drinks*	£35.6	£65	£4,222	95%	£3,736	£8,072	5.8%	12.5%

Figure 8.11 continued

	Brand	Category	Grocery Sales	Retail Sales	Total MEAL	% TV	Adj MEAL	Est M&A	Adj Meal as %	Est M&A as %
55	Vitalite Margarine	Edible Fats	£34.1	£38	£3,243	96%	£2,880	£4,709	7.6%	12.4%
56	Domestos Bleach	HH Cleaners	£33.7	£37	£3,191	90%	£2,776	£5,210	7.4%	13.9%
57	Oxo Cubes	Condiments	£33.4	£37	£2,822	40%	£2,032	£3,880	5.5%	10.5%
58	Spillers Prime	Pet Food	£33.0	£37	33,702	85%	£3,165	£5,121	8.6%	14.0%
59	Cadbury's Roses	Confectionery*	£31.6	£57	£2,263	100%	£2,037	£4,568	3.5%	8.0%
60	McVitie's Homewheat	Biscuits*	£31.5	£57	£271	98%	£242	£763	0.4%	1.3%
61	McVitie's Digestive	Biscuits*	£31.2	£57	£383	97%	£341	£973	0.6%	1.7%
62	VS Wash & Go	Personal Products	£31.1	£57	£6,581	100%	£5,923	£12,446	10.5%	22.0%
63	Kenco	Coffee	£30.3	£34	£5,980	100%	£5,382	£8,288	16.0%	24.6%
64	Pal Dog Food	Pet Food	£29.4	£33	£3,002	75%	£2,477	£4,085	7.6%	12.5%
65	KitKat	Pet Food	£29.1	£32	£2,188	100%	£1,969	£3,299	6.1%	10.2%
66	McVitie's Penguin	Confectionery*	£28.4	£52	£1,262	92%	£1,106	£2,594	2.1%	5.0%
67	Surf	Detergents	£27.5	£31	£5,768	85%	£4,932	£8,820	16.1%	28.9%
68	Snickers	Confectionery*	£27.5	£50	£3,250	90%	£2,827	£6,243	5.7%	12.5%
69	Findus Lean Cuisine	Ready Meals	£27.4	£30	£1,990	85%	£1,701	£3,857	5.6%	12.7%
70	Heinz Weight Watchers	Ready Meals	£27.3	£30	£2,707	97%	£2,410	£5,359	7.9%	17.7%
71	Gillette Sensor	Personal Products	£20.0	£36	£6,364	59%	£4,954	£10,507	13.6%	28.9%
	Average		£52.1	£66			£4,353	£7,917	5.8%	10.6%
	Median						£3,447	£6,666	5.3%	10.2%

* – categories whose grocery to non-grocery retail sales ratio = 55:45

Source: The Added Value Company

Figure 8.11 continued

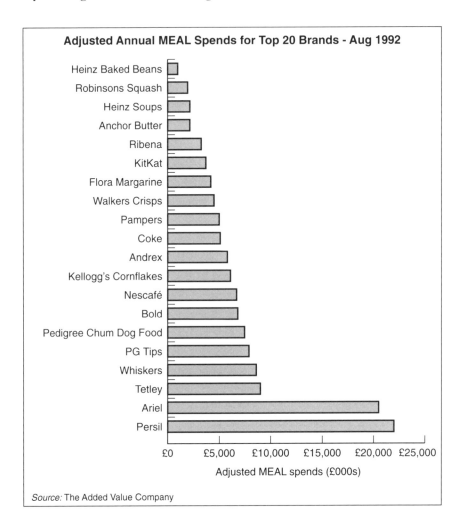

Figure 8.12

In the case of Heinz soups and beans, advertising declined dramatically. However, in the case of soups retail sales actually increased, while in the case of beans they remained stable. Anthony O'Reilly's remarks about trench warfare in the supermarkets suggest that below-the-line activity increased in relative importance in the period.

In the case of Coke, advertising spend decreased by over 50 per cent yet sales grew by over 35 per cent. This is presumably connected with the long-term strength of the brand coupled with short-term sales promotion activity.

On the back of an advertising spend increase of over 100 per cent, Persil increased sales by 27 per cent and re-established itself as the number one

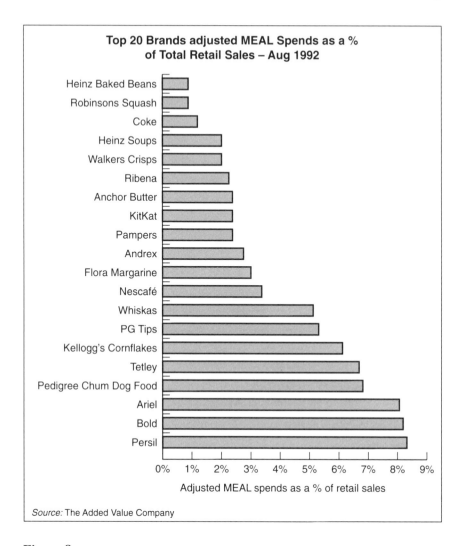

Figure 8.13

brand in the UK. Persil brand management would presumably give their eye teeth to know the optimal correlation between increased advertising and increased sales when setting subsequent budgets!

Andrex, PG Tips, Tetley, Ariel, Bold and Daz, all in sectors with relatively low own-label presence, aggressively increased advertising spend to retain market share and brand loyalty.

We are unlikely to get full explanations of these relationships. What we are left with is a broadbrush picture of the scale and impact of different budget levels, and their effects on brand growth.

Advertising Spend and Retail Sales Growth Trends for Top 20 Brands

Brand	Estimated Retail sales 1992	Estimated Retail Sales 1990	Estimated Adj MEAL 1992	Estimated Adj MEAL 1990	Sales Growth 1992 – 1990	Ad Spend growth 1992 – 1990
Persil	£264	£208	£22.3	£11.1	27%	102%
Daz	£87	£67	£7.1	£4.1	31%	71%
PG Tips	£151	£148	£8.2	£5.0	1%	63%
Bold	£87	£54	£7.1	£5.0	62%	44%
Tetley	£134	£106	£9.1	£6.7	26%	34%
Robinsons Squash	£224	£175	£2.1	£1.6	27%	34%
Andrex	£214	£197	£6.1	£4.7	9%	31%
Flora Margarine	£146	£122	£4.5	£3.5	20%	30%
Ariel	£249	£209	£20.3	£16.0	19%	27%
Kellogg's Cornflakes	£102	£85	£6.5	£5.3	21%	22%
Ribena	£145	£111	£3.4	£2.9	30%	19%
Pedigree Chum Dog Food	£113	£115	£7.8	£7.9	−2%	−2%
KitKat	£154	£145	£3.8	£4.0	6%	−3%
Nescafé	£198	£207	£6.9	£7.5	−5%	−8%
Anchor Butter	£93	£97	£2.3	£2.7	−4%	−14%
Whiskas	£167	£198	£8.5	£10.4	−16%	−18%
Heinz Soups	£112	£96	£2.3	£2.9	17%	−22%
Walkers Crisps	£227	£163	£4.6	£6.1	39%	−24%
Heinz Baked Beans	£116	£116	£1.1	£1.8	−1%	−40%
Coke	£431	£319	£5.3	£11.3	35%	−53%

Note: Brands listed by ad spend growth

Source: The Added Value Company

Figure 8.14

CONCLUSION

The process of internal budget definition remains an imprecise one which is gradually struggling to become better informed and more scientific. Each company needs to develop accurate brand cost and earnings information, to improve activity based accounting systems and to get a clearer idea of the absolute amounts and conventional splits relevant to its specific marketplace. Consultancies like The Added Value Company are lining up to give companies the required industry specific picture.

Once these elements are in place strategic questions remain to be answered. Would a radical increase in marketing or advertising expenditure in a given sector fundamentally shift the sector dynamics? Would a decrease in advertising and marketing expenditure really make any difference other than to boost the bottom line? Is it possible to alter the mix and timing of marketing and media techniques to get a competitive advantage with lower marketing costs?

The next chapter looks at some of the efforts which are being made to help answer these questions and to improve the quality of campaign planning.

Bibliography

WPP Group PLC, Annual Report and Accounts 1993

Company Image & Reality, David Bernstein, Holt, Reinhart and Winston Ltd, 1984 ISBN 0 03 910574 1

The Advertising Budget, Simon Broadbent, NTC Publications Limited/Institute of Practitioners in Advertising, 1989, ISBN 1 870562 35 6

The Effective Use of Advertising Media, Martyn P. Davis, Century Business, 1992, ISBN 0 7126 5497 6

Spending Advertising Money, Simon Broadbent/Brian Jacobs, Business Books Limited, 1984, ISBN 0 09 155971 5

9

THE RISE OF THE CAMPAIGN PLANNER

'Unhappy the general who comes on the field of battle with a system'
Napoleon 1st

INTRODUCTION

In the last chapter we looked at some of the internal factors which affect the budget setting and control process. Is there a fool-proof system for determining budgets? Are we edging closer to a more robust and scientific approach? Are there outside specialists who can help in the process? What are the obstacles and problems to be resolved?

It is clear that in determining the best use of marketing funds there continue to be a number of significant imponderables:

- which messages and creative approaches are most effective?
- which channels are most appropriate for the target audiences?
- what are the prevailing rules in the specific sector?
- what is the optimal percentage split between marketing techniques?
- what is the ideal timing of each activity?
- how do different channels interact with one another?

We looked at one consultancy's attempts to quantify the amount and split of resources needed to tackle specific consumer marketing campaigns. The resulting tables were based on empirical evidence and informed guesswork, and did not pretend to offer anything other than broadbrush figures. At present, there are few client companies with a more precise way of defining the amount or disposition of marketing communications budgets. Yet refining the process holds out the possibility of both cost savings and greater efficiency.

This chapter looks at the possible development of a more systematic, informed and objective approach to campaign planning, across all marketing communications disciplines. Napoleon advised against entering the field of battle with a predetermined system; flexibility and pragmatism are crucial to victory. However, he clearly believed in the need for an experienced general, commanding the respect of his troops, planning campaigns at both a strategic and a tactical level. As the marketing communications battle becomes more complex, integrated and risky who will take the role of general?

At present there is no simple answer, although as a matter of principle the answer should be the client marketing manager or director. Generally it is agreed that campaign planning is an essential function of marketing management, and in most companies the decision-making process is primarily internal. In huge blue-chips, like British Telecom and Shell, dedicated campaign planning and control units exist. In large manufacturing companies the marketing manager, advertising manager or media manager get together to plan the campaign. In smaller companies campaign planning falls to the marketing or product manager.

The problem is that marketing management moves and is promoted so fast that many companies experience serious dislocation. Decisions are often taken by relatively inexperienced marketing management, and the safe decision is often to leave the basic campaign parameters identical from year to year.

How can a product manager with only a few years experience be expected to know and understand all available communication techniques and their effects on one another? In practice, responsibility for planning optimal budget allocations, and for planning the weight and timing of marketing communications, falls to a number of different people, both internal and external. Reliance is often placed on the agency to comment and advise on overall marketing campaign plans. Yet in many cases this is like Little Red Riding Hood asking the Wolf for directions.

Some agencies claim to be 'channel neutral', and therefore able to offer genuinely independent advice. They try hard to be objective, in particular those agencies which have espoused the concept of total integration. Many have tried to put structures in place to achieve integrated campaign planning. For example, O&M has introduced the idea of a *campaign co-ordinator,* sometimes referred to as Client Service Director, to balance the various elements of multidisciplinary campaigns. Unfortunately, as Mike Walsh, the chief executive admits, it is hard to maintain the structure; '. . . the concept was so popular with clients that the first two individuals we put in the role in the US were poached by Microsoft and Sears!'

Others argue that there is an inevitable bias towards specific disciplines, most obviously advertising. In addition, can an agency group with its own products to sell ever be so channel neutral that it advises against spending at all? Would it advise a company to put budgets into product or service enhancement, or into trade and consumer discounts, rather than into tangible communications? Even supposedly integrated operations like KMM have a vested interest in high-profile marketing communications.

Some companies tackle the campaign planning issue by convening a round table of different agency experts to discuss the shape and direction of the communications campaign. Individual disciplines propose initiatives and make bids for parts of the budget. The image of sharks in a feeding frenzy springs to mind.

A third alternative, for which there is growing evidence, is that a new type of discipline will develop, that of the independent *campaign planner*. The need for a wide range of experience, and objectivity, will tend to favour external consultants rather than internal personnel, although, as O&M's experience demonstrates, in the very largest organisations such campaign planners already exist and will continue to flourish.

There are a number of areas where such campaign planners could come from; the burgeoning agency selection and monitoring sector could produce them, retired agency gurus could fit the bill, or companies could poach the likes of O&M's campaign co-ordinators. However, it seems most likely that the new discipline will grow out of the media function, particularly in the independent media sector.

This chapter begins by looking at the growing importance of the independent media sector and the trend towards centralised media. It then turns to the possibility that the analytical skills, research orientation, computer literacy and objectivity of the media independent sector will lead it down the route of total campaign planning.

GROWTH OF THE MEDIA INDEPENDENT SECTOR

Media independents have been around in the US and Europe since the late sixties. To begin with they were characterised by aggressive buying skills, low overheads and low commission rates. Today, the independent sector is more likely to be equated with media research, media innovation, communications planning and broader marketing skills.

The first UK media independents appeared in the early seventies. For example, TMD, now the leading media independent in the UK, was set up in 1972. Many others followed, during the seventies and eighties, as 'à la carte' agency provision became the vogue. The 1976 Office of Fair Trading ruling, which banned standard 15 per cent commissions, and opened up the media process to more direct deals, gave an impetus to the independent sector. However, for many years media independents were scorned by full service agency people as pirates on the fringe of the advertising business.

Both business and cultural factors had driven high quality media people away from full service agencies. At the business level, media people could see that the engine of agency profits was high fixed commissions on advertising budgets; they felt they could offer more effective buying and lower commission rates without any loss of quality. They had also become tired of being treated as the boring backroom boys, juggling with numbers and going last in agency presentations; 'If time runs out before lunch just bike the media charts over to the client, love.'

Their escalating growth rates throughout the eighties demonstrated that clients were on the side of the media pirates. Media independents are now a major force in the market.

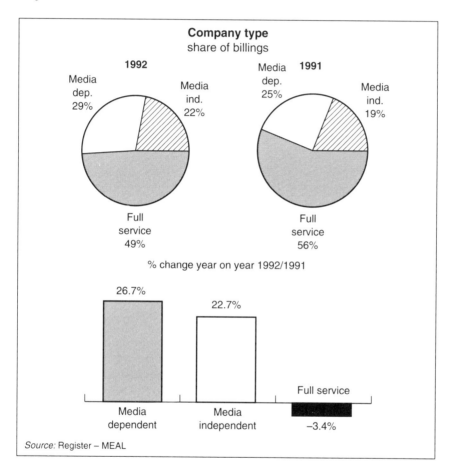

Company type
share of billings

1992

Media dep. 29%

Media ind. 22%

Full service 49%

Media dep. 25%

1991

Media ind. 19%

Full service 56%

% change year on year 1992/1991

26.7%

22.7%

Full service

Media dependent

Media independent

−3.4%

Source: Register – MEAL

Figure 9.1

Even though they account for less than a quarter of total media billings in the UK their growth rates remain strong and their ideas dominate the media scene. In fact, their methods have been adopted by the full service sector, to prevent further erosion of market share. Many full service agencies now run their media operations as totally separate subsidiaries or as media clubs, with several agencies putting buying volume under one roof.

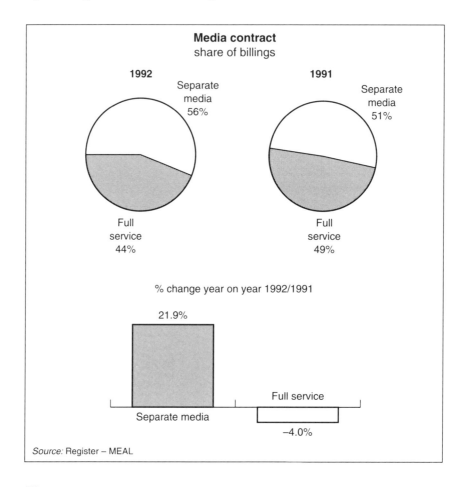

Figure 9.2

The centralised media buying concept, with all brands from one manufacturer being bought by one agency, is just one of many new media ideas which have been driven forward by the independent sector (see Figure 9.3).

From the late 1980s the independent influence became global. Carat is the world's largest independent media company with a staggering 12 per cent of the European media buying market. This is double its nearest full service agency rival (see Figure 9.4).

It is possible that the creation of media dependents and media clubs will halt the advance of the complete independents like Carat. However, it is almost certain that the number of full service advertising accounts, which now account for only just over 40 per cent of the total advertising cake in the UK, will continue to decline. In the opinion of Tony Ayers, Chief

Figure 9.3 Share of media billings* Jan–Dec 1992 versus Jan–Dec 1991 (TV, press, radio)

	Jan – Dec '92 £	% Total billings	Jan – Dec '91 £	% Total Billings	Yr/Yr % Change
Media contracts					
Total media billings*	4,461,816,151	100.0%	4,088,715,472	100.0%	9.1%
Type of company					
Full service only	1,938,863,051	43.5%	2,018,887,151	49.4%	–4.0%
Separate media	2,522,953,100	56.5%	2,069,828,321	50.6%	21.9%
Centralisation					
Media independent	965,883,537	21.6%	787,003,085	19.2%	22.7%
Media dependent	1,292,264,743	29.0%	1,019,783,440	24.9%	26.7%
Full service	2,203,667,875	49.4%	2,281,928,950	55.8%	–3.4%
Split within comp. type					
Total	614,902,081	13.8%	575,038,202	14.1%	6.9%
Cent. at media ind.	138,063,247	3.1%	92,494,546	2.3%	49.3%
Cent. at media dep.	326,392,764	7.3%	297,248,130	7.3%	9.8%
Cent. at full service	150,446,070	3.4%	185,295,526	4.5%	–18.8%
Not centralised	3,846,914,070	86.2%	3,513,677,270	85.9%	9.5%
Media independent					
Total	965,883,537	100.0%	787,003,085	100.0%	22.7%
True independent	796,093,551	82.4%	679,176,870	86.3%	17.2%
Affiliated	31,726,739	3.3%	15,331,669	1.9%	106.9%
Cent. at media indep.	138,063,247	14.3%	92,494,546	11.8%	49.3%
Total	2,203,667,875	100.0%	2,281,928,950	100.0%	–3.4%
Full service					
True full service	1,938,863,051	88.0%	2,018,887,151	88.5%	–4.0%
Media independent	114,358,754	5.2%	77,746,273	3.4%	47.1%
Cent. at full service	150,446,070	6.8%	185,295,526	8.1%	–18.8%
Total	1,292,264,743	100.0%	1,019,783,440	100.0%	26.7%
Media dependent					
True media independent	144,563,037	11.2%	98,518,092	9.7%	46.7%
Affiliated	821,308,942	63.6%	624,017,218	61.2%	31.6%
Cent. at media dependent	326,392,764	25.3%	297,248,130	29.1%	9.8%

* Excludes Creative/Creative & Planning

Source: Register – MEAL

Carat's European competitors

In Europe Carat is the largest media buying organisation. The analysis below is based on articles from the press and industry analysts.

Company	Affiliations (Ownership)	No. of Countries (1992)	1991 Billings US$ bn	1992 Billings* US$ bn	Market Share
Carat					
Independent	Carat (Aegis)	14	5.6	6.5	12%
TMP	JWT, O&M (WPP)	9	1.7	3.4	6%
Club	BBDO, DDB (Omnicom)				
EURO-RSCG	Euro-RSCG (Havas)	11	2.4	2.7	5%
Agency Specialist					
ZENITH	Saatchi, BSB	13	2.4	2.7	5%
Agency Specialist					
INITIATIVE	Lintas	14	2.1	2.1	3.5%
Agency Specialist	(Interpublic)				
UNIVERSAL	McCann	12	1.8	1.9	3%
Agency Specialist	(Interpublic)				
EQUMEDIA	DMB&B, Grey, Leo Burnett	8	1.2	1.8	3%
Club	Y&R				
OPTIMEDIA	Publicis, FCB	9	1.1	1.7	3%
Agency Specialist					
Total Market		**16**		**55.3**	**100%**

Source: James Capel Feb 93/Advertising Age/M&M Europe

* At 1992 average exchange rates

Figure 9.4

Executive of Media Audits, the leading media monitoring consultancy, 'In the future, media accounts will be moved separately from creative accounts in the majority of cases.'

Apart from their traditional reputation as keen buyers the media independents have invested heavily in research; for example, in 1992 Carat spent over $18 million on media research. Although the ability of European media groups to provide research may be hit by the Loi Sapin in France, the need for, and commitment to, research will continue. The independents are providing increasing quantities of high quality information and are exploring new ways of delivering communications impact for their clients.

In fact, as media continues to fragment, as new TV, radio, satellite and print media develop, and as new interactive media are brought onto the market, the independents are turning increasingly to communications planning and consultancy. CIA, a major, quoted media specialist, has been particularly active in the consultancy area, through its Billett Consultancy. CIA is keenly promoting the concept of integrated communications planning to its clients. Initiative Media has also been active in this area and Patterson Horswell Durden, a young, fast-growing media independent, has created Second Opinion, a specialist consultancy subsidiary, to advise its clients on wider marketing and communications issues.

The independents argue that in terms of media and marketing strategy they can be more professional in defining a communications mix, and more objective in the way campaign budgets are allocated, than any other player in the agency sector. They are genuinely 'channel neutral' because they simply plan and buy; they have no vested interests in specific media or in the delivery of specific creative disciplines.

The business, media and analytical skills are in place. In addition, the media independent sector is looking for more business from its clients and a more central role in the direction of brands marketing. The conditions are right for the development of a wider campaign planner role.

AGENCY AS PRINCIPAL

As traditional relationships between agencies and their clients unravel it is interesting to consider the issue of 'agency as principal'. The reason that media contractors were always happy to pay agencies a standard commission was because credit risks and administrative hassles are high when media deal direct with clients. Agencies act as a filter and carry the credit risk. In law, agencies are responsible for the payment of all space booked on their clients' behalf. In fact it is surprising how many agencies either intentionally or unintentionally overshoot credit ratings, and even credit insurance limits, on their clients. Some try to 'manage' dodgy clients, whom they want to work for creatively, but for whom they cannot get credit insurance cover.

From the agency's point of view principal status means that it must maintain healthy balance sheet ratios to qualify for recognition by the media associations, the Independent Television, Radio, Newspaper Publishers and Periodical Publishers Associations. In the absence of a solvent agency balance sheet personal guarantees from directors are sometimes required to secure recognition.

The traditional benefit to the agency of principal status used to be access to standard commissions, but, as the media debate and the growth of the independent sector have eroded revenues from this source, it becomes increasingly hard to see what there is in it for some agencies. It creates administrative hassles, credit risks, and working capital requirements, all of which are costly. These are often used as reasons why agency remuneration should be at a decent level, to cover the running costs and bad debts. But in many cases agencies face the risks without the rewards.

As media is progressively hived-off, from traditional full service agencies into media dependents and independents, these problems will become more of a media than a full service agency issue. Administration, credit control and working capital management are all key strengths of the media independent sector, so the problems are gravitating towards the place where they can be most effectively dealt with.

MEDIA BROKING

The logical extension of the 'agency as principal' concept is for an agency to buy media space wholesale and sell it retail to its clients. Theoretically, the agency only passes space onto its clients at market price. In addition, the agency provides a service by taking media liabilities onto its own books, and running uncovered risks, until the space is sold. Is this a nice idea to ensure supply of prime space, or an opportunity for nasty agency abuses?

In Anglo-Saxon markets the thought that agencies might buy cheap and sell dear has always antagonised clients. Probably rightly, clients have always felt that agencies never take real risks, simply buying according to predictable demand patterns. Marketing people in the UK have always argued that unsold media space inevitably gets offloaded onto gullible clients. It has always been felt that conflicts of interest proliferate when agencies have a vested interest in persuading clients to take space they don't really want or need, simply to square the agency's books. As a result of these feelings the UK system has always been transparent, with a highly developed media auditing and monitoring sector.

The Loi Sapin

However, in France traditions are different, and until recently it was considered quite normal for agencies to act as media brokers, taking *sur commission* on wholesale space. In fact, the growth and profitability of the French advertising industry depended on the substantial profits agencies made from this source. The most prolific were the poker playing Gross brothers who built Carat Espace into a European media empire on the proceeds.

By 1991 75 per cent of the £5.2 billion French media market was bought through only four media buying groups, Carat, Euro-RSCG, Public Media Service and The Media Partnership. This compared with only 18.5 per cent of the £5.6 billion UK media market bought through the top four UK buying points.

Unfortunately for the French advertising world, the Socialist Government of Pierre Beregevoy began to suspect that some of the sur commission was finding its way back into the political process. It therefore passed the Loi Sapin in March 1993 to make the media buying process totally transparent. French clients now have right of access to underlying media invoices, and to rebate of all discounts. Agency super profits have dried up.

Perversely, the law has affected small- and medium-sized agencies at least as dramatically as the big boys. According to the Association des Agences Conseils en Communication (AACC) the Loi Sapin will cut average agency revenues by 20 per cent in 1993 and will result in massive layoffs in the French advertising industry. Ironically many clients had already compensated for sur commission by cutting standard remuneration levels. It will take some time to restore these to their original levels. Pressure is being applied to modify the law, to allow direct media commissions for agencies. However, it is likely that the French advertising industry will take several years to adjust, and it is unlikely that the demand for transparency will disappear. In fact, the Loi Sapin has created a wider call for transparency throughout the EU and in the Brussels headquarters of the EU itself, which is considering European rules along the lines of the Loi Sapin.

Another consequence of the Loi Sapin, which has been widely discussed, is the possibility that French agencies will develop new marketing services and agitate for greater integration, as they seek to restore income levels by providing a broader range of marketing services to their clients. At the media level this creates one more argument for the development of the campaign planner role, as impoverished media groups look for additional fee income.

CENTRALISED MEDIA

Much of the growth in marketing budgets during the 1970s and 1980s was caused by the dominance of network television, and media inflation rates which ran significantly ahead of general price inflation (see Figure 9.5).

This created a strong incentive to tackle media costs, and one way large clients attempted to do this was by pooling their media business through one buying point. Gradually, as the benefits of media centralisation became clearer, the concept was taken up by smaller and smaller clients. Several factors, some valid others not so valid, have rapidly propelled many clients towards centralised media buying.

Many agree that by centralising media buying clients can often secure better deals and discounts, from increasingly powerful publishing and broadcasting conglomerates. Despite governmental and regulatory action the media continue to be concentrated in the hands of fewer owners – although many have yet to co-ordinate the offerings of their disparate networks. This

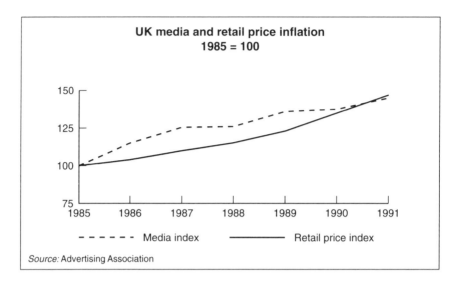

Figure 9.5

media concentration is expected to continue, further reinforcing the trend towards centralised buying. Particularly in the TV market, and increasingly in the Press market, the scope for package and bulk buying has increased.

As media owners become increasingly involved across a range of media, and as they spread around the globe, the 'weight of money' argument will become more and more relevant. The argument is particularly strong in countries like France where the power conferred on the big buying groups has been huge, although with the passage of the Loi Sapin this may subside.

It is argued that when a company's media buying is handled through one buying point the chance of brands from the same company bidding for space against one another is removed. Blocks of TV airtime can be booked for several brands at the same time and allocated internally afterwards. At the international level it is suggested that multinational brands need media allocation and buying strategies across national boundaries, which can only be done effectively by centralising media buying through one of the large, international media buying groups.

The growth of the media independent sector has heightened the debate about centralised media. Independents have always prided themselves on their aggressive buying skills, and now offer the logistics and research to deliver quality planning and buying as well as the most cost-effective campaigns.

There is also the issue of overheads. By appointing one media team in one agency to handle all media buying, the costs of running several teams can be eliminated. So there are potential savings through bulk buying, through noncompetition, through greater efficiency and through overhead reduction. For a company like SmithKline Beecham centralising media buying is highly beneficial. In the words of Roger Scarlett-Smith, Vice President of Marketing of SmithKline Beecham Consumer Healthcare Division.

> *'We moved to centralised buying and found it to be highly beneficial in terms of cost and complexity. It reduced the number of contact points that we had and generally resulted in a better deal. One company knows it is carrying the onus for media buying and with the correct motivation and the correct review I think we have achieved a major advantage.'*

On the other side of the argument are those who say that different brands within a company portfolio often have little in common with other brands owned by the same company. If the brands are not trying to communicate with the same target audiences or are using different media, what is the point in centralising the buying? If the brand has a fragmented, multimedia spend the benefits of mass TV or Press buying are less relevant.

For example, it is doubtful whether centralising media would be a good idea for a company with three different marketing divisions, targeting different types of product into different consumer markets, in different regions. Even relatively small clients may gain some advantage by separating media buying from the creative agency. However, short-term financial gains may be outweighed by long-term loss of agency enthusiasm or effectiveness of the campaign. In Roger Scarlett-Smith's words,

> *'I think some of the convenience advantages apply down the scale, but the rationale for moving to centralised media-buying is to achieve more clout in the marketplace. Without a critical mass companies are never going to achieve that clout, no matter how much they centralise.'*

It is argued that as integration of marketing disciplines becomes more important, the commodity approach, epitomised by centralised media buying, becomes counter-productive. It is said that as media inflation moderates and as media fragments, the imperative for centralised buying may decline. The choice of media available to clients has broadened and the task of media selection has become more skilled, more complex and more intimately connected with the creative process.

Media people are increasingly expected to have an understanding of brand strategies across all communication channels; if they are to innovate in brand communications they must work very closely with all the other agency disciplines.

Some agencies have tackled the need to integrate media planning into the total communication strategy by leaving the media planning function with the creative agency, while putting the media buying into a centralised arrangement. Buyers simply execute buying briefs defined by the media planners in the creative agency. Whether this works for smaller creative agencies is open to question, because media planners need to keep in touch with the media marketplace. However, larger agencies have the scale to make it work.

Another perceived disadvantage of centralising media buying is the problem of complacency. In the words of Tony Ayers, Chief Executive of Media Audits, the leading media monitoring firm in the UK,

> '. . . historically, the best media results have been obtained by frequently changing the media buying team. A cynical recipe for success is to have one buying team for two years, change it the next year and create a stimulus among the agencies, the suppliers, the marketing executives, and the media owners. One of the current perceived advantages of centralisation is the ability to get a lower commission from agencies. That's a very false premise, because gaining 1 per cent on commission can be completely offset by losses in media efficiency. Once commission savings have been eroded through complacency, and once the agency starts to push its commissions back up again, marketing people will need to inject competition back into their media buying. The choice of a single supplier for media buying is a classic example of putting all your eggs in one basket. Once you've had the basket for three years you don't know whether it's the best one any more.'

Clearly if agencies are buying in competition and being comparatively audited they are more likely to maintain a consistently high-buying performance. Once the media has been centralised there is a danger complacency may set in. However, there are many other centralised operations waiting to pick up work from any media buyer who goes off the boil.

The international advantage of centralised media buying is clearly irrelevant if the brand is just a local or a national brand, even if the ultimate holding company has many local or national brands across the world. Most companies also give national profit responsibility to national marketing directors, so transnational media buying can be difficult within the culture of many marketing companies. Meanwhile, on the supplier side, there still isn't much pan-European media selling, although there is multimedia owner selling in the UK.

At present the vogue for centralising media buying is strong. For many companies with coherent brand portfolios and huge media budgets the arguments for centralising are often clear cut. There may come a time when there are too few major players in the market leading to account conflicts and a slow-down in the process. But that is some way off.

For small clients with integrated, multimedia campaigns and relatively low budgets the argument for keeping media budgets with the rest of the communications mix are also clear cut. It is those companies in the middle where the debate will flow backwards and forwards. Again in the words of Tony Ayers,

> *'At the moment there's a strong move towards media-centralisation but in time we will see some of those centralisations breaking-up and going off to one or two specialist companies who offer a better service. Some may even return to a full service basis.'*

MEDIA MONITORING

In keeping with the Anglo-Saxon ethics of transparency and accountability the media auditing and monitoring business has been established in the UK for longer than anywhere else in Europe.

In response to large clients who wanted a greater insight into their media buying performance Media Audits was set up in 1976. Clients recognised a major area of marketing expenditure which was fast-moving, complex and specialised, and which they did not understand. They sought third party help and assistance at each step in the media process:

Advertising strategy

What are the opportunities? What are the implications of different strategies?

Media brief

How should the brief be drafted? What do all the media terms mean? What are the research and buying opportunities?

Media strategy

Is the agency strategy the optimal one for the target audience and media?

Media planning and forecasting

Do the tactical media recommendations best fit the agreed media strategy?

Media buying

What deals are available in the market and do they suit the client's needs?

Media evaluation

The agency may be buying well against ratecard but is it buying better than the competition? Is the space of the required quality and have the media objectives been fulfilled?

By providing these services throughout the media buying cycle Media Audits has grown to 45 staff, a turnover of £3.5 million, over 100 advertiser clients and a growing network of affiliated offices in Europe. Thirty five of the top 100 UK advertisers, 90 of the top 300 UK brands and 38 of the top 100 pan- European brands use its services to monitor the buying performance of their media agencies.

Media Audits' main competitor in the UK, Barsby Rowe, has grown at an equally rapid pace – it has 30 staff and has handled over £140 million of centralisation review work. Thirty of Barsby Rowe's clients are amongst the UK's top 100 advertisers. Both consultancies now offer media auditing services, training for marketing management, selection advice in the appointment of centralised media shops, media planning advice and general media consultancy. In addition, as the sector has become more sophisticated the consultancies have added new media related services. For example, Media Audits has a product called QUAD – the quantitative advertising division, which relates media exposure to shifts in advertising awareness, brand awareness, image, consumer preference and purchase intention.

This and other added value consultancy services now offered by the monitoring firms go some way to defuse the historical criticism of the media auditing fraternity. It was a constant agency refrain that they reported on only the crudest cost measures of the media buying process, ignoring or misunderstanding qualitative issues. For many years Media Audits was the butt of constant criticism from media people. The difficulty was knowing whether the criticism was sour grapes from people who simply resented the idea of being checked up on, or whether the criticisms were valid.

As the emphasis in media buying has moved towards qualitative effects rather than quantitative buying performance the monitoring consultancies are attempting to provide a more three-dimensional appraisal of media buying performance. Agency antagonism has subsided if not entirely disappeared. As the media market continues to fragment and as marketing programmes become more integrated there will be a growing emphasis on consultancy rather than simple cost measures.

The advantage of media auditing consultancies is that they are totally independent, objective and confidential. Those companies which have not used them should seriously consider the new perspective they can bring to the media planning and buying process. In the words of Tony Ayers,

> *'Many companies spend large amounts of money on advertising, but traditionally have not scrutinised their investment with the rigour which they*

apply to similar sized capital projects. We provide a means for general managers, who are not expert in media, to assess the specialist work done for them by agencies or media-buying companies.

'In many cases we are more critical of the client than of the agency. Planning should, but often does not, flow from marketing objectives through the media brief to a media strategy, and then to the tactical media plan. The target audience is very rarely defined precisely, so many campaigns have built-in wastage. The media plan must implement the media strategy properly, but sometimes there is a mismatch because advertisers don't understand the media language. Media has become like a medieval guild – the guild members retire to the top of a tower to produce an alchemical formula, then won't explain how they are doing it, what the objectives are or anything about it! We are there to try and make our clients demand more and understand more of what they get.'

SHIFT FROM QUANTITY TO QUALITY

In the past, media, particularly TV media, was bought largely on price and on crude quantitative measures; ratings, costs per thousand and opportunities to see. The emphasis was very much on buying below the station average price on the *'pile it high, sell it cheap'* philosophy. This suited the nascent media independent sector, which was particularly adept at buying TV media cheaply.

Quantitative measures were also the easiest measures for the media auditing consultancies to monitor. It was often suggested that the focus on competitive price, rather than qualitative measures, by consultancies like Media Audits, reinforced the lowest common denominator in the media environment. It was said that the lowest cost route discriminated against those agencies which bought their media against other criteria; positioning in specific breaks, times of day, programmes with higher audience involvement, or higher editorial quality. Despite adverse media cost comparisons some agencies consistently went for quality rather than quantity.

As the difficulty of reaching audiences has increased, as the need to motivate consumers becomes more pressing and as campaigns incorporate multimedia executions, demanding greater consumer involvement, the balance of opinion has begun to shift away from the lowest cost to the highest quality approach.

Ray Kelly, the Chief Executive of Carat UK, comments *'If all you're doing is competing for the lowest costs you're losing sight of the reason why you're advertising, which is to sell more product or communicate something to the consumer.'* Quite a change in attitude for the head of a media buying operation which built its reputation on low overheads and aggressive buying.

In financial terms, the old style of buying was more obviously and crudely measurable. The new style of buying makes the assumption that ultimate sales will be higher because consumers become more involved with the communications. This should translate into higher sales, but the relationship is not easily researched or tracked. However, the intuitive belief that quality media buying is ultimately more productive in marketing terms is now finally being systematically researched.

RESEARCHING MEDIA SALIENCY

Serious studies are at last beginning to be commissioned into consumer behaviour. For example, one of the more ambitious projects has been undertaken by Armand Morgenzstern of Carat. He has developed a consumer *memorisation model* as a way of making qualitative decisions about media selection, and the optimal combination of media.

Beta scoring and the 'memorisation model'

For many years, two conundrums had irked media planners; not only in the UK, but across Europe. Firstly, what were the relative benefits of 'burst' vs 'drip' media campaigns? Secondly, the incomparable measurements of the various media produced apparently huge differences in 'costs per thousand' when reaching specific target groups.

For example, posters offer massive coverage of any target group, with spectacularly high frequency of opportunities to see, at very low costs per thousand. On the other hand, the cinema medium shows a relatively low coverage of many target markets, at low average frequency of 'opportunities to see', and at apparently high costs per thousand. Intuitively, a media planner rationalises these differences, by pointing out the different impact levels of the media. Posters have a low impact/attention value, cinema has a much higher impact/attention/recall factor. But how different are these values? And, if media planners could only quantify the differences, how might they apply such factors in the media planning process – other than purely subjectively? Might the differences in costs outweigh the benefits of impact – or vice versa?

To help answer these questions Carat companies, in France and Belgium, developed computer models which examined the reach, frequency and impact values of the various media, their inter-relationships, and the effects of the timing and distribution over time of the advertising activity.

The result was what Carat has called the 'memorisation model'.

Applying the memorisation model

A typical client might well ask the question: 'With an advertising investment of £2 million, what additional volume of my product will I sell to the consumer?'

Although the media planner fully understands the client's objectives the frustrating limits of the tools available to the media planner mean that the answer to the client is likely to be: 'With an advertising budget of £2 million, x per cent of the target group will have at least y opportunities to see/hear', in order to translate the advertiser's requirement into an actionable media strategy.

Media plans are *exposure minded*, marketing plans are *sales minded*: two starkly opposite extremes. Classic criteria for media planning have been focused on media exposure levels. When media planners say 'x per cent of the target audience has at least y opportunities to see/hear', what they actually mean is exposure to the media used, and not to the advertising message or what the take-out is from the advertising message. However, selecting the various media on the basis of their quantitative performances is virtually impossible. An 'opportunity to see/hear' does not have the same value for magazines, newspapers, television, radio, cinema or outdoor.

The final intermedia decision often depends upon such unquantifiable judgements as expertise, experience, intuition, creative aspects, and *'gut feeling'*. In other words, *'I think'*, rather than *'I know'*.

The question which Carat has tried to answer is whether media planning needs to remain a matter of subjective judgement and of qualitative expertise in integrating the various aspects of the advertising process? If Carat's memorisation model can be shown to have a solid empirical foundation the answer could be 'Yes, but the level of subjectivity can be greatly reduced'.

If the model can quantify the value of an exposure in each medium, the media planning process may become more objective and move closer to the sales measurement criteria needed by marketing people. In other words, when a media planner says 'An exposure to a 30 second TV commercial has more impact than, for example, a full colour page in a magazine', can this be quantified? How much more impact? The memorisation model may be a major step in the right direction.

The memorisation concept

The 'memorisation' concept reflects the percentage of people, within the target group, who remember the brand, plus at least one element of the advertising copy or visual, after the first exposure, to a new message, appearing in an exclusive medium. The percentage is also referred to as the *beta score*.

Carat has found the beta score to be an efficient way of quantifying the value of an advertising exposure within a medium, and between the various media. A media exposure is judged by its ability to produce memorisation in the target groups, in other words to maximise its beta score.

This raises two questions. How can beta scores be defined, medium by medium? How can beta scores be integrated into a practical, useful media planning system? To define beta scores, country by country, Carat set up impact research in each country.

In Belgium, existing sources of impact research were used. In the case of newspapers, 832 advertisements had been tested, using 'day after recall' incorporating recognition and attribution methods. Among these were 265 advertisements where new messages appeared exclusively in newspapers. The sample base was 17,000 interviews amongst readers of the last issue in which the advertising message had appeared. Similar research covered magazines, television, outdoor and cinema. These research sources led to the following beta scores currently applied by Carat's media planners in Belgium.

Beta Scores used by Carat's Belgian Media Planners

Medium		Average Beta Scores %	Min %	Max %
Newspapers	($1/4$ page, mono)	28	0	75
Newspapers	($1/2$ page, mono)	35	3	69
Television	(30 seconds)	27	9	70
Cinema	(30 seconds)	70	N/A	N/A
Radio	(30 seconds)	5	N/A	N/A
Magazines	(Page, colour)	19	6	46
Magazines	(d.p.s., colour)	27	6	46
Posters	(20 sq. meters)	0.5	0.03	13
Posters	(2 sq. meters)	0.4	0.1	8
Posters	(36 sq. metres)	3	0.4	61
Posters	(15 sq. metres)	1.8	0.4	35

Source: Carat Belgium

The wide variability around the average beta scores underlines the crucial importance of creative aspects, as well as of initial brand awareness.

Carat has also found that beta scores cannot be exported from one country to another; for example:

Beta Score Comparisons: France and Belgium

Medium		France %	Belgium %
Magazines	(Page, colour)	10	19
Television	(30 seconds)	14	27
Posters	(4 × 3 metres)	2	0.5

Source: Carat Belgium

The inevitable question is whether the differences are due to social or structural differences between European countries? Or whether the differences are the result of different research methods?

Integration in the planning model

There is also a need to examine the multimedia effects: the conjoint beta scores for a mix of media.

Armand Morgenzstern has carried out various experiments in France to formalise the process of memorisation, and of memory decay. His research demonstrates how impacts develop over the campaign period, the different functions of the various media, and, most importantly, the variations in impacts which can be achieved by alternative plans at identical budget levels. This disciplines the media planner into going beyond the classic *'opportunities to see/hear'* criteria, and directs him to a qualitative examination of the longer- term effects of alternative media plans.

Carat believes that the memorisation model can be applied to multimedia plans, not simply to single-medium plans.

Example of a multimedia campaign

This example uses three media: television, cinema, and radio. A media planner might consider, as three of his options, the use of a) television only, b) television and cinema, or c) television, cinema and radio, for the same media budget.

With a target market of 16 to 24 year-old adults, his original outline plans might be summarised as:

Media	Plan A TV only	Plan B TV & Cinema	Plan C TV, Cinema & Radio
Budgetary split	100%	75%:25%	50%:25%:25%
Gross Rating Points split	450	340:84	230:84:494
Net cover by medium (total)	82%	75%:40%	70%:40%:83%
Beta scores	15%	15%:70%	15%:70%:5%

The beta scores used are hypothetical but reasonable, based on Carat's French and Belgian experiences.

In terms of input to the memorisation model, it is necessary, for each wave of activity, to enter the net coverage, average frequency of opportunity to see/hear and beta scores.

The resultant lay-down of advertising activity of the three plans would be as follows:

Plan A

WEEK NUMBER   1 2 3 4 5 6 7 8 9 10 11 12 13 14 15

TV ONLY   X - - X - - X - - X - -   X - -

Reach/frequency

TV: 50% net cover @ 1.8 opportunities to see/hear per wave

Plan B

WEEK NUMBER   1 2 3 4 5 6 7 8 9 10 11 12 13 14 15

TV   X - - - - X - - - - X - - - -
CINEMA   X - X - X - X - X - X - X - X

Reach/frequency

TV: 50% net cover @ 2.3 average opportunities to see/hear per wave
CINEMA: 9.6% net cover @ 1.1 average opportunities to see/hear per wave

Plan C

WEEK NUMBER 1 2 3 4 5 6 7 8 9 10 11 12 13 14 15
TV   X - - - - - - X - - - - - - -
CINEMA   X - X - X - X - X - X - X - X
RADIO   - X - - - X - - - X   - - -   X -

Reach/frequency

TV: 50% net cover @ 2.3 average opportunities to see/hear
            per wave
CINEMA: 9.6% net cover @ 1.1 average opportunities to see/hear
            per wave
RADIO: 41.2% net cover @ 3.0 average opportunities to see/hear
            per wave

Under this set of input criteria, which plan will the model suggest as that giving greatest effectiveness, in terms of both the distribution of the recall and memory decay rates, and of the overall average memorability/recall over the 15-week campaign period?

Before looking at the model's answers it should be emphasised that different results would be obtained by simply retiming the advertising effort by, for example, using cinema and or radio as in Plan C before using television, or by different levels of 'pulse' over the campaign period, all within the same budget.

However, given the restrictions of this experiment, the memorisation model gives the following results:

First, the average memorisation of the campaign alternatives would be:

Plan A   :   16.2%

Plan B   :   21.24%

Plan C   :   22.46%

The three-media Plan C achieves better overall memorisation than either of the alternatives considered.

Looking at the contributions to the overall memorisation figure made by each medium to the average, they are:

Plan A	:	Television	16.2%
		Total	**16.2%**
Plan B	:	Television	11.44%
		Cinema	11.15%
		Total	**21.24%**
Plan C	:	Television	7.3%
		Cinema	11.15%
		Radio	6.27%
		Total	**22.46%**

It can be seen that the total average effects are not the simple sum of the individual contributions made by each medium: the total is less than the sum of the parts. The model is suggesting that the effect of any one of the media will be duplicated to a certain extent by another. Nevertheless, the model also insists that the use of three media is advantageous, relative to the use of two, or of the single medium of television.

Caution in using the model is essential. Using average beta scores does not necessarily allow for the specific creative aspects of particular campaigns. This problem can be solved by commissioning specific research, or pretesting advertising recall and effectiveness.

In the UK, Carat is working to validate the model using Millward Brown and Mass Observation tracking studies. The memorisation model is being adapted to suit the individuality of the British media marketplace and it is planned that the model will be in everyday use by Carat media planners.

Wider implications of beta scoring?

There will almost certainly be arguments about the validity of a method like the memorisation model and its related beta scores. Cynics regard it as so much gobbledy gook with little to offer. In Ray Kelly's words,

> *'It sounds like the answer to life, the universe and everything. But strangely while we in the UK are still arguing about whether it means anything our French colleagues argue about whether the beta factor should be 0.117 or 0.119.'*

Similarly there will be debates about the intermedia choice, the choice of 'burst/drip/pulse' timings of advertising activity within any campaign period, the effect of PR and promotional activity and the quality of the creative messages. Such considerations as the environment of a medium – its 'rightness' for a campaign – and of its eventual ability to sell the product, will always be subject to discussion.

However, what is really interesting about Carat's work is the attempt to apply more discipline to the everyday practice of communications planning rather than simply to go for lowest cost media buying. It is of significance that such a major player as Carat is looking at the different impact/memorability values of each medium, the relationship between communication channels and the abilities of consumers to retain and react to messages over time. There is a genuine attempt to bridge the gap between conventional media buying methods and broader client marketing and sales objectives.

Applying beta scores to nonadvertising communications?

In a wider context it is easy to see that if the methodology matures similar techniques could be applied in planning campaigns involving other techniques. For example, will it be possible to derive beta scores for sales pro-motion, direct marketing or public relations activity? What are the relative beta scores for advertorials as opposed to editorial or advertising? What are the relative beta scores for personalised letters, brochures or newsletters? Would it be possible to gauge and quantify the impact of PR campaigns at different weights on the beta scores for a specific media campaign?

If the model is taken into such areas it could help to bring a quantifiable discipline to techniques for which there are few reliable measures. It could also help to assess the relationship between techniques in more complex campaigns and to ameliorate the process of integrating marketing communi-cations disciplines. Above all, it could help clients to more accurately and efficiently plan the allocation of marketing budgets between all channels, not just the advertising channel.

UNDERSTANDING CONSUMER BEHAVIOUR?

Opinions differ widely as to the relative effectiveness of different promo-tional techniques within the marketing mix. Is advertising, direct marketing, sales promotion, or public relations more cost-effective than any of the other techniques? Which produces the best result for each unit spent? Of the advertising media available, which is most effective? Are different tech-niques more relevant for different products at different stages in their lifecycles, at different times of year, with different audiences and so on? How do the different techniques interact with and amplify one another?

In many cases the debate seldom surfaces, because in many organisations budgets simply evolve over time. Radical changes in budget split rarely occur to allow a clear comparison of the relative effectiveness of the main promotional techniques. However, every now and then special circum-stances prevail.

Radical changes in budget split

For example, Macleans Milk Teeth, the entry-point for children into the Macleans toothpaste brand, had a full marketing programme including adver-tising in women's magazines and mother and baby press, together with PR support. However, the only activity that seemed to have any response was sampling to mothers in the 'Bounty baby-bag', a sampling device distributed to new mothers in hospital. As a result, SmithKline Beecham cut out every-thing except sampling of this kind, and sales increased. This one activity achieved awareness, trial, endorsement and, to some extent, advertising.

SmithKline Beecham had a similar but opposite experience with Ribena, the vitamin enriched children's blackcurrant drink. In one particularly successful year the company was running short of blackcurrants, so all promotional activity, including added value packs and price discounting, was stopped, although advertising was maintained. The company found that sales actually carried on growing faster than before.

In the Macleans case the nature of the product and the concern of the new mother dictated that product sampling was crucial to acceptance. Whereas with Ribena, the product was already well-known and accepted by the housewife and the children who drank the product, so discounting and special offers were much less relevant to consumer loyalty and sales.

In other circumstances, weight of advertising may be so low for a given task that there is little point in advertising at all. Unfortunately, the nature of the advertising agency/client relationship tends to militate against objective advice in such situations because agencies get paid if money is spent and not if it isn't. What is needed is far more research insight into consumer behaviour and how it is affected by different communications techniques and channels. Marketing management needs to be prepared to finance research to help plan which communications channels to use and the relative weight of each channel?

Some pointers from America

As the largest, most dynamic and arguably the most competitive marketing culture in the world, America is often seen to lead the marketing services industry. Does it give any pointers to the effectiveness of techniques and how to allocate budgets?

One aspect of the American market which does not apply to anywhere near the same extent in the UK is the opportunity to promote through the retail trade, with all sorts of in-store activity. As a result US manufacturers spend a larger proportion of their budgets in this area. By contrast, in the UK many supermarket items have very limited promotional opportunities. Sainsbury, Tesco, Boots and the other majors have their own promotional vehicles which manufacturers can buy into or not. If they want to launch on-pack offers in-store many will be rejected because the distribution systems and the merchandising layouts won't allow them. In the USA there is a much more fragmented retail marketplace with a wide variety of promotional activities available.

Virtual blanket couponing, particularly freestanding press inserts, are also very common in the US, but this technique has not really taken off in the UK. Many US companies seem to feel that they need to coupon heavily to keep in the swim, and the technique has achieved a momentum of its own. In the UK on-pack and door-to-door coupons are relatively common and redemption rates are high, but indiscriminate press couponing has so far not taken off. The UK Sunday papers have been experimenting with books of coupons but the technique creates another cost to the business, whose bene-fits have not been proved. As a result many US companies are questioning indiscriminate couponing and UK companies may have learnt an expensive marketing lesson vicariously from the US experience.

Even in the US consumer products, direct marketing is still in its infancy. However, the growth of huge consumer databases, both proprietary and commercially accessible, is gradually making the concept of one-to-one con-sumer dialogue through direct marketing an increasingly realistic option. The ability to recall huge amounts of data on individual consumers is making the concept of personalised, lifetime relationships a reality. As a result, budgets for the development, maintenance and use of large consumer databases is taking a growing proportion of many marketing budgets in the US. There is also a growing number of direct sales organisations, utilising new technology, for whom direct communication with the consumer is a fundamental part of the business and therefore of huge significance within the marketing budget. Public Relations is also taken far more seriously in the US and much larger budgets are allocated to marketing PR.

However, in all these areas the US experience is often little better informed in terms of consumer reactions to different techniques than it is in the UK. Investment in different techniques is often dictated by pragmatic factors or by practical observation and 'gut feel'.

Charting the unknown continent

Below-the-line may be more important in the US, but there is little which objectively evaluates the relative impact of different techniques or the opti-mal mix of the various techniques in the marketing plan.

Despite their importance, many of the questions about consumer res-ponses to different types of marketing activity remain unanswered. It is fre-quently said that more research needs to be done to evaluate the impact of different marketing techniques on the consumer but the number of variables involved, the complexity of the issues and the costs have put many off the track. There are many continuous studies from Nielsen, AGB and others which track sales data, but few, if any, tracking studies which comprehen-sively explain how purchasing decisions were arrived at or how they could be influenced.

In the growing climate of accountability and with the need to make mar-keting budgets work harder the unknown continent of consumer behaviour is likely to be explored more thoroughly in the next decade.

What makes the consumer tick?

Frazer Thompson, the Director of Marketing for Lagers at Whitbread, makes the point,

'In the past, marketing departments had a lot of their own qualitative research data and media buying research looking at Opportunities To See, Ratings, Coverage and Readership Habits of target audiences. But there was little in the way of large scale, pooled qualitative research into how consumers perceived brands, how advertising and promotions affect those perceptions, what kind of creative approaches work best, how consumers make their brand choices and how all these factors change over time.

'In the absence of more qualitative analysis the tendency among many media people has therefore been to buy on price rather than quality. Those that have bought on quality have tended to base their judgement on intuition rather than hard data. We have always supported the quality argument. For example, it seems logical that a TV viewer is more likely to concentrate on the screen, and be receptive to advertising messsages, in a gripping thriller like Prime Suspect *than a low concentration family show like the* Generation Game. *But it is almost impossible to support this kind of view analytically in the absence of robust, continuous studies.*

I believe that in the next few years we will see a lot more money invested in large scale consumer omnibuses which track behavioural responses to advertising, promotions and the brand buying decisions that result.'

If it allows us to understand the mechanisms of consumer behaviour and their responses to a mixture of communications techniques, it will be money well spent.

A NEW ROLE FOR MEDIA STRATEGISTS

At an ISBA conference, in July 1993, Chris Dickens, the Worldwide Media Director of Young & Rubicam, presented a paper which outlined two growing trends, one towards media fragmentation the other towards marketing services integration. He made the point that the arrival of new interactive media, and the opportunity for individual communication, meant that the traditional, mass market media function would rapidly become an anachronism. He argued that media people would have to devise fully-integrated communications strategies to reach target audiences and would have to become much more aware of, and involved in, brand marketing strategies. In his words,

'Some media specialists are already much more involved in the entire marketing process, and boundaries between media and communication disciplines are no longer discrete. They are merging and overlapping with increasing regularity, and as communication strategies replace advertis-

ing strategies, PR, promotions, advertising, direct, sponsorship, and events, managers all need to collaborate more to create the optimum solution. To achieve this we will need to develop a new breed of media specialist; truly alert to all the options, fully understanding of the marketing context and involved throughout the development and execution of communication strategy. No longer can the media department's role be a simple planning and buying one. Media people must now become communication strategists. Their skills, knowledge and ability to evaluate alternatives are needed at every stage.'

He provided several examples of the way this type of strategy might work. For example, he gave the hypothetical example of sponsoring a ten-part wine series on the BBC – apparently a limited communication opportunity, given the strict rules on sponsor credits. However, more heavily-branded transmissions around the world, the use of footage for in-flight and in-store videos, the opportunity to print an adaptation of the script for use as a newspaper part-work, the opportunity to use both videos and printed materials as premium promotions, the opportunity to include material on PC or CD discs, potential radio sponsorship tie-ins, and a host of PR, sales promotion and merchandising applications could transform the basic idea into a multimedia campaign.

This is a perfect example of the type of campaign for which the new breed of campaign planner will be needed. Close to the client, fully conversant with marketing objectives, aware of the different media and the promotional techniques which can be integrated with them, channel neutral and objective in the definition of total budgets and the disposition of total budget between different techniques.

Chris Dickens went on to say that in fulfilling this new role,

'Success becomes even more dependent upon a new depth of knowledge of both the brand and the consumer that much of today's research is unable to fulfil. Tomorrow's communication strategists will need to be supported by a significant amount of new research. Much greater focus will be placed on consumer dynamics and their behaviour towards different communication vehicles. We need to know more than just what the consumer thinks, we need to know how he or she behaves.'

In the future campaign planners, from a media background and armed with both media and consumer research, will define whole programmes of marketing communications activity. They will be the conscience of the brand and the guardian of the marketing budget.

CONCLUSION

Nothing is ever simple, and conclusions are never black and white. As in the past there will go on being many influencers and decision-makers in the planning process described in this chapter. However, as the media mix becomes more complex, as the independent media function becomes more sophisticated and as clients search for an objective voice I believe there will be an expansion in the role of the media specialist. They will be the pragmatic generals of the marketing communications battlefield.

10

EXTERNAL AGENCY MANAGEMENT

'When we found a rattlesnake in the factory we used to just kill it; now we bring in a consultant'
Lee Iacocca

INTRODUCTION

Two of the great problems facing the marketing services sector in the last few years have been an increasingly hostile client environment and a constant attempt to deconstruct the services provided by agencies. These trends fit with the need to be more accountable, and with a shift towards greater specialisation. There has been particularly strong pressure to 'unbundle' agency services, to both enhance quality and to pay less for the component parts. In-house provision and direct purchase of creative services are just two manifestations of this process.

However, the results can sometimes be counter productive and damaging to the overall effectiveness of the marketing budget. What are the alternatives? What are the relative pros and cons? How can this process be reconciled with the need for greater integration and global co-ordination of marketing activities? Deconstruction may be the right economic answer in the short run, but does it damage long-term marketing performance? Insistence on petty cost control may save money, but will it kill the creative spark which is the key ingredient for success? Can in-house creative resources produce the same results for less money?

The answers to these questions of external agency management and control are of fundamental financial significance. This chapter explores some of the alternative options and their financial implications.

INTERNAL OR EXTERNAL RESOURCES?

The criteria

There are a number of issues to be addressed internally before deciding whether and to what extent the marketing communications process can be handled internally or externally. For example:

Frequency

Are the marketing activities involved regular or irregular features of corporate activity? Can they be bought in from time to time or are they needed on an ongoing basis?

Budgets

Is the amount involved of major corporate significance? Would the budget be of interest to an external agency of the appropriate type, either as a whole or as a fragmented budget?

Saliency

How critical is the quality and potency of marketing communications to corporate or marketing success? Can risks be taken with regard to the professionalism, resources and commitment of the approach chosen?

Expertise

Does internal management have the temperament and experience to handle either the internal or the exernal creative route?

Specialism

How specialised is the business? The more specialised, the more viable an in-house route may be, and the smaller the number of external agencies which fit the bill.

The options

There are a large number of companies which handle a wide range of executional functions in-house. For example, many retailers have internal public relations, design, print-buying, promotional and even advertising departments. Many large financial services and industrial companies have creative services units soaking up a wide range of creative assignments from around their organisations. By contrast, some companies produce nothing in-house, as a matter of deliberate policy. Between these two extremes the available options are:

Total in-house

This route tends to be more appropriate for specialist companies, with lower budgets, often in business-to-business or small, specialist niche markets, with a very low reliance on above-the-line advertising.

Partial in-house

This pragmatic approach is adopted by many companies, particularly in the areas of low risk graphic design. Major exercises like corporate identities, annual reports and advertising tend to be bought from specialist, external agencies.

Internal buyers

An experienced creative or account handler is sometimes appointed as an advertising or creative co-ordinator, to buy-in services as required, basing decisions on a working knowledge of the creative services market. In the past, it was common for many large companies to have both a print buyer and an advertising manager. Today many companies have saved money by abolishing the functions and by merging them into other marketing positions. In many cases budgets and workflows no longer justify the roles, and the responsibility commonly falls to brand management. However, many companies which should have in-house buyers, but do not have them, are losing large amounts of money as a result.

In the words of David Wethey, Managing Director of Agency Assessments, one of the most respected agency selection and management consultancies,

> 'A whole cadre of advertising managers has disappeared from the industry. Every company used to have an advertising manager. These people were purchasers, they knew facts and figures; for example, how much a page in The Express cost. They also had 15 or 16 printers at their beck and call. Agencies didn't rip them off, because they couldn't.'

In the case of British Telecom the purchasing role lives on in The Customer Communication Unit (CCU) which has 100 staff and deals with millions of pounds worth of marketing spend each year. It sits between BT product managers (the clients) and external agencies, writing briefs and vetting the process of agency selection and work execution.

But many companies do without, sometimes with unfortunate results.

External buyers

Another solution is the appointment of a consultant to act as go-between and adviser. Many ex-agency people, particularly from an account management background, provide this kind of service, often coupled with strategic advice on a whole range of marketing communications issues.

For example, Bruno Lloyd-Lyons, who spent many years managing large consumer advertising agencies, and was latterly vice chairman of Publicis, now runs a Consumer Strategy & Communication consultancy. He acts as a knowledgeable insider to the marketing services process. In his words, *'I work with Chief Executives and marketing management at the highest level, recommending strategies focused on consumer needs and advising on the use of outside resources.'*

The advantages of the in-house route

The main advantages of an in-house route to creative execution are:

Culture

Internal staff are imbued with the internal culture. They know the market and the products. It won't take them a week to understand what a with-profits life policy is, how the latest hardware product differs from the last one, or how the vitamins in the new food supplement benefit the consumer. They also know what will and will not 'fit in' and how the 'dramatis personae' within the company will react to different marketing and creative routes. This can save a lot of time and aggravation.

Continuity

Everyone is aware that the marketing services business is a young and mobile one, and there is nothing more irritating than having constantly changing teams. It's an appealing thought that creative staff will remain in place for long periods, to avoid 'learning curve' problems and unnecessary changes in creative direction – often change for change's sake.

Consistency

In-house staff are far more likely to adhere to the dictates of internal design, corporate identity and creative guidelines. They are much less likely to propose 'unfruitful' routes which have been explored, researched or used on previous occasions.

Control

Priorities can be set by management, not filtered through an agency's management system, which may have a wholly different set of priorities. With a major marketing initiative looming who wants to rely on an external firm to 'deliver the goods'? For example, how many apochryphal stories are there of agency creative directors finishing the creative work on the way over in the taxi?

Security

The chances of a security lapse are inevitably higher with an agency than with an in-house unit. Planners conducting 'confidential' qualitative research groups, creatives bragging about their latest work at the 'creative circle', callow account men becoming legless at a well-known brasserie, despatch men spouting off at the pub, and creative suppliers inadvertently biking confidential artwork to the wrong client are just a few of the many security lapses which could 'blow the gaff' on a new product launch, a new corporate identity or a major new advertising campaign.

Marketing services agencies are generally leakier than the average strategy consulting firm, merchant bank or firm of accountants, and many clients have spent sleepless nights worrying about being trumped by the competition as a result of a careless agency. 'Loose talk costs lives', and in this context they are likely to be in the marketing department.

Price

Depending on how the work is handled, the marginal costs incurred by an in-house department are likely to be lower. Agencies inevitably have the economies of scale to buy many external creative services more cheaply, but a lot of creative work can now be executed using in-house computer and desk-top publishing systems.

Accountability

There can be no doubts about the costs and composition of charges if the in-house unit is run by the same finance department.

The disadvantages of the in-house route

The main disadvantages of taking the in-house route are:

Staff turnover

Creative people like variety and dislike overbearing clients dictating to them. They want to move around, learn from experienced seniors and develop their careers. Whether really good creative people hang around in-house depends to a huge extent on the ability of the organisation to provide these stimuli. Many are unable to do so and lose their best people. When there are plenty of good people on the market, as there have been for the last few years, this may not pose huge problems, but as the economy takes off, and as the supply of talented and experienced people dries up, the situation can become more difficult.

Creativity

Nothing stultifies creativity more than repetition, either of the same problem or of the same product. This is an almost inevitable consequence of working in-house, although some organisations are large enough to avoid the problem.

Imagination

The best creative solutions often come from taking a completely fresh look at the problem. As many in-house staff are weighed down with the learned experience of what will and will not work, the opportunity for experimentation with unconventional or controversial approaches is constrained. They also become too close to the problem and can't 'see the wood for the trees'.

Objectivity

It can be hard for an in-house team to be entirely objective about its own work, and the internal marketing team's judgement may be compromised for the same reason. What can they say if they hate the work?

Time

Does the management of a retailing, financial or industrial company have the time, skills and inclination to manage an in-house function? How can managers, focused on the core business, motivate people in such specialist areas? How can they manage the problems of 'moonlighting', freelancing and poor morale?

Fixed costs

While costs may be lower for some bought-in items, and while the level of time costs for employees may be lower than for equivalent agency teams, the fixed establishment costs of in-house units are often high, and the utilisation rates may be very low from time to time.

Trends?

Because each company has its own priorities, which change from time to time, there is no clear short-term trend in the move towards or away from internal or external creative functions. During the recession some have moved further down this route, buying-in talent which has dropped-out of the impoverished agency sector. Others have concluded that in the climate of cost cutting and rationalisation closing, hiving-off or selling in-house units makes more strategic sense. Such moves are either followed by a period of tied supply to the former in-house function, or alternatively of buying as cheaply as possible in the cut-throat marketing services environment of the moment.

At one extreme is the in-house consolidation of creative work by some large retailers. At the other, is the divestment of full-service, in-house agencies by firms like Lever Brothers and Siemens. In a sense Rover has recently done the same with KMM, the agency created by its former Managing Director.

Which of these routes is most appropriate is often best assessed by an external consultant, objectively defining the optimal course.

WHAT CAN DIFFERENT AGENCIES DELIVER?

Personality

In *Liberation Management* Tom Peters writes, 'We tend to think of ad agencies as zippy. Yet many mature agencies have developed the same symptoms of advanced bureaucracy . . . that mark dying industrial outfits.' The fact that a business is apparently in a dynamic environment doesn't prevent it becoming ossified, unoriginal and managerially unwieldy. As agencies have grown they have tended to go down these routes and there is a constant struggle to regenerate them. But the fact is that agencies, like people, go through lifecycles and develop very definite corporate personalities. Some clients feel more at home with one life stage and personality than another. A few of the possible agency types could be characterised as follows:

- teenage rebel
- smart alec graduate
- trained professional
- arrogant jetsetter
- arthritic uncle

Agency names immediately spring to mind for all these characters. Each has a very definite personality and attracts people who fit that personality. Worse still they mould people to the corporate personality, so that after a while individuals cease to be themselves and become an extension of the corporate ego. Clients need to be sure they choose a compatible corporate mould.

Analysis and advice

Some marketing services agencies are great at strategy and weak at execution; deeply intelligent, analytical planners devise strategies which the creatives either can't or won't execute. Others are quite the reverse, with the creative director leaping for the magic marker before the client has left the room; the planning and creative briefs are then written to fit the resulting campaign. Great agencies manage to create a synthesis of the two.

In the coming decade the balance will move further in the direction of the marketing thinkers. The ability to provide strategic marketing advice will become a major priority as the marketing environment becomes more complex. The understanding of brands, and the ability to contribute to brand equity, will also become more and more essential.

Creativity

Creative excellence will be required more than ever in the coming decade to help differentiate brands and services in an increasingly crowded marketplace. In the words of Burt Manning, Chairman and Chief Executive of J. Walter Thompson, writing in 'Advertising in the 21st Century'.

> '. . . the discriminator between equal marketing investments will be creativity. Creativity in strategy. Creativity in the core idea. Creativity in execution.'

Different agencies define creativity in different ways, some meaning the physical act of producing artworks or commercials, others meaning a whole mindset to the client's market and products. Some mean mechanical creativity restricted to one discipline; advertising, direct mail, sponsorship or public relations. Others are more eclectic in their approach. It will become increasingly apparent in the next decade that the broader concept of creativity will be what is expected and needed to produce the required solutions for client marketing problems.

The recent case of Classic Coke awarding its US advertising to the specialist creative shop Creative Artists Agency highlights the risk agencies run if they take their eye off the ball of the most tangible and immediate expression of creativity – the visible product. The WPP 'Annual Report and Accounts', 1992 describes the situation in the following terms,

'A great deal of interest has been aroused by Coca-Cola's decision to appoint Creative Artists Agency, the leading Hollywood talent agency, to create this year's advertising for Classic Coke. Some have speculated that this decision indicates more than a client's temporary dissatisfaction with its agency and heralds a major change in the role of agencies, with a large number of clients defecting to CAA or its competitors.

While advertising industry leaders have been quick to dismiss the competitive threat, Coca-Cola's move certainly highlights some of the challenges facing agencies. However important international co-ordination may have become, an agency's prime and central function continues to be the provision of imaginative strategies and outstanding creative solutions.

On occasion, cumbersome client or agency structures and approval systems militate against clear and vigorous decisions. Agencies must ensure that size does not begin to impair agility. Agencies must be sure to keep in touch: both with a rapidly changing youth culture and with the talent that exists in the world of entertainment. The finest directors, musicians, editors, photographers and special effects people will never be found on the payrolls of agencies: but agencies must know where they are and be able and ready to marshal them on their clients behalf.'

In the words of Donald Keough, former President and Chief Operating Officer of the Coca-Cola Company, quoted in *Advertising Age* on 12 April 1993.

'What we have simply done is to say we are not going to be limited in where we go for creative access . . . you know, the move to Creative Artists Agency was not a cataclysmic event in the Coca-Cola Company. It was simply an effort to link up with a very bright person in (CAA Chairman) Michael Ovitz and his associates, to open up a pool of creativity to put their arms around the ultimate star, which is Coca-Cola.'

The urge by clients to cut out the middleman – conventional agency management – certainly has financial savings implicit in it. However, creative people are not notoriously good at working within a defined budget, working to time, understanding the nuances of the marketplace, listening to hard research or thinking how their work will tie in with other corporate and marketing objectives. These are issues which the conventional account handling structure, if it is working properly, is there to manage on the client's behalf. Sometimes regarded as a breed of parasites on the creative process, agency management can often seem like sublime impresarios when they have been dispensed with.

Geographical reach

Some agencies are happily parochial, others aggressively expansionist. In both cases co-ordinated networks are being established worldwide so that clients have a choice of co-ordination styles. Some networks are proprietary to one or other agency group. Others are co-operative groups of independent local operators, although the scope for discord and poor liaison between independent companies tends to favour the proprietary networks.

As larger client companies expand into new territories and new product fields, and as central control of client operations increases, there will be a growing commercial advantage for centrally controlled, international agency groups. Smaller clients may opt for the looser type of network.

Client conflicts will inevitably occur more frequently worldwide and as a result parallel, competing agency networks will be developed. However, as clients become more attuned to the idea of joint ventures with competitors in their own business environments the scope for flexibility and compromise will grow among the larger clients and their international networks.

Clients looking for national or transnational account co-ordination clearly have a larger selection of agencies to choose from than those companies looking for Pan European or Global account co-ordination.

Multinational Agencies

Group	Agency	No. of countries	No. of clients in more than ten countries
WPP	Ogilvy & Mather	57	28
	J. Walter Thompson	48	19
Omnicom	BBDO	59	21
	DDB Needham	56	13
	DMB&B	42	7
	Leo Burnett	48	11
	FCB Publicis	51	17
	Grey	52	24
Interpublic	Lintas	46	13
	McCann-Erickson	82	33
Saatchi & Saatchi	Saatchi & Saatchi	50	18
	BSB	39	17
	Young & Rubicam	55	21

Source: *Advertising Age*

Figure 10.1

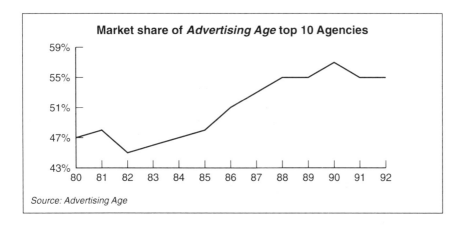

Figure 10.2

In fact, at the very top end of the business the number of agencies genuinely able to provide the required service continues to decrease and concentrate. The 1992 WPP Annual Report and Accounts makes the following contention, 'For clients, market pressures and worldwide expansion have further increased their requirement for agency partners able to provide strategic and creative resources internationally; yet there are only 13 agencies able to service clients in more than 40 countries.'

In the accountancy sector mergers have seen the number of credible international firms dwindle to only five or six. A similar pattern appears to be developing in the marketing services sector. In financial terms internationally co-ordinated agencies and campaigns can often be more expensive. Apart from the limited supply of suitable agencies and the inevitably high overheads, co-ordination time costs are significant and the apparent time savings resulting from central co-ordination are often illusory. There can be savings in terms of creative origination, but the biggest financial benefit to the brand is having effective marketing communications.

Integrated solutions

Some agencies like WPP and Saatchis provide integrated and co-ordinated marketing services within their networks, although most have been slow off the mark. In the words of Joe Cappo, senior Vice President and Publishing Director of Crain Communications, Inc., the publisher of *Advertising Age*, in 'Agencies: Change or Die' *Advertising Age* 7 December 1992,

> *'What (advertising agencies) have not done, with a few exceptions, is plunge into the concept of integrated marketing their clients need to*

*survive and thrive through these changing times. All of these various ele-
ments must be co-ordinated, and precious few large agencies are doing it.
Strangely enough, many small and business-to-business agencies regularly perform this service for their clients.'*

Some agencies intentionally do not aspire to integration of marketing services. The benefits of integration are significant, but how the integration is
achieved depends upon whether the client has a single buying point for all
activities and whether the integration is planned internally or externally.

SINGLE SKILL OR TOTAL INTEGRATION?

Greater integration and co-ordination of marketing services will almost certainly be a fact of life in the future. The demand for greater integration has
come from clients like Rover which have grown tired of the inefficiencies of
the old nonintegrated approach. It is on the lips of many clients and is
increasingly being repeated by agency senior management. It is a business
argument which has been won.

However, the issue has not been resolved as to whether the integration
should be:

- managed by internal marketing management
- co-ordinated by specialist, external campaign co-ordinators
- handled by multidisciplinary agencies
- handled by a range of specialist agencies working to one brief.

The argument will continue and there will be no simple answer. Where on
the spectrum of options a particular company falls depends on the quality
and depth of its marketing management team. In the words of David Wethey
of Agency Assessments,

*'It very much depends on the capacity of the marketing director to
manage his marketing communications. The need for one-stop shopping
is in inverse proportion to his skill and sophistication as a manager of
marketing services.'*

With a strong and experienced internal marketing team the need for an
external campaign co-ordinator or an integrated, multidisciplinary team
from one agency inevitably decreases. In addition, the question arises of
whether one agency can master all the marketing disciplines or whether it is
preferable to use specialists in each category; specialists who know how to
integrate their input with other specialists?

In the opinion of Peter Gummer, Chairman and Chief Executive of
Shandwick, the largest independent public relations network in the world,

'Integration should happen at the client end, not at the supplier end. A lot of multiservice agency concepts went wrong in the eighties because the central proposition was a load of nonsense, driven by the need to keep earnings up. We've done a lot of things wrong and a few things right – one being to defend the purity of our offering. The only problem we face is a client without a centralised function to which we can report.'

Many in the PR world endorse this view, based on the different nature of the disciplines. Others point to the success of Burson Marsteller within the Young & Rubicam Group, or Hill and Knowlton within the WPP Group.

Whether the services are delivered within one group or from several the key is quality of delivery. Every element of the marketing mix needs expert attention but it also needs to be integrated with the rest, whether pack design, promotional, public relations, media buying or advertising. Individuals have to be creative in their own right, and create work to meet specific objectives, but also have to understand the overall business context that they are operating in.

SELECTING AND MANAGING AGENCIES

Safe sex and the consultancy business

In the swinging sixties and permissive seventies clients used to put their business up for pitch, choose an agency and jump into bed together. Personal chemistry was the critical factor and many of the simple, mechanical details of agency service were not properly verified. The idea of checking 'the agency promise' in detail was like demanding proof of virginity; simply too embarassing for words. If the relationship failed the client would be out on the streets again, looking for another partner.

As with sex, the 1980s and 1990s were and are far less promiscuous, and clients can't be too careful about the partners they choose. For AIDS read foreign competition and recession. Companies are now in the position where they cannot afford to make mistakes with their agencies. Slip-ups not only result in lost budgets but cause time delays, incorrect brand positionings and lost market share. Tolerance of marketing department errors in agency selection has evaporated among the wider management team.

This trend has coincided with a large number of experienced agency and marketing people being on the job market with nowhere to go. As a result the agency marriage broking and guidance business has taken off. In the words of David Wethey of Agency Assessments, *'Why go on a series of blind dates when you can have marriage guidance.'*

A wide variety of consultancies are now available for marketing directors to call upon; creative review, selection, remuneration, training, production, media and more. For example, in the UK, client selection consultancies include The Advertising Agency Register and Agency Assessments and Stratagem; Strategic consultancies include SCAN and McClaren Associates; Production consultancies include Production Link in the prepress area, and Focus on Film in commercials. The extent to which these consultancies have been accepted by the marketing services community varies. The Advertising Agency Register, run by Lindy Payne since 1975, has always been well-liked by agencies and clients. Running as more of a discreet dating agency than an aggressive selection service, Lindy Payne is more like a well-informed agony aunt for clients. At the other extreme Focus on Film took a particularly aggressive line on film production when it was launched in 1991, suggesting that huge discounts were there for the taking if the commercials production area could be put under professional management. The commercials industry and the AFVPA went for its throat and savaged it at birth. Others have met with varying degrees of success.

The consultancy business is not likely to be a one-day wonder, created by the recession. As the agency world fragments and becomes more complex the need for explanation and intermediation increases, particularly for marketing management without an intimate knowledge of the agency world. In the words of Tony Ayers, Chief Executive of Media Audits,

> *'Quite a lot of marketing directors come from a sales background, and the agency world is very alien. The need for a consultancy is an admission of weakness. However, it's an admission of strength to recognise weakness and deal with it.'*

Not surprisingly, the consultancy business began in the US with bias towards cost and remuneration. One of the first consultancies there was Cantor & Achenbaum. According to David Wethey Al Achenbaum was a formidable operator and was feared by many agencies. Morgan-Anderson is another leading US consultancy which specialises in assessment techniques and remuneration. There are many, more aggressive, remuneration and cost-oriented consultancies in the US, which largely justify their existence through cost savings.

By contrast SCAN, which has been advising blue-chip clients since 1978, was set up in Holland to service large international conglomerates like Unilever and Heineken; its approach is more cerebral and involved in the marketing process than some of the US consultancies.

Agency Assessments' selection process

As an example of the systematic approach being brought to agency selection and review by consultancies like Agency Assessments, the following is the 15-step approach used by David Wethey for his clients:

- decision to proceed with agency review
- set selection criteria
- establish selection process
- management review
- develop consideration list of agencies
- invite agencies to participate using questionnaire
- evaluate responses
- develop long list
- ask for strategic responses based on briefing document
- evaluate responses
- pick short list
- visit short list
- present, select, negotiate
- final selection
- phase I contract.

With the advice of Agency Assessments the client allocates scores to agencies as follows:

First stage evaluation – capabilities questionnaire	20 points
Second stage evaluation – response to briefing	20 points
Third stage evaluation – chemistry meeting and agency tour	20 points
Fourth stage evaluation – presentation	60 points
TOTAL SCORE	120 points
Fifth stage evaluation – contract discussion	* GO * NO GO

The key elements of the presentation scoring are as follows:

Enthusiasm, energy, build-up and initiative	–	10 points
Team capabilities, chemistry, overall effectiveness, ability to work together	–	10 points
Strategy, understanding, thinking	–	15 points
Ideas, programmes, recommendations	–	25 points
TOTAL SCORE	–	60 points

According to David Wethey agencies get a written questionnaire with a request for a written response, typically within two weeks. Shortlisted agencies receive an intimate brief on what the company is looking for, what the brand is about and where it's been, with research appendices. Some questions are logistical. For example, who is going to work on the business? What is their experience? How does the agency expect to be remunerated? Marks and scores are awarded on credentials and the documentary response, resulting in a short list no longer than four.

Managing the ongoing relationship

Facilitating the selection of a new agency is the critical entry point for many consultancies. However, making the best of existing relationships, advising clients on assessing performance, setting appropriate remuneration levels and comparing service quality are of growing significance. Training and coaching of marketing management in how to deal with agencies is also increasingly important. David Wethey of Agency Assessments comments that,

> *'Marketing people are supposed to be expert in advertising and the other marketing communication skills, and yet they've never taken a "driving test" in it. They've also got to do the rest of their job and they are judged pretty harshly.'*

With this in mind, he claims that,

> *'Unless I am physically restrained, I always go beyond the marketing people. I always talk to financial management, sales, manufacturing and other people in a client company, to try and put the marketing department into perspective. One of the most important factors I have found is that marketing people tend to be more recently arrived. Another thing is the latent unpopularity of marketing people. They are seen to be less expert, better paid, with a nicer lifestyle, and to be relatively superficial. I try to recommend agencies which fit the whole corporate culture.'*

Relationship versus process

Where it comes to performance appraisal external measures include brand share, sales and market research. Internal performance appraisal covers process on the one side and relationship on the other. More and more good agencies are introducing process determinants into their own review procedures. In the past, many agencies had review boards and they are being revived to look at process in account planning, process in creative, process in media, process in management. In David Wethey's opinion, 'It's essential to separate the relationship from the process, because my experience is that a poor interpersonal relationship can survive a good process, but not vice versa.'

In many ways, consultants help agencies because they ensure that all agency management issues are handled objectively and professionally. They inject realism into the brief and avoid wasteful pitching by agencies with no chance of success.

However, some clients attempt to delegate too much to their consultants, for time and political reasons. For example, Rupert Howell, Managing Director of Howell Henry Chaldecott Lury, is reputed to have turned down the opportunity to pitch for a client which wanted the whole selection process to be handled exclusively by a consultant. In a recent *Marketing Week* report on the subject, Tony Hillyer, NPD Director of Bass, commented, 'Its like lamp-posts and drunks – you should use consultants for illumination, not support.'

Whether the selection and management of agencies is ultimately handled by the marketing team or a hired gun there seems no doubt that the amateurish approach of the past has gone for good.

NEGOTIATING WITH AGENCIES

There are those who believe negotiating with agencies is about as easy as picking water up with chopsticks, and this may have been true in the past. However, the last few years have seen an increase in the openness and honesty of the process. Professionalism in the process has been injected via a series of publications and training courses from the trade bodies on both the client and the agency side.

In determining the nature, depth and cost of an agency relationship some of the key considerations are as follows:

- which agency services are needed?
- what are sensible staffing levels?
- what are the campaign media – press, radio, television, outdoor?
- is there a need for integrated disciplines – sponsorship, PR, direct, promotions?
- what is the timing and frequency of activity?
- is there a need for international co-ordination or activity?

The time, effort and resources needed to operate a simple, regional press campaign in a single tactical burst will be infinitely different from a multimedia, through-the-line, international campaign at strategic and tactical levels.

Member Agencies

Year	1988	1989	1990	1991	1992
Number	260	265	275	245	230
Billing average	14,423,077	16,415,094	16,181,818	17,061,224	17,934,782
Billing total	3,750m	4,350m	4,450m	4,180m	4,125m (est)

Extracts From IPA Analysis of Agency Costs

	1988	1989	1990	1991	1992
Number of agencies in the analysis	115	101	106	84	100
Billing					
Average	29,785,708	39,204,547	38,338,730	44,279,753	42,001,000
Total	3,425m	3,960m	4,064m	3,719m	4,201m
% of billing	91.34	91.03	91.32	88.97	101.84
Gross Income					
Average	4,510,787	5,648,576	5,372,280	6,058,796	5,314,000
% of billing	15.14	14.41	14.01	13.68	12.65
Staff costs					
Average	2,293,647	2,889,375	2,821,951	3,343,496	3,116,000
% of total costs	59.49	58.94	59.06	59.25	62.98
% of gross income	50.85	51.15	52.53	55.18	58.64
Av salary	20,109	23,551	24,830	27,795	28,396
Av number	117	122	117	117	101
Av number – cars	39	45	41	45	37
Total costs					
Average	3,855,296	4,901,966	4,778,152	5,642,541	4,948,000
% of billing	12.94	12.50	12.46	12.74	11.78
% of gross income	85.47	86.78	88.94	93.13	93.11
Net profit (before interest etc)					
Average	655,491	746,611	594,127	416,225	366,000
% of billing	2.20	1.90	1.55	0.94	0.87
% of gross income	14.53	13.22	11.06	6.87	6.88

Source: IPA

Figure 10.3

In a different context, consideration should be given to the ownership of copyright in any work produced. The ownership of copyright usually rests with the agency unless it has been assigned to the client. More trouble is often caused by copyright issues than by straight-forward financial haggles when client/agency relationships break up, as is shown by the prolonged dogfight between Barclays Bank and the now defunct Hook Advertising, over copyright in the 'Rabbit' mobile phone brand name.

Staff Costs – All Agencies

	Total % of Staff Costs 1991	Total of % Staff Costs 1992
Wages and salaries	79.29	80.83
Bonuses	2.57	1.12
Profit Sharing	1.21	
Social Security i.e. national insurance	7.88	7.71
Pension premiums, contributions, and pensions paid	4.30	3.72
Agency temps and freelancers	2.34	2.01
Recruitment and head hunters fees	1.69	0.74
Severance	0.73	2.42
TOTAL STAFF COSTS	100	100
Numbers of returns used	100	94

Source: IPA

Figure 10.4

THE COSTS OF RUNNING AN AGENCY

Advertising

Each year the Institute of Practitioners in Advertising in the UK publishes a breakdown of agency running costs based on returns from all its member agencies. This indicates, in depth, what it actually costs to run an agency and what the level of profit is across the advertising industry as a whole (see Figure 10.3).

Because it is used as a reference point by Agency Managing and Finance Director, for comparison and better management, great effort is taken to ensure that the figures are accurate and consistent from one year to the next. They are consequently put together and reviewed by chartered accountants. In fact, until fairly recently the IPA Agency Cost Survey was a confidential, internal document. However having suffered incessant accusations in the eighties that the industry was obscenely profitable it was decided to publish summary information. It is interesting to note that in the legal and accountancy professions it is only fairly recently that firms have been prepared to even publish their total fees. The idea of disclosing cost structures or profitability levels is quite unthinkable. Yet the agency world, stung by what it sees as unfair criticism, has opened its books.

The IPA hopes that by publishing this information it will create a less emotional climate for pursuing sensible discussions about remuneration levels and this seems to have been the case – at least up to a point.

Wages and Salaries by Function – all agencies

	1991		1992	
	% of wages and salaries	Average no. of employees	% of wages and salaries	Average no. of employees
Management	9.86	3.82	9.14	3.45
Account Management	25.81	27.98	24.68	22.90
Planning and research	5.03	5.08	5.67	4.85
Media	9.04	11.12	9.88	10.36
Creative	21.25	17.69	22.22	16.46
Mechanical production, traffic printing	6.41	9.45	6.14	8.03
TV, Radio and Cinema production	3.54	4.71	3.28	3.82
Finance, accounts & data processing	7.68	12.59	7.03	10.51
Secretaries	4.37	11.15	4.85	9.55
Office Administration	2.87	7.76	3.85	7.31
Other Staff not included in the above	4.08	5.19	3.26	3.64
TOTAL WAGES AND SALARIES	100.00	116.54	100.00	100.88
Average cost per person	£27,795		£28,396	
Number of returns used	51	51	67	67

Source: IPA

Figure 10.5

What the cost statistics show is that, consistently over a long period 60 per cent of agency costs have been directly related to personnel (see Figure 10.3 and 10.4). During the recession, as billings and remuneration levels have dropped the cost percentage has remained stable and as a consequence the numbers employed in the industry have dropped by over 30 per cent (see Figure 10.5).

Interestingly, the mix of functional staff numbers and costs has remained stable. This suggests that either agencies have found the perfect operating model or the industry is stuck in its ways and may be ripe for restructuring.

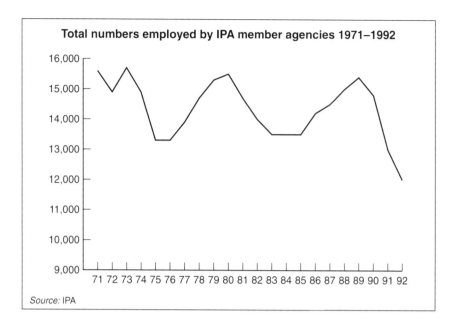

Figure 10.6

Other marketing services

No other trade body in the marketing services sector is as systematic in the data it collects or as open in its disclosure policy as the IPA. However, it is a reasonable assumption that agency cost structures in such people-oriented businesses are broadly similar.

Key cost components

The primary costs will always be personnel and accommodation. Agency computer systems are becoming more costly but, unlike other people businesses which handle large amounts of their client's money, like the wholesale banking business, IT remains a small cost component in the agency business. Training should be a major cost line for all agencies, given the fact that they only have ideas and advice to sell, and that staff are both young and rapidly promoted. However, in the recession, training is an area which has universally suffered in the battle to control costs.

New business pitching and research costs represent a large proportion of every agency's net profits, although they have reduced of late as belts have been tightened. There is evidence that even when the recession is over the endless succession of unstructured pitches, with too many agencies on the list will decline, particularly among more professional clients. Speculative creative pitching will remain low as the selection process becomes more professional. More clients will accept that credentials are appropriate at the first selection stage only, with project fees being paid when shortlisted agencies are asked to produce speculative creative recommendations.

Credit control is another large element of agency costs. Bad debt write-offs, and interest costs arising from financing work in progress and receivables, can be substantial. This is an area which separates the sheep from the goats in agency management, with well-run agencies billing in advance, running negative work in progress and receiving cash from clients before paying suppliers and media. Many full service agencies have been less efficient in this area than the media independents, many of which make up to a third of total net profits from interest income.

Entertaining and other costs form the basis for a perennial debate between agencies and their clients. Where should overheads stop and chargeables start? For example, even for items like travelling, subsistence, couriers, taxis and transmission costs there are long discussions over whether they should be 'in the fee' or not. In a vacuum these issues seem insignificant but apparently minor costs can come to represent a large slice of agency profits if not clarified.

Long-term profitability

Many agencies have found it hard to break even, let alone make sensible profits in the last three years, and survival has become the test of success. It has always been a false impression that advertising and other marketing services agencies made huge returns, either on turnover or on capital employed. However, with the pressures of recent years it has become even truer that these are tough, low margin businesses.

Ironically, while most sensible commercial people prefer to do business with suppliers making satisfactory profit margins, enabling them to reinvest, the logic of industrial and raw material supply relationships does not always extend into the marketing services sector. As long as recessionary pressures continue, and until the negative reactions caused by the production debate subside, there will be continued pressure on agency margins.

AGENCY ACCOUNTING AND COSTING SYSTEMS

Most agencies have the following computer systems at their disposal:

- media – for planning, buying and evaluation
- work in progress – the 'job bag' system for collating production costs

- general accounting – including profit and loss account reporting
- payable and receivable systems – for managing agency working capital
- time reporting – to process and analyse time sheets
- client profitability – to estimate gross and net profit attributable to each client
- Forecasting – to predict future profits and cashflows.

These are all vital tools in agency management and are provided by a variety of suppliers. Many of them are specifically written and provided for the agency sector, most notably by Donovan Data Systems, the eponymous US-UK company with a virtual monopoly on agency systems. They are not cheap and they are not simple to install and run. Highly skilled computer and finance people operate them.

Yet for some reason agencies are generally pathetic at integrating these systems to generate useful management information. This high turnover industry is notorious for late and inaccurate financial reporting and for the paucity of internal information to indicate where resources are being allocated and where profits are being made. The trouble is that you can lead a horse to water but you can't make it drink. Few managers and staff in agencies take the need for accurate and timely financial information seriously, with the notable exception of media companies, which tend to be highly disciplined and profit conscious.

In the absence of financial understanding and a wish to report internal profitability managment information will always be weak. The prime problems are:

- accurate definition of time spent by staff on individual clients
- reasonable overhead allocation policies to activity and client profit centres
- effective costing and cross-charging of noncore agency services.

Getting creative people to fill in timesheets is notoriously difficult, although for some reason they are both fast and accurate when it comes to expense sheets! At a time when activity based costing and tight cost control are fundamental to making clients competitive, similar disciplines are only gradually evolving in agencies.

WPP under Martin Sorrell, the ex-Finance Director of Saatchis, is a good example of an agency which has always been rigorous in terms of financial reporting. When they were taken over by WPP both JWT and O&M were instilled with financial discipline from the top down. Saatchis always had an edge in the area of financial control, which allowed it to grow faster than many of its competitors. Unfortunately, many agencies are less focused and therefore less efficient.

Given the demand for greater transparency and fairer remuneration it is perhaps surprising that few clients take any interest in agency accounting and management information systems.

METHODS OF REMUNERATION

'Pressure on agency remuneration has continued, as clients have moved from pure commission to fees and agencies have had to bear the increased costs of multinational co-ordination.' – WPP Annual Report and Accounts 1992.

The fragmentation of the business, the move towards greater transparency and the recession have all ensured that the subject of agency remuneration has never been more topical. In a sense, the amount of interest the subject has excited is out of all proportion to its importance. The real issues are whether the creative ideas make a quantum difference to the client's business, whether production is expertly planned and responsibly managed, and, above all, whether media is planned and bought effectively. However, the distrust stimulated by the excesses of the eighties will not go away, and the subject remains a matter of contention.

Traditional commission system

Historically, media owners gave agencies 15 per cent commissions for booking press media space and for taking the credit risk on their clients. The same system was adopted by the commercial TV and radio contractors and has continued. For certain regional press the commission rate has reduced to 10 per cent, and many large clients now negotiate over-riding discount levels direct with the media. However, the banning of fixed commissions in the US in 1957 and in the UK in 1976 made little difference to the fundamental operation of the commission system, because it suits media owners. It is simple and easy to operate. They do not have to administer, or take commercial credit risks on, a large number of individual clients; they just deal with a few agencies.

However, pressure has gradually increased from clients, for disclosure of commission income levels, and a closer equation between agency time and resource requirements and the level of agency income. The wish for clients to understand and negotiate the required *resource package* has shifted the emphasis away from traditional commission.

In many cases this has suited agencies which have been able to more sensibly plan the *timing of remuneration*. This has made the matching of agency incomes and costs much more systematic, as income has tended to move away from the vagaries of the media schedule. In the past, agencies might earn no commission for long periods, then when the media campaign broke large quantities of revenue came flooding in. If the media campaign was deferred, or cut, all hell broke loose.

Coincidentally, the increasing trend towards *front-end fees* has had the additional benefit of providing a creative accounting tool for imaginative agency accountants. The ability to negotiate *front-ended fees* provides the perfect way for fast-growing agencies to manipulate their current year earnings to keep investors happy.

Alternative remuneration methods

There are many different systems for defining remuneration. The US has had more experience of these than any other country because automatic media commissions have been disallowed there for longer. The American Association of Advertising Agencies has been tracking different patterns of agency remuneration since automatic fixed commissions were banned in 1957. It has identified eight separate methods used by its members which are classified under four broad headings.

Commission arrangements

1 Media commissions only.
2 Media commissions plus production markups.
3 Media commissions plus production markups plus fees for specific add-on services.

Commission and fee

4 Retainer fee plus some element of commission.
5 Commission arrangement but with guaranteed minimum profit percentage and a controlled maximum profit percentage.
6 Minimum fee arrangement plus commission to the extent that it exceeds the agreed fee.

Fixed fee

7 A fee agreed in advance with all markups and commissions rebated.

Cost plus

8 The fee is agreed after the event based on work done with all markups and commission credited.

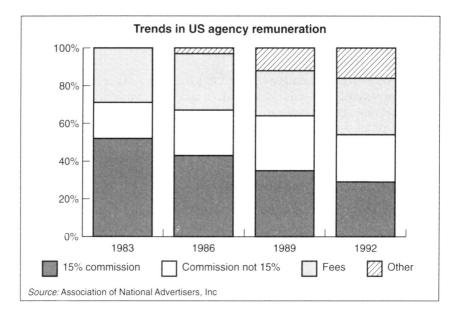

Figure 10.7

The shift in remuneration patterns in the US is illustrated by Figure 10.7.

But while there has been a shift away from a fixed percentage of spend towards a more flexible method of calculating remuneration there is evidence which suggests that this has led to an increase in percentage remuneration, particularly at lower budget levels, with 15 per cent seeming to represent the base level of actual agency remuneration (see Figure 10.8).

A report on 'Negotiating with agencies and suppliers', published by the ISBA in 1991, seemed to suggest that clients should begin remuneration debates at 8 per cent, on the first million of expenditure, and reduce the percentage as the spend increased. This ruffled feathers at the IPA and led to a heated dialogue. Particularly at the lower end and where service levels are high it is often the case that even conventional 15 per cent commission is inadequate to cover required service levels.

Hourly based fees

As agencies have unbundled, and become more transparent in the recession, there has been a significant impetus for hourly-based fees to be the prime method of remuneration. Many accountants like this basis because it seems to equate with other professional services and it is easy to check an invoice against a timesheet. But in David Wethey's words,

General average by agency size groups

Percentage of gross income to billing

1960 – 1966 – 1978 – 1983

Agency size (Annual Gross Income)	1960 %	1966 %	1978 %	1983 %
up to $300,000	20.7	22.1	26.8	27.4
$300,000 – $750,000	18.6	20.5	23.3	27.3
$750,000 – $1,500,000	17.3	18.8	21.1	27.2
$1,500,000 – $3,000,000	17.1	17.7	20.1	23.8
$3,000,000 – $6,000,000	15.1	16.3	17.3	22.0
$6,000,000 – $13,500,000	15.2	17.5	16.3	20.1
Over $13,500,000	15.2	15.2	16.2	15.7

Source: AAAA

Figure 10.8

'If the commission system is badly deficient, because it doesn't pay agencies for what they do, and pays them for what they don't do, the hourly-fee system is equally lunatic, because it incentivises the agency to use as many people as possible for as long as possible to produce a commercial or a strategy. In other words, you're incentivising people to be slow and inefficient.'

Payment by results

In recent years, and in line with the demand for accountability and results, there have been calls for some form of payment by results. The main argument against this method is the uncertainty and instability it creates. There are huge problems of definition and verification. In the words of Bob Willott, a partner in Willott Kingston Smith, an accountancy firm specialising in the marketing services sector, 'It would be fatal to bring this in as a standard basis for calculating agency revenues. It would be suicide for both parties because of arguments over subjective judgements. It might be appropriate on very rare occasions.'

A number of agencies have produced remuneration systems with a results-based element, but the common view is that results-based systems are too complicated and subjective to form the central element of advertising remuneration systems. They are a useful addition rather than a serious alternative to fees and commissions. There is growing evidence that major advertisers are taking this view. They set a base remuneration level by reference to total budget spend then have a 'top-up' payment based on predefined performance measures. This has the benefit of ensuring a reasonable level of income to support the agency cost structure and a strong incentive derived from an additional payment when campaign results have been measured.

For example, according to the WPP Annual Report, at least three major multinational packaged goods companies – Kraft General Foods, Nestlé and Unilever – all revised their remuneration arrangements in 1992 and in general settled on levels equivalent to 13 per cent, with further bonuses of up to 3 per cent dependent on performance.

Many large, steady-spending clients prefer a remuneration system which incorporates a mixture of flat percentage together with rewards for success in the agency. As the brands grow there is more wealth to be spent through the agency and bonuses provide a long term incentive to the agency.

Remuneration systems and objectivity

One of the fundamental problems with all systems connected with volume of expenditure on advertising or other media is the disincentive for the agency to be totally objective about the need to spend.

Although there are totally objective agencies many rarely advise their clients against spending, and as a result are often not consulted about whether money should be spent or not. This limits the relationship between agency and client, and militates against a genuine partnership. Some companies like Procter & Gamble tackle the issue by having a very tight roster of agencies with informal guarantees that if there are three of them they will have an agreed proportion of the P&G business internationally. If they lose one account they will gain another, and they know they can plan on a constant cash-flow from the client. They gain the confidence to say 'don't advertise on this', or 'delay your advertising on that' and they become more intimately involved. The regularly-shifted account, or the account under threat, militates against this kind of relationship. Other agencies opt for the fee-only route as a means of demonstrating total objectivity.

Conclusion

No one method will replace the traditional commission system. As ways of using agencies become more sophisticated the methods of remuneration will also become more sophisticated and variable. However, it seems probable that financial people will have to become far more involved in the definition of an acceptable agency return at different spend and activity levels. This will often be in conjunction with specialist agency consultants.

It also seems probable that while slavish adherence to time-based systems will not become the norm, more attention will be paid to internal time and costing systems as benchmarks against which agreed remuneration will be measured. Results-based bonus payments will also become far more common as a supplement to basic remuneration. This may be in the form of additional one-off payments at the end of a campaign, or by way of premium rates, where a time-based approach is adopted.

THE VALUE OF CREATIVITY

As agency remuneration methods become progressively more systematised and related to time and costing systems one question remains unanswered by the accountants and the consultants; what is the value of creativity? Can it ever be quantified by a standard costing system? Nick Phillips, the Director General of the Institute of Practitioners in Advertising, uses the analogy of Michelangelo and the Sistine Chapel.

In the sixteenth century the Pope wanted to demonstrate his power and influence by building the grandest chapel in Italy, as a venue for impressing and influencing key opinion leaders. As all great ceilings conventionally incorporated the 12 Apostles the ceiling had to be painted with the biggest and most magnificent fresco of the Apostles. He selected Michelangelo from 19 contenders and asked for an oblong fresco in double quick time. Michelangelo decided that a conventional picture of the Apostles would not fulfil the Pope's underlying purpose. It would lack the required majestic power and originality, even if it met the precise brief he had been given.

So he spent four years on his back painting the prophets, mythological figures and heroes of the Old Testament around the margins of the ceiling, and at the centre he painted the Creator and the created, fingers just touching, linked by a spark of dynamic energy. What inspiration, what glory. Michelangelo and the Sistine Chapel ceiling have passed into history.

Yet the Pope used to climb the scaffolding and hit Michelangelo with his papal staff because he was displeased with the progress of the work. He was peeved that it had not been finished on time. Imagine if he had employed a Sicilian accountant to monitor the amount and quality of paint used and the need for Roman rather than Florentine assistants. Imagine if he had queried the cost of clips and bolts on the scaffolding to ensure that the artist wasn't wasting money or 'on the take'.

Agency people like to think of themselves as latterday Michelangelos, with the philistine client using his papal staff and financial adviser to quench the creative spark. Putting aside the self pity, they have a valid point that brilliantly conceived ideas may not take long to devise but have huge value, and that supreme craft skills cannot be bought and sold with materials costs as the key criterion.

The increasingly mechanistic approach to remuneration could result in a backlash, where creative agencies simply refuse to discuss costs. The price is what the market will bear. At present the market is not tight enough to make this a feasible option for many agencies, but as supply tightens in the recovery the situation may change.

The lesson in terms of financial control of marketing activity is that qualitative issues need to be handled sensitively. The purchasing manager's attitude to 'least cost' may not result in the most effective results in marketing terms.

PRODUCTION COST MANAGEMENT

While we are on the subject of 'what the market will bear' it is timely to consider the issue of production cost control. In the 1980s it is alleged that many agencies overcharged production costs as a way of achieving additional margins. Some tried to post-rationalise the abuse as a way of increasing puny agency margins to an acceptable level. It would have been better if they had just been more open with clients in the first place, demanding fair rewards for the required resources. Unfortunately, many did not and the resulting scandal set back client/agency relations.

The Parkway bubble

Some point to Parkway as an example of the excessive production margins of the 1980s. In 1987, Parkway PLC was feted as a new player in the fast growing and highly profitable area of pre-press production – the production of films and plates for the advertising business. Parkway was launched on the USM and became a stock market darling. Profit margins were high, acquisitions were made at a breathtaking rate and the company expanded world-wide. It won the USM company of the year award in 1988 and looked like being the marketing services phenomenon of the 1990s. Then something went wrong and the bubble burst. Some joked about the wisdom of accepting the poisoned chalice of business awards, which had cursed other entrepreneurial stars – Sophie Merman of Sock Shop being one.

Some felt that Parkway's phenomenal growth had depended too heavily on close relationships with a small group of agencies, and that there would be margin pressure if agencies bought pre-press production services more aggressively.

Many clients were beginning to believe agencies had not been aggressive enough in buying on their behalf, and had divided loyalties. In the case of Parkway, the implication was that high margins, funded out of client production budgets, had launched a stock market phenomenon. Client tempers were beginning to fray.

The missing link

As the debate got into full swing much worse accusations were hurled about. 'Rip-off', 'hidden discount', 'hidden margin' and 'back hander' were all used in the heated exchanges of the early 1990s.

In 1991, Bob Holt, ex-Production Director of Saatchi & Saatchi, raised the temperature several degrees by resigning from Saatchis and setting up Production Link, a production consultancy. He argued, and in many cases demonstrated, that agency production margins of anywhere between 200 per cent and 500 per cent were commonplace, and that it was not unusual for agencies to double-charge for insertions, or charge production costs on cancelled insertions. He argued that overcharging was not only the result of inefficiency or inaccuracy, but also an agency conspiracy to deliberately and systematically milk their clients, who were either too ignorant or too trusting to stop the abuse.

He built up an impressive client list; not only could his fees be paid for out of cost savings but clients could satisfy feelings of righteous indignation by putting their agencies through the wringer. On top of all this he offered the opportunity of achieving higher levels of production quality and efficiency for the same or for less money.

As 'poacher turned game-keeper' he was both loathed and feared by those who had been supplementing revenue by marking-up production. Unfortunately for potential detractors he was too experienced and respected within his own trade for his opinions to be rubbished as the ramblings of a disgruntled or ill-informed junior. He had been production director of one of the largest agency groups and had been responsible for various important production innovations. For example, describing himself as a 'printer in the advertising world' he came up with a special fading ink for a motor neurone disease poster campaign, where the creative idea required the image to fade over the period of a month. He succeeded in producing an ink which did this – a world first.

He was also chairman of the Association of Print and Packaging Buyers. In fact, he claims to have been driven to action primarily for craft reasons. He was particularly aggrieved that production qualities could have been higher, at a lower cost, if so much had not been taken in hidden margins. Nothing was left to invest in improving quality standards.

Part of the woodwork

After several years of evangelising Bob Holt and Production Link are now accepted features of the advertising scene. He accepts that agencies have radically revised their margin policies and estimates that prepress production charges have dropped by half in the last two years. Obligatory supplier discounts to agencies have virtually disappeared.

So how can his services still be justified. He cites a number of reasons:

- conducting random production audits for clients
- helping to persuade clients to use the highest quality suppliers and processes by negotiating directly to get the best deals
- explaining complex production processes
- generally improving production quality standards
- negotiating with suppliers who notoriously overcharge agencies to cover costs
- a commitment to reduce costs

It may be wishful thinking but Bob Holt forecasts, '. . . that most clients will ultimately either handle their own production work or will use an independent production consultancy like Production Link'. He plans to enter the TV production market and believes that the days of unsupervised agency activity in this area are over.

That there is still scope for improving agency production buying skills is echoed by Roger Scarlett-Smith of SmithKline Beecham. On the subject of agency sourcing of printed materials, he comments, 'On one insert we found that by buying the paper ourselves, we could save £70,000 on a total budget of £200,000. We buy a lot of paper in-house. Paper is a well-known commodity item, which we buy in bulk for packaging and with the correct specification we can go out to our suppliers and get a very good price. As major buyers of media, agencies should be able to negotiate a good price. They seem to be excellent at competitively negotiating media, but in terms of production they are lousy. In defence of my agencies, I think it is more to do with incompetence than corruption or deviousness!'

The area of print buying is one of the areas where many clients have their own in-house buyer, print department or a third-party print consultant to advise on buying policy. With hundreds of thousands and sometimes millions at stake the client who is not professionally managing this function is foolhardy. According to Bob Holt all areas of agency production buying will ultimately be subject to similar rigour.

THE QUEST FOR TRANSPARENCY

In May 1993 Bartle Bogle Hegarty, one of the most highly respected agencies in London, launched its Business Practice statement. It set out a number of interesting concepts. The idea of an agency 'salary' rather than commissions or strictly time-related fees; the idea of incentives for 'measurable over achievement'; the idea of total financial transparency and disclosure; the idea of Annual Account Audits conducted internally, and Client Satisfaction Surveys conducted externally; the idea that if third-party consultants were to audit BBH then BBH should retain the right to audit the consultants, and pass judgement on their competence.

Some trade journalists found the document verbose, and its launch rather pretentious – with a see-through cover on *Campaign*. However, the initiative was a genuine attempt to recapture the high ground in relations with clients. It demonstrated the willingness of first-class agencies to respond to client demands for impeachable practices.

RE-ENGINEERING THE AGENCY PROCESS

The fact is that in the next decade there will need to be major changes in the way agencies operate. Just as client companies are being driven by forces which they cannot prevent, and are harnessing those forces to gain a competitive edge, the same is increasingly true in the agency world.

At the technological level there will be much greater integration of agency processes, both within agencies and at the interface with clients, suppliers and media. There will need to be far higher investment in technology to achieve this.

At the supply level clients will increasingly interfere in the purchasing chain in a number of areas; media, paper, print, production, film and so on. Large clients buying in bulk will dictate supply to their agencies.

At the service level there will be a growing need for integration of marketing services by agencies. Many more disciplines will need to be delivered by the same account handling team in the way that KMM delivers all services to Rover.

At the same time there will be a need to discriminate between agency services more clearly, and only supply those services to clients which they want and need. This implies far more effective agency information and accounting systems. The agency of the next millenium will be far more flexible than the average agency of today. It will look at the individual client's value chain and seek to mirror what the client wants delivered, rather than what the agency wants to deliver. At present agencies lecture their clients about transforming outdated production or sales cultures into customer focused marketing cultures.

The cobbler will increasingly need to look after his own shoes. Those agencies which do will benefit the way retailers have done in their sector, with increasing customer satisfaction, market share and widening margins.

Bibliography

WPP Group PLC, Annual Report and Accounts 1992

Costing Systems for Advertising Agencies, Arthur Andersen/IPA

Rewarding the advertising profession, David Haigh/IPA

11

FUTURE TRENDS AND DEVELOPMENTS

'What we look for does not come to pass; God finds a way for what none foresaw'
Euripides

INTRODUCTION

Predicting the future is never a particularly sensible move. According to Edmund Burke 'You can never plan the future by the past'. Looking into the future has been compared with looking into an opaque mirror. All you can see is the blurred image of a worried face. The future almost always proves us wrong. For example, who foresaw the rapid breakdown of the Soviet bloc? Even those who did could never have predicted its precise effects on the European economy. However, this book set out to review factors currently affecting the strategic control of marketing finance, and it would be incomplete without at least some attempt at crystal ball gazing. What are the implications of issues discussed for the future of marketing finance? In this final chapter some of the apparent outcomes are considered. Several trends and developments seem to stand out like the nose on your face. Or is it just a trick of the mirror?

TRENDS IN PROJECT CONTROL AND EVALUATION

Internal review

One of the most striking trends seems to be the increase in financial controls and methods of evaluating marketing projects. As the risks get greater and the costs of failure get higher the need for accountability increases. Ken Miles, the Director General of the Incorporated Society of British Advertisers (ISBA), believes that accountability is one of the most powerful and growing trends in the marketing world. In his words,

'Many finance people in companies regard the marketing and advertising areas as ones in which the rules of accountability are not as well followed as those in most parts of manufacturing or service business. There are not many companies which apply the same level of stringency to marketing decisions and marketing communication budgets as they do to other areas of activity. I know of an increasing number of companies which are bringing their purchasing people into the marketing field, not to do the buying but to see whether there are ways in which more realistic controls can be introduced, with the co-operation of marketing people rather than over their heads. This will become much more widespread not only in this country but internationally as well. I hope everyone in the communications business recognises this and goes with the trend rather than trying to fight it.'

As a result more and more emphasis is already being placed on internal and external monitoring. One example of the approval and review procedures which are proliferating is the system of project review at Whitbread. Frazer Thompson, the Marketing Director for Lagers at Whitbread, describes the project evaluation system at the company,

'Every project we undertake begins with a project approval request *and ends with a* project completion review. *Both the PAR and the PCR include detailed financial analysis in addition to qualitative data. They are flexible documents but always incorporate key marketing and financial information. PARs and PCRs are taken very seriously and are prepared by marketing managers in close co-operation with marketing accountants, who are assigned to every project.'*

The standard Whitbread project approval request (PAR) is structured as follows:

MARKETING PAR

1 PROJECT SUMMARY

PAR NUMBER:
PROJECT NAME:
LOCATION:
NATURE OF PROJECT:
TOTAL PROJECT COST:

2 PROJECT AUTHORISATION

PAR NUMBER:
PROJECT NAME:
BRAND:

AUTHOR:

PROJECT EXPENDITURE: **£000**

research and development
capital investment
finance
production
stock keeping
advertising and promotion:

media space
production
sponsorship
public relations
point of sale
design
promotions
counter-mountings
other (specify)

_____

TOTAL PROJECT COST   **£** _____

PROJECT TYPE:

risk of not doing it:
risk of project failing:
date for Post Completion Review:
Budget Code Funding:

AUTHORISATION   **DATE**

Project sponsor
Finance director
Sponsorship manager
Marketing manager
Marketing director
Investment committee

3 APPRAISAL COMMENTARY

Background rationale:
Project detail and timing:

4 CASHFLOW SUMMARY

Financial year	199x					199y				
Quarter	1	2	3	4	Total	1	2	3	4	Total

**Detailed
Cashflows**

5 FINANCE COMMENTARY

6 SUCCESS CRITERIA

Criterion	Means of measurement	Timing	By whom

7 PROFIT AND LOSS ACCOUNT IMPACT

Income	199x	199y	Risk	Assumptions
Detailed revenue projections				
Total				
Detailed cost projections				
Total				
Net effect				

8 ASSESSMENT OF RISK

Project revenues:
Project costs:

9 CRITICAL PATH

Detailed project timetable:

The post completion review covers each of the areas defined in the PAR in some detail and is formally considered and evaluated by senior management.

Brand equity monitoring

This sort of marketing/finance approval and reporting system is becoming more and more common. Marketing managers are increasingly being expected to work within financial and business planning frameworks, and the reviews are becoming financially more sophisticated. If internal brand valuation and brand equity reviews become the norm there could also be periodic reviews of the whole brand along the same lines. Interbrand has already installed brand diagnostic, monitoring and evaluation procedures and manuals in more than one major multinational, and the trend seems likely to continue. Interbrand's brand manuals set out in detail financial templates for measuring brand profitability and cashflows, and structures for systematic analysis of brand equity development. They are a useful guide and support for marketing managers, for it is marketing managers not financial managers who will be expected to complete them. The resulting reports will be used by senior management to assess how well brands are being maintained and developed. They will also form the basis for a range of internal decisions, from brand extension and brand licensing to the promotion of brand managers. This will create internal pressure for more detailed, accurate and timely analysis of brand related financial data to make reviews meaningful and comparable. It will also create a need for financially literate marketing managers working in integrated teams. Some of the key criteria they may consider will be:

- capital investment
- revenue costs of campaigns
- budget size and split
- price and consumer demand analysis
- market share statistics
- sales volumes
- sales conversion rates
- costs per consumer or respondent
- distribution profiles
- cashflows
- profitability
- brand awareness and saliency
- future development opportunities
- brand asset values.

The sort of criteria which in a less formal way every small businessman and entrepreneur considers every day of his working life. In fact, it is being recognised that marketing and brand managers are effectively the managing directors of their own business segments and should be expected to account for their business in financial terms.

External analysis

The number of external measures by which marketing campaigns and brand activity can be monitored is also growing apace. At the most basic level is the data now being made available on a weekly basis from electronic point of sale (EPOS) systems. This information, when properly analysed and cross-referenced to marketing campaign information, can be invaluable in calculating which marketing expenditure actually produces results. In addition to sales data there will an increasing variety of advertising and brand awareness tracking measures. Some of these will be far more directly connected with sales patterns than a lot of current awareness tracking studies.

For example, in the US the advertising market is dominated by *ARS persuasion shift testing*, whereby people are invited into a theatre to judge a finished commercial as part of a pilot programme with adverts in the middle of it. They are asked their purchase intentions for a range of brands beforehand; they circle brands on a shelf and then they are asked to make a similar brand choice later. The difference in their choice before and after seeing the adverts is taken as an important measure of how good or bad the advertising is. This research method has been validated in marketplace activity but tends to drive American advertising towards hard-edged competitive claims with little or no attempt to charm or amuse. In many cases little attempt is made to create any degree of empathy or warmth towards the brand. It's difficult to measure the effect of charm or humour, and 'if you can't measure it, don't do it' is now the way many Americans approach their advertising. Persuasion shift testing produces a more aggressive type of advertising but it results in measurable sales benefits over the short-term. Admittedly the US advertising industry is importing more subtle UK planning methods to rectify the situation, because of the questionmark over long-term empathy towards the brand. However, it seems probable that there will be a two-way trade, with far more hard-nosed research methods becoming common in the UK.

There will be many other new research techniques. Carat's search for a meaningful 'memorisation model', and other attempts to genuinely understand the relationship between marketing activity and consumer behaviour, will proliferate. The key will be tangible sales effects of marketing activity both short- and long-term. In the search for new techniques even Media Audits is developing monitoring measures. The main development Tony Ayers, the Chief Executive of Media Audits, sees is,

'something that will link our expertise with media data through to the ad-tracking data that companies undertake with companies like Milward Brown and NOP. Their research measures the effectiveness of advertising campaigns. There are two elements in creating shifts in consumer awareness: the creative vehicle and the media vehicle. We think our ability to

analyse the media vehicle should let us strip out the contribution media makes to shifts in awareness. This will leave a purer measure of the creative end-result. This ought to help in planning media campaigns – answering questions about "burst" or "drip", and about weights of advertising, helping to identify how many exposures are necessary to create different end-results. Media is essentially about delivering coverage and frequency of target audiences, getting people to see ads a given number of times. Tracking studies are to measure awareness of the advertising, the results of the advertising, like attitudes to the brand and propensities to purchase. We've done some interesting work on awareness as a first measure leading into propensity to purchase. We hope our new research techniques will help reveal different trigger levels and different patterns of advertising necessary to influence both brand awareness and propensity to purchase.'

Statistical methods

These and other new types of monitoring research will be introduced. They will be supplemented by statistical analysis conducted by econometricians like OHAL. For example, Scott has been working with OHAL to monitor the success of its Andrex 'Puppy' campaign since 1974. Andrex is the brand leader in toilet tissue, with twice the market share of its major competitor. The 'Puppy' campaign has been running since 1969 and its appeal and sales power have been constantly refined by reference to statistically valid test sampling. For example, in 1974 Andrex was being supported by three equal bursts of advertising each year, giving 1,200 television rating points (TVRs). While this formula had apparently been successful in sales terms, Scott was interested to know whether a continuous schedule would produce more effective sales results than bursts. A continuous advertising test was therefore constructed in four TV regions, with bursts running in four 'control' regions. The test showed that in the regions with a continuous advertising schedule sales increased over the control region by between 5 and 7 per cent. Continuous schedules were therefore introduced nationally.

Great care needs to be taken when designing, constructing and evaluating statistical tests of this sort. How much difference does the distribution profile make? Is there any competitive activity? Have stocking patterns been changed or disrupted in any way? There is never a simple uplift in sales which can be evaluated from the test to the control regions. Sales graphs gyrate around the basic sales line and the background noise of sales variations has to be eliminated using statistical methods. To illustrate this point here is an OHAL analysis of a basic sales graph showing the contribution to total sales of different elements in the mix.

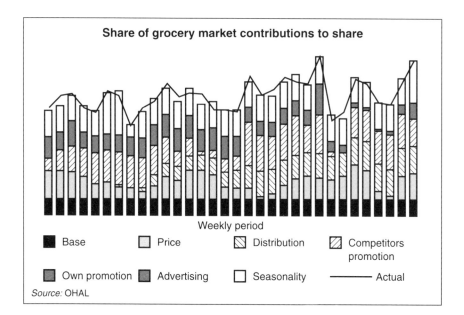

Figure 11.1

One of the most important questions underlying this kind of analysis is whether the samples are statistically valid. The number of months duration and the number of test areas from which conclusions can be drawn have to be carefully related to ensure the validity of the prime result, the 'standard error' and the 'level of confidence' which is to be placed in the result. In one case OHAL showed that measuring a 3 per cent sales uplift with a standard error of 4 per cent at a 90 per cent confidence level required a test sample of either one site for a 12-month period or 12 sites for one month. The higher the number of test sites or the longer the duration of the test the greater the level of confidence which can be obtained in the results. It is not simply a case of looking at two clean sales graphs compared with two marketing spend profiles. In fact, the great thing about detailed store by store weekly EPOS data is that it now makes statistical sampling techniques far more achievable for the average company. Where sales data used to be received monthly, in aggregate form and long after the event, it is now available in readily digestible form on a regular basis. More companies should and will be using it.

During its relationship with Scott OHAL has consistently used these techniques to assist marketing management develop and refine the advertising and marketing programme for Andrex. For example, in the early 1980s it analysed the proposition that an increased weight of advertising would result in increased sales and profits for the Andrex brand. A test was constructed in three areas with a 50 per cent uplift in advertising weight to 200 TVRs per month. Breakeven was a 2.5 per cent increase in sales. The predicted sales increase amounted to 4 per cent. As a result Andrex increased its weight of advertising to 200 TVRs nationally.

In the mid-1980s there was some concern that the 'Puppy' campaign had run its course and that a new creative approach should be developed. A new 'Puppy' route was developed with the puppy appearing in fairy tales. However, OHAL testing methods demonstrated that this creative route was not sales effective and a new route was developed. How many statisticians have told the creative department what to do?

Another proposition which OHAL evaluated in the mid-1980s was the idea that because own-label products were improving in quality, and because toilet tissue was being sold in larger packs with lower purchase frequency, a higher consumer *opportunity to see* (OTS) 'trigger' level was required, to convert consumers to the Andrex brand. The issue of 'trigger' levels is one of the most important concepts in the whole media planning process but one which is often left in the shadow of media jargon and complexity. Here is a typical matrix of TVRs related to OTS distribution.

OTS distribution

Percentage of target audience seeing at least N adverts

TVRs	N = 1+	2+	3+	4+	6+
100	56	26	11	4	1
200	71	47	31	19	8
300	77	58	43	32	18
400	81	65	52	42	26
600	86	73	62	55	39
% change from					
200/400	14	38	68	120	225
300/600	12	26	44	82	117

Based on typical housewife ITV/Ch4 schedule

Source: OHAL

Figure 11.2

What is the level of OTS which incites the average consumer to buy a product? The answer is inevitably connected with the creative work and the recall of past advertising (see Figure 11.3).

However, OHAL claims that after many years of sampling it is able to fairly accurately predict the required 'trigger' level for a given brand; (see Figure 11.4) a typical value is three OTS with variances around the core

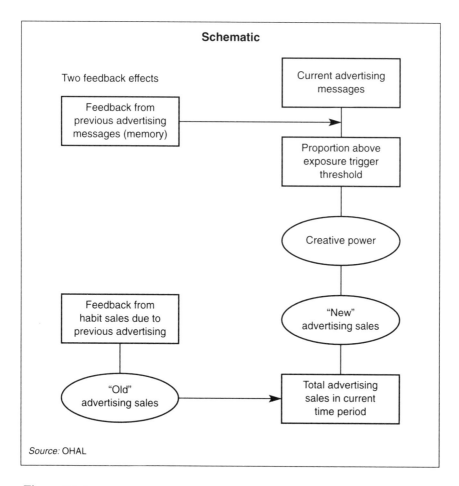

Figure 11.3

figure. In the case of the Andrex 'Puppy' campaign consideration was being given to heavyweight 'burst' advertising. A test was devised in two areas with 600 TVRs a month for two months. Results were evaluated using Adlab, the TCA Panel, and sales deliveries into individual outlets. Using its statistical sampling methods and taking all other data into consideration OHAL concluded that higher burst weights would have no significant sales benefit and monthly weights returned to 200-300 TVRs.

In the late 1980s and early 1990s OHAL assisted in the selection of the most sales effective advertising treatments. 'Little boy', the advertisement with a little boy stranded in the loo as the Labrador puppy runs off round the house with his long, strong Andrex roll, topped the *Marketing* AdWatch table for a record number of weeks. The campaign has been hugely success-ful in sales terms and has won an IPA Advertising Effectiveness Award.

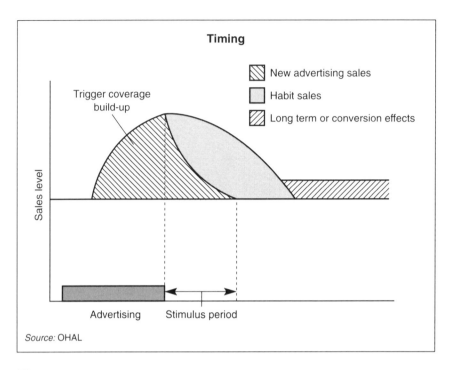

Figure 11.4

OHAL has moved on into the evaluation of spot lengths and daypart mix.

The lesson from this long-standing relationship is that econometric modelling techniques, defining meaningful relationships between marketing activity and sales effects, has helped in a long sequence of decisions to improve advertising and promotional effectiveness. Scott has been able to take all available opportunities without making costly mistakes. It has been able to define objectively which promotional decisions contribute most to profitability. In addition, knowledge of the effects of different techniques has been maintained through many changes of marketing management.

Monitoring single and multimedia campaigns

Interestingly, the techniques applied to Andrex are also applicable to multimedia campaigns. For example OHAL recently tested a multimedia campaign for a national clearing bank, to establish which mix of marketing techniques produced the highest level of customer activity in the branch network. The bank's regions were used as discrete test areas with different marketing mixes being used in each region. OHAL sought to establish whether advertising alone or a mixture of advertising, direct mail, public relations and in-branch sales promotion had the most profitable effect. The results have been used to refine marketing plans and budgets.

OHAL has also used similar techniques with single medium campaigns involving no advertising. For example, it used statistical sampling methods on behalf of a public transport operator to determine whether a huge annual brochure drop would result in a profitable increase in travelcard subscription sales. The costs of the annual brochure drop had risen to £700,000 and the operator naturally wanted to be sure that sales resulting from it were profitable. Four weekly sales data were supplied for every outlet for the preceding two years and similar data were supplied during the test period. Thirty four outlets were 'silent' with no brochure drop, 167 outlets were 'active'. OHAL calculated that the brochure drop resulted in £1.5 million of additional sales, with a standard error of plus or minus £500,000 at a 95 per cent confidence level. The percentage probability that the brochure returned a profit was 99.9 per cent and the apparent return on investment was 100 per cent.

Of course there are limits to what can be achieved with statistical methods. It is very difficult to evaluate anything unless it has a statistically significant activity level or commercial benefit, and in order to achieve this it often has to be a large activity. It's easy to evaluate a national coupon or sample drop, and quite clearly worth investing money in evaluation techniques. Similarly with advertising it is possible to measure effectiveness in terms of sales and awareness, and it's worth spending money to track them. Other elements are much less easy to evaluate, like good pack design as opposed to functional or poor pack design. Good design is worth a lot of money, but how can you tell? You can measure preference, but how much does it add in terms of sales value? In the marketing areas where statistical methods are most valid there will be a big increase in demand.

Effectiveness awards

The techniques described so far are for the internal use and control of marketing organisations. In addition to such measures there has been a massive upsurge in activity by marketing trade organisations to reward and promote effective marketing practice. There have always been awards for successful campaigns but in the past they have tended to relate to narrow definitions of creative success. However, the Institute of Public Relations, the Public Relations Consultants Association, the Institute of Sales Promotion, and the Direct Marketing Association all now have highly competitive awards for good practice. Such awards are no longer simply to massage the egos of prima donnas, but to mark out those consultancies and agencies which have made a real contribution to the marketing success of their clients. Of these awards the most high profile is the biannual Institute of Practitioners in

Advertising's (IPA) Advertising Effectiveness Awards. These are published in a widely-read book series as *Adworks*.

In fact, the IPA Advertising Effectiveness Awards are currently in the process of structural change. The six awards categories are being replaced by three new categories with an increased emphasis on through-the-line and direct response entries. For the 1994 awards there will be three categories: products or services that are new or have no significant history of advertising; new campaigns from previously advertised brands that have resulted in significant short-term effects on sales or behaviour; and campaigns that have benefited a business by maintaining or strengthening a brand over a long period. There will be special prizes for case studies featuring integration of marketing techniques, best use of direct response, best multicountry campaigns, most ingenious use of limited funds, best use of media planning and best use of innovative, strategic or executional thinking.

One important aspect of awards like these is to demonstrate to clients that agency services are not simply about creative people knocking out ads. In the words of Nick Phillips, the Director General of the IPA,

> '. . . advertising effectiveness is not only about creative execution, it is about the process. The planners, researchers and the people who link in the consumer view are not just a bunch of egg-heads, they are an essential part of the process. The account handler is an essential interface, a union of left and right brain, where strategic thinking, analysis and understanding of the consumer come together with intuitive brilliance and creativity.'

There is also some speculation that the awards should be run in conjunction either with the Incorporated Society of British Advertisers or one of the marketing trade bodies. This would reflect the practice in other countries and would emphasise the shift towards a serious marketing purpose rather than simply an agency focus. However, while Ken Miles, the Director General of the ISBA, recognises the importance of similar award schemes in Europe he prefers to tacitly endorse what the IPA has achieved rather than to get directly involved in the effectiveness awards. As long as they reinforce the need for accountability, integration and sales effectiveness rather than more ethereal agency concerns he feels they will be doing their job.

PROMOTIONAL CAMPAIGN MEASUREMENT

Following on from Ken Miles' comments it is fair to say that the increase in awards issued by marketing trade bodies is matched by a similar increase in effort and expense invested in finding ways of measuring the effectiveness of different promotional techniques. From the IPA, with its Advertising Effectiveness Awards, to the Association of Media Independents, which has been involved in a number of research studies showing the impact of advertising media on product sales, through to the Public Relations Consultants Association (PRCA), with its backing for Precis, a PR evaluation system, there is a frenzy of activity in terms of campaign measurement.

Coincidentally the Director General of the PRCA is a chartered accountant who was Managing Director of Army and Navy stores for many years. Colin Thompson spent a number of years pulling the PRCA back from the brink of bankruptcy and is now helping to put the PR industry into a more businesslike frame of mind. In his view *'the PR business has been held back by the fact that most PR people are wonderful at developing the art of PR but hopeless at managing businesses.'* According to him, *'many don't even know the difference between cashflow and profit.'* He believes this lack of serious business discipline has held the industry back from taking its rightful place in the marketing mix. He cites studies in the US which indicate that every pound spent on PR is worth five pounds spent on advertising. *'If you are going to shoot a person it's easier to kill them with one bullet. You don't need to bombard them with thousands of missiles. As target audiences and media fragment, PR will become far more important, particularly as PR management is becoming more professional.'* His view of the client end is that, *'I think there is going to be a major change. Accountants need to appreciate what marketing is all about. You have to spend money to make money, you can't just look at cost-savings as a way to improving profitability as many companies have in this recession. You have to invest to expand and investments don't generate profits in six months.'*

One of the major growth areas over the next decade will be promotional monitoring and evaluation techniques stimulated by the actions of people like Colin Thompson in the different trade bodies.

TRENDS IN PROMOTIONAL SPENDING

That the emphasis is shifting within the marketing mix is endorsed by Willott Kingston Smith, a chartered accountancy firm specialising in the marketing services sector. Willott Kingston Smith research suggests that two trends will gather pace.

One is the switch from advertising into other brand building disciplines like direct marketing, sponsorship, sales promotion and public relations. The other is the fact that they will more often be delivered in an integrated way.

SCENARIOS FOR THE FUTURE

A recent internal conference at The Added Value Company summarised the consultancy's views of the future in the following table:

The past	The future
Marketplace	
Predictability	Discontinuity
Market consolidation	Market fragmentation
Homogeneity	Heterogeneity
Organisational structure	
Mergers and takeovers	Unbundling
Conglomerates	Cores
Vertical	Flat
Integrated	Networks
Centralised	Decentralised
Departments	Areas of expertise
Individuals	Project teams
Permanent arrangements	Temporary arrangements
Organisational style	
Long-term planning	Flexibility
Quantity	Quality
Prescription	Empowerment
Procedures	Values and culture
Management	
Implementers	Entrepreneurs
Unsupported	Information systems
Single discipline	Multi-disciplinary
Knowledge	Skill
Lifetime practice	Continuous development
Brand managers	Marketing project heads
Marketing	
Mass markets	Niche markets
Mass media	Targeted media
Customer penetration	Customer retention
Customer feedback	Customer dialogue
Brand portfolios	Corporate brands
Brand proposition	Brand personality
New brand development	Brand leveraging
Standard products and services	Customised products and services
Product features	Added value
Internal selling	Internal marketing

This neatly summarises many of the trends and developments discussed in earlier chapters. Within this broad framework a number of possible developments will be particularly relevant at the interface between marketing and finance.

Change in human resource strategies

There will be a marked shift towards flatter management structures with more flexible working structures and an increase in the use of freelance consultants, temps and home workers. There will be much greater emphasis on a smaller number of 'gold collar' workers, who will expect a far greater level of experience and understanding from their agencies and consultancies. Above all there will be an increase in the number of multifunctional managers working in fully integrated teams with other disciplines. More financial managers will be trained in marketing and vice versa. Psychometrics, improved training and internal communications will be used to more effectively select, develop and manage the 'talent intensive' organisation of the future. These developments will be costly but productive.

Investment in new technology

We are on the brink of an explosion of IT investment in the marketing function, driven by the finance function as it seeks to get a grip on marketing finances in the same way that other business areas have been brought under financial control. Systems are rapidly coming to maturity, primarily in mechanical areas like customer database management and salesforce management, but increasingly in more intelligent areas of analysis and decision support. Data analysis and reduction specialists will proliferate to help understand and utilise the wave of new information which will soon be available to the average marketing manager.

Corporate re-engineering

It may seem just another fashionable management gimmick, but corporate re-engineering is likely to have a longer lifespan than many fashions, because a number of underlying trends are pushing for it to happen in many organisations. The growing flexibility of staff and the move towards greater team working both militate in its favour. IT is a major driver and catalyst. Competition is forcing the pace, so that companies which do not fundamentally address the way they deliver their products or services could find themselves priced out of business.

Extension of brand valuation

Brand valuation will not die nor fade away but will be used in an increasing number of corporate transactions. As the joint venture culture and the incidence of licensing, franchising and co-branding increases the relevance of brand valuation as a benchmark for cross-charging royalties between affiliated companies will grow. It will also be used in investor relations, acquisitions and ongoing brand management. There will be an added impetus from companies seeking to optimise tax planning opportunities and a corresponding interest will be taken by tax authorities worldwide to ensure that fair value is received from corporate taxes paid by domestic and foreign businesses.

Financial disclosure of marketing information

Given the increasing importance of marketing to corporate health, and the importance of brands in particular, it will be increasingly necessary for shareholders to know much more about the stewardship exercised by management over valuable marketing assets. It may well be that the accountancy profession will prevent the disclosure of home grown brand valuations on balance sheets. However, more disclosure of advertising and promotional expenditure, market share information, brand profitability and marketing developments in the annual report will give shareholders a better idea of the health or otherwise of their investments. There are obvious dangers that commercially sensitive information will become available to competitors but it seems likely that in future forward thinking, blue-chip, marketing organisations will disclose much more about their marketing performance. This will be tied in with a need to justify performance to shareholders who will no longer accept inadequate returns on capital.

Evolution of the brand manager

Although recent financial history has graphically demonstrated the value of brands there has been a delay in recognition of the brand manager's importance as custodian of the brand. In future the brand manager as all-round business manager will come into his or her own. The seniority and capabilities of those involved in managing and directing brands will increase as will their role within the business. Brand management will develop a flatter structure, relying more heavily on a range of highly skilled external services and consultancies. Brand managers will increasingly come from MBA or similar analytical backgrounds and have the breadth of experience to manage total brand strategy at a business as well as at a promotional level.

Innovation at a premium

The habit of endless brand extension and price increases without new product features or benefits will have to be broken. The threat of own-label will not go away; it will intensify as retailers develop not just one own-label range but several at different levels in the marketplace. 'Manufacturer labels' will die under this onslaught, and only true brands with genuine and defendable product benefits will hold their own. The sales function will reinvent itself as a means of reinforcing existing distribution channels and of creating new ones, using interactive technology and direct-to-the-consumer techniques. Investment in new products, innovative distribution and robust brand building strategies will be the price of survival, not optional extras.

Evolution of the campaign planner

A new campaign planning discipline will grow out of the media planning function to accommodate not only an increasingly fragmented media scene but also client demands for genuinely integrated campaigns, incorporating above- and below-the-line disciplines. The role will be fed by a much more extensive range of research methodologies concentrating in particular on consumer attitudes and brand purchasing behaviour. Quality will prevail over quantity in media selection. Campaign planners will work with Campaign co-ordinators who may come from the client side but will frequently work on the agency side, drawing on extensive experience to integrate campaigns. Integration of campaigns will become the typical rather than the exceptional way of running campaigns, although one stop shopping will not necessarily be the norm.

Re-engineering the agency process

The structure of agencies is as much a throw back to the last century as the empire and the class system. Their commission and management structures are legacies of the nineteenth century, and inherent conservatism is holding up their evolution into structures more compatible with the needs of the late twentieth century. Despite this conservatism various trends will continue. The trends towards media independence and centralisation will gather pace. Agency services will be unbundled and will be delivered to clients on a task-oriented rather than on a standard package basis. Within those agencies which do offer a full range of executional functions the traditional ways of separately providing agency disciplines will become less pronounced, with agencies providing a range of services integrated more effectively with one another. There will be a reduction in the culture of separate profit centres and a thinning of account co-ordination personnel, who will be skilled at handling a wider range of executional outputs. There will be a much closer integration between agency and client in terms of both internal market information and external creative work, much of which will be driven by further advances in information technology. The creative continuum between client, agency, production house and media will develop further. There will be a further erosion of the traditional commission system with time based fees becoming more common, supplemented by success related bonuses. Transparency will become the rule rather than the exception.

Re-engineering the marketing function

The necessity to meet client needs effectively in an increasingly dynamic and open marketplace will lead to both corporate and marketing re-engineering. As information technology makes the integration of business processes a realistic possibility there will be a major change in many organisations and the demarcation lines between marketing, sales and finance will blur. This will be a painful process in many instances but a liberating one for those individuals, with both analytical and creative skills, who will increasingly staff the marketing function.

CONCLUSION

When Nostradamus put down his pen after predicting the end of the world he must have wondered whether his predictions would come true. Many did, but the world is still here. I may not have predicted the end of the world, but to many marketing and agency people the introduction of greater financial accountability at all levels may seem like it. The nature of marketing practice will change significantly. To paraphrase those immortal words from Star Trek, 'It will be life Jim, but not as we know it'. Marketing will change dramatically in the next decade and finance will be both one of the reasons for the change and part of the change process. Strategic control of marketing finances will be central to corporate control. Companies which can achieve the synergies available from integrating marketing and financial processes will be the ones which are still alive and kicking at the millenium.

INDEX